A Welsh
Building Rugby
1990 to

Ian Golden

London League Publications Ltd

A Welsh Crusade
Building Rugby League in Wales 1990 to 2009

© Copyright Ian Golden. Foreword © John Dixon. Introduction © David Watkins.

The moral right of Ian Golden to be identified as the author has been asserted.

Cover design © Stephen McCarthy. Photographs © the photographer or contributor of the photograph. No copyright has been intentionally infringed.

Front cover photo: Celtic Crusaders celebrate after scoring a try in their historic win at Bradford in 2009 (Photo: Ian Lovell)
Back cover photo: Gareth Dean in action for Wales against Papua New Guinea in 2007 (Photo: Ian Lovell)
Title page photo: Wales 2008 under-18 squad which beat France in the European Nations Cup Final in Prague. (Photo: Courtesy Andy Lindley.)

A CIP catalogue record for this book is available from the British Library.

First published in Great Britain in October 2009 by:
London League Publications Ltd, P.O. Box 10441, London E14 8WR

ISBN: 978-1903659-47-2

Cover design by: Stephen McCarthy Graphic Design
                                  46, Clarence Road, London N15 5BB

Layout: Peter Lush

Printed and bound by: the MPG Books Group,
                                  Bodmin and King's Lynn

This book is dedicated to Tony Duggan, Damien Quinn, Jace Van Dijk, Mark Dalle Cort, Josh Hannay and Darren Mapp.

Foreword

It was May 2005 when I was first asked whether or not I would be interested in taking on the role as head coach of a new rugby league club that was starting up in Wales. The fact that the club had the stated ambition to rise from the National Leagues to Super League in the space of just three years had real appeal. This seemed (and in hindsight most naively) to me at the time an opportunity to be part of 'bringing' the game I love to Wales.

Like most antipodeans I was well aware of Wales' standing in the rugby union international community and of some of the famous Welsh based names such as Pontypool and Llanelli (although it's not until recent times that I've had any hope of pronouncing it). I was also aware that rugby league as a sport was confined almost solely to northern England and that for Wales to compete internationally it was dependent on the Welsh based players who lived and plied their trade playing professionally in England.

What I as unaware of was the number of people in Wales who have rugby league as their sport of first choice and the fact that rugby league has been part of the sporting landscape of Wales for the past 100 years. What I was also unaware of were the previous attempts to establish rugby league at an elite level here in the principality in more recent times.

In this book Ian Golden has highlighted the state of rugby league in Wales over this period. It includes the rise and demise of the Cardiff Blue Dragons, the contribution of Wales to international rugby league such as in tournaments like the 1995 World Cup, the contribution of Welsh players to the Great Britain international teams, through the advent of professionalism in rugby union in Wales and rugby league switching to a summer code, to the formation of the Celtic Crusaders and the introduction of Super League to Wales. The book also highlights the key contribution of those off the field, people like Mike Nicholas who have never let go of the dream of rugby league being a major sport in the Welsh psyche.

For my part I would like to thank all those who have played a part in the rise and hopefully further rise of the Celtic Crusaders and those who have supported the club through the joys of our triumphant rise through the National Leagues to our tribulations as the new boys in Super League.

While the first season was a challenge for us on-and-off the field, the three year licence gives the club a wonderful opportunity to establish rugby league in Wales as a sport of real significance. I hope when Ian writes another book in 10 to 20 years time he has a stellar story to tell.

I hope all readers enjoy this book.

John Dixon

(Photo of John Dixon by Peter Lush)

Acknowledgements

Thanks to all the interviewees for giving their time out to speak to me, to Tony Rees and Gary Baker for their journalism tips, to Anthony Seibold for approving the Crusaders chapters, to Siân and Tony Couch for proofreading, to Peter Lush and Dave Farrar for agreeing to publish the book, to Ian Lovell, Peter Lush and Robert Gate for providing the photos, to the Rugby Football League for permission to reproduce programme covers, to Michael O'Hare for sub-editing and to the staff of MPG Biddles for printing the book.

Also, thanks to people like Mike Nicholas, Danny Sheehy, Wayne Williams and Leighton Samuel for making rugby league in Wales possible and last but not least to all fans who have stuck with Welsh Rugby League through thick and thin.

About the author

Ian Golden always liked sport from an early age and despite following Cardiff City Football Club from the 1980s, was never put off liking it. He first started watching rugby league from around 1989 when Jonathan Davies moved up to Widnes and can remember being a closet Widnes fan during that era. He has followed Wales Rugby League since its reintroduction in 1991 and has rarely missed a game, when his god-daughter Kirsty was being christened on the same day that Wales took on New Zealand in 1993, it was a debateable decision on which event to attend but on that occasion, the Vetch Field lost out! He started following Cardiff Demons from 2001 and started to write reports for them a year later. He was appointed press officer for the Welsh national side in 2003, a post he still holds, and was given the job as press officer for the Crusaders from their inception. Holder of a degree in journalism, Ian, for his sins, has also written for and edited a number of Cardiff City and Wales football fanzines. In his spare time, he also enjoys radio broadcasting for local community station GTFM as well as supporting the England cricket team where he was a founder member of the infamous Barmy Army in 1994. He is engaged to Siân Couch, who writes the Welsh language reports for Crusaders for both the club's website and Welsh language newspaper, *Y Cymro*.

Introduction:
Rugby League – The Welsh way, the way it was, the way it is

Rugby football, like no other sport, has always had two ways of expressing itself. Union was the so-called amateur sport and league was the paid version with no wing forwards, or flankers as they are known today. Almost 170 full Welsh internationals were induced to go north in the first 100 years of the professional game while countless other Welshmen gave up the chance of winning that priceless Welsh cap to seek fame and fortune among the mines of Lancashire and Yorkshire. Some succeeded and became legends in that other game of rugby while some found the going too tough, played out their contracts and returned home. A few simply took their money and ran (mostly home).

A rugby player in Wales was idolised and became public property, a nation's pride – others were idolised throughout the world. In our country we grew up wanting to wear the red jersey from birth and play at what was the old Arms Park, but to be left out of the team representing your country made the option easier to take the money. Although a certain amount of stigma was attached by officialdom in Wales to those who took the route north, Welsh rugby enthusiasts have continued to follow their progress with interest. Today, no longer are the players who are attracted to rugby league made to feel like social outcasts by the public and their former clubs, and are congratulated on their achievements in what is no longer just the 'Northern game'.

While money has always been and will always be the first consideration for players to change codes, the union code can now offer more and the player doesn't have to uproot his family to earn a living playing rugby. There is no doubt that players in the past sought the easy way out if they didn't see their chances of representing Wales in rugby union so the money and the route north was a good alternative.

When I'm asked by supporters which game I enjoyed more, I always find it difficult to give an answer without discussing the pros and cons. Despite my previous enjoyment of spending 10 glorious years at Salford, my first cap for Wales in rugby union and my six seasons and 200 plus games for Newport RFC will forever be my greatest achievements. But to play rugby league and be part of the culture will always stand out in my rugby career. To captain Wales and Great Britain in both union and league is something that I will always cherish. There is no doubt in my mind that the two games are as different as chalk and cheese, the similarities being that you score tries and kick drop-goals, conversions and penalties. I believe that it is more difficult for a player to go from league to union than it is from union to league. To ask a rugby league player to jump in a line-out or push in a scrum would be too much to ask! But then, would you ask a union player to tackle and distribute the ball and run as fast as a threequarter. Would they? Could they?

The Salford club when I joined in 1967 was a wonderful place, full of supporters who could discuss, criticise and assist with your game as they saw it from the terrace or the stand. Salford's average gate at the time was between 12,000 and 14,000 and they were rivalling Wigan, St Helens and Leeds. Now we have the chance to do this down here in Wales which I think is marvellous.

We've seen a lot of changes in the last 20 years. The Welsh national side was reintroduced in 1991 which saw many of the top stars playing league in Wales and becoming heroes once again and then, of course, in 1995 rugby union turned legitimately professional which made a massive difference.

There are now more opportunities to earn a living playing rugby with top sponsors coming in for the bigger clubs. What's more important now is that players have a choice. They learn to play both rugby union and rugby league in schools and when they are older, they can make a decision which sport to carry on playing. It's marvellous to see clubs like Newport Titans and Bridgend Blue Bulls playing rugby league throughout the summer – that gives many players the opportunity to give both sports a try. There's plenty of enthusiasm there and it's opened a few people's eyes.

In the old days you couldn't go into rugby league and come back, you were banished completely from any association with rugby union. You didn't even have to get paid, even if you competed in a trial game, you were out. Now I'm pleased that everything's changed. Now people don't have to worry about it, they're more inclined to see what they can do in either sport. I've watched some of the games at Newport Titans and they've been a very good quality of rugby league. It's been because of teams like them that we have Celtic Crusaders here today. We've tried the professional game in Wales a number of times, but only now do we not have the fear that someone is going to look over your shoulder and stop you playing the game of your choice.

The future of Welsh Rugby League depends entirely on the amount of support that the Crusaders can get and whether or not the players want to take the plunge and go and play. The Crusaders' average gate in their first season in Super League has between 3,000 and 4,000 and that's very good and it can only grow and I think that their change of location to Newport will only strengthen them. I think people now are more prepared to watch rugby league now than ever before especially with Super League making it more popular and attractive. I'm certainly proud to still be playing a role in rugby league today and I hope it continues to grow.

David Watkins

(Photo of David Watkins by Ian Lovell)

Wales Rugby League Timeline – Major Events 1989 to 2009

1989: Wales enter the Student World Cup for the first time and finish fifth out of eight. The original North Wales Coasters club is formed.
1990: Widnes play Wigan in the Charity Shield at the Vetch Field in Swansea in front of 11,178 fans.
1991: The Welsh national side makes its comeback after seven years in the wilderness beating Papua New Guinea 68–0. 11,442 were at Swansea to watch. Wales 'A' beat Moscow Spartak in the curtain raiser. Cardiff Institute College win the Student Championship for the first time. Wales Students beat England and Ireland to become the first British Student Champions.
1992: Wales play two matches against France and one against England. Wales Students reach the semi-finals of the World Cup in Australia.
1993: Wales take on the touring Kiwis in Swansea and are unlucky to lose 24-19.
1994: The RFL announce that Wales will compete in the 1995 World Cup, their first for 20 years. The touring Australians visit and beat Wales 46–4 at Ninian Park. Wales 'A' play their first full international, losing 14–10 to England.
1995: Wales win the European Championship after beating England and France, and reach the semi-finals of the World Cup. They also visit Philadelphia and play two matches against USA. Rugby union allows professionalism which leads to most of Wales's stars returning to the 15-man game.
1996: Wales enter the World Nines in Fiji and win the Bowl Final. Super League starts – an on the road match is played in Cardiff between Sheffield Eagles and St Helens. South Wales RLFC are formed and enter a side in Division Two finishing sixth but are wound up after one season. Wales beat France but lose to England in the European Championships. Wales Students win the Plate competition in the Student World Cup.
1997: Wales play no matches for the first time in seven years. Cardiff Demons, Wales longest running club, are formed and play matches in the RFL's Academy Leagues. North Wales Coasters disband.
1998: Super League 'on the road' matches are played in Cardiff and Swansea. Despite good attendances in both games, a Super League franchise is given to Gateshead as Wales is ignored. The Welsh side returns to take on England but lose 15–12. Cardiff Demons Academy reach the Division Two Grand Final but lose 39–30 to Hunslet Hawks.
1999: Wales lose to Scotland and Ireland in a Tri-Nations Tournament. Cardiff Cougars, an amalgamation of Cardiff Demons and UWIC, start a Challenge Cup run with an away win in Durham. Wales co-host the Student World Cup and finish seventh out of 12.

2000: Cardiff reach the third round of the Challenge Cup before losing 90–0 to Keighley Cougars. Super League is played in Newport for the first time with Warrington Wolves beating London Broncos 28–18. Wales reach the semi-finals of the World Cup again and give Australia a fright after leading at half-time. Rugby League is played at the Millennium Stadium for the first time.

2001: Wales take on England in Wrexham's first ever international. Cardiff Demons and North Wales Coasters enter the Rugby League Conference.

2002: The first ever 'A' Home Nations tournament is played with Wales beating Scotland, Ireland and England to take the title. Wales take on New Zealand at the Millennium Stadium.

2003: The Rugby League Challenge Cup Final is played at the Millennium Stadium for the first time. London Broncos beat Widnes Vikings 40–18 in a Super League in Aberavon. The Welsh Conference starts and Bridgend Blue Bulls are unbeaten throughout taking the Welsh and British titles. Wales 'A' retain the Home Nations Championships. The European Championships are reborn after a break of seven years. Wales also take on Australia at Bridgend's Brewery Field.

2004: Cardiff Demons win the National Rugby League Conference Shield competition. Wales 'A' win their third successive Home Nations title.

2005: Celtic Crusaders are formed to play National League Two in 2006. London Broncos play their third Super League game in Wales drawing 24–24 with Hull FC in Bridgend. Wales Students finish sixth out of eight in the Student World Cup. Brynteg High School of Bridgend win the British Year 7 Champions Schools Final. Bridgend Blue Bulls win the Welsh and British Rugby League Conference titles. Wales "A" win their fourth successive Home Nations title. The full Wales side reach the Final of the European Nations Cup but lose to France in Carcassonne.

2006: The Welsh Rugby League become self-governing for the first time and drop the three feathers for a dragon logo. Celtic Crusaders reach the Final Eliminator of the National League Two play-offs but lose by a golden point drop-goal to Swinton Lions. Wales 'A' lose their grip on the Home Nations with England winning the title.

2007: Millennium Magic is staged in Cardiff for the first of two years. Celtic Crusaders take on Brisbane Broncos in a friendly and later win National League Two. S4C show four of their matches live. Bridgend Blue Bulls win their fifth successive Welsh title. Wales 'A' regain their Home Nations title and also take on France for the first time at this level, winning 22–18. The Wales senior side fails to reach the World Cup Finals after losing to Lebanon in Widnes.

2008: Celtic Crusaders are awarded a Super League licence – they finish second in National League One and lose the Grand Final to Salford City Reds after extra time. Crusaders Colts, their second string side, win the Conference National. Valley Cougars from Nelson win the Welsh Conference breaking Bridgend's stronghold. Wales "A" win the Home Nations again. Wales under 18 win the European Championships. Wales Students reach the semi-finals of the World Cup. Seven Welsh players are selected for Great Britain under-18s.

2009: Celtic Crusaders play their first season of Super League while their under-18s win the National Youth League. Wales Students, Wales 'A' and Wales under-18s are all crowned as British Champions. Five Welsh players tour Australia with Great Britain under-18s, Mark Wool from Pontyclun is captain. Blackwood Bulldogs win the Welsh Conference.

Publisher's note: Celtic Crusaders RLFC have been supportive of this project. However, the views expressed in it are those of the author, and not necessarily of the club.

Contents

1. Early years   1
2. League returns   11
3. South Wales and Super League   31
4. The 2000 World Cup   45
5. Building a base   59
6. Rebuilding in Wales   79
7. 2005: Development and decisions   93
8. Launching Celtic Crusaders   109
9. Champions   125
10. 2008: Promotion   141
11. A Welsh rugby league structure   159
12. International disappointment   175
13. Into Super League   191
14. Super League wins and more   211

Appendices
1: Cardiff Demons by Simon Davies   234
2: Development in Wales by Anthony Seibold   240
3: Statistics and Records   245
Bibliography   260

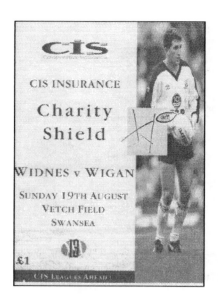
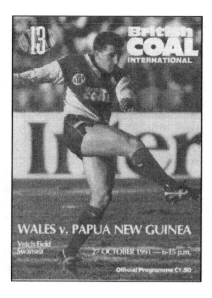

Programmes from three important matches in the 1990s
(Courtesy Rugby Football League)

1. Early years

Celtic Crusaders' historic 30–24 win at Odsal over the Bradford Bulls on 17 May 2009 was the first win by a Welsh club in an elite league in rugby league. The previous Welsh clubs had played either when the game had only one division for its professional sides, or in the Second Division in the 1980s.

Two tries from Luke Dyer clinched the win at one of rugby league's historic venues. But the game in Wales can trace its roots back over 100 years, when clubs in Merthyr Tydfil and Ebbw Vale joined the Northern Union...

*****

The formation of the Northern Union in 1895 was the culmination of almost 20 years of divisions within rugby football. The determination of the south of England establishment to keep control of the game and hold back its development in working class communities in the industrial north had seen suspensions of clubs and players for alleged breaches of the game's rules on professionalism. The RFU refused to accept the idea that players should have the right to claim 'broken time' payments to cover loss of Saturday morning earnings when travelling to play for their clubs. The leadership of the RFU was also determined to stop commercial development of the game, and opposed competitions such as the Yorkshire Cup, which attracted huge crowds, and the development of leagues in Lancashire and Yorkshire.

Similar breakaway factions occurred from RFU-aligned rugby unions in New Zealand and Australia in 1907 and 1908 respectively, and formed associations known as 'Rugby Football Leagues'. The Northern Union later changed its name to the Rugby Football League in 1922 and thus, over time the sport itself became known as rugby league.

Over the following decades, the rules of both codes of rugby were gradually changed, and now rugby league and rugby union are distinctly different sports.

In the Northern Union, the first minor rule change, awarding a penalty for a deliberate knock-on, was introduced in 1897. The line-out was also abolished and the value of all goals were reduced to two points. Nine years later, the number of players on each side was reduced from 15 to 13 while rucks and mauls after a tackle were replaced by the play-the-ball. All these rules were designed to make the game faster and more attractive to watch. This was important for the Northern Union clubs, who had to pay their players, maintain their grounds to accommodate large crowds, and fight off the rise of association football, which was competing for their supporters.

One reason that Northern Union rugby didn't take off immediately in Wales is that the English Rugby Football Union turned a blind eye to Welsh clubs paying their players (an act known as shamateurism) otherwise they knew that rugby union would be destroyed in working class Wales, which would put a huge dent in the international game.

At the time, the Welsh didn't care which organisation they played under because both games had the same rules, but it was obviously far easier to carry on playing against Welsh clubs and to pay their players. Had the RFU not turned a blind eye then it is likely that Wales would have turned to Northern Union. Had the RFU lost rugby in South Wales, and the south west of England, which had close links with the game in Wales, they would have been left controlling a rump primarily based around London.

A key incident was the Arthur Gould affair in 1897. The Welsh rugby international had a testimonial awarded to him in the previous year and was awarded the deeds to his house (but no actual money). The RFU declared Gould a professional and then banned all clubs and players from playing against him. Because of this, in February 1897 the Welsh Rugby Union withdrew from the Rugby Union International Board and was ready to join up with the Northern Union. But by August a compromise was reached as the RFU realised that their control of rugby was at stake. They continued to ignore the payments issue until top player Dai Jones publicly walked out on Aberdare to rejoin his native Treherbert because he wasn't getting enough money. Half of the Aberdare committee were banned and formed the Merthyr and later Aberdare Northern Union clubs.

These clubs were just two of six that were formed in the early part of the 20th century in South Wales. The edition of the *Merthyr Express* dated 7 September 1907 was an historic one advertising not only Merthyr's first ever match against Oldham but also previewing Ebbw Vale's trip to Keighley. There was even a paragraph talking about the "All Black professional movement" that was "being formed in Sydney

OLDHAM F. C.
Official Programme.

OLDHAM v. EBBW VALE
AT
WATERSHEDDINGS, OLDHAM.
Saturday, October 1st, 1910.

by Mr Albert Baskiville, the honorary secretary of the New Zealand Football Club". These events would also have great significance for professional rugby in Wales and the international game as a whole.

Neither Welsh club was given much of a chance of winning their first match. Ebbw Vale's Keighley adventure wasn't glamorous either because they had to make a 12-hour overnight journey on the 10pm Friday night train to Yorkshire in order to play on Saturday afternoon.

The *Merthyr Express* dated 14 September said that the team had "an enthusiastic send-off" and that "the GWR station was packed with supporters and well-wishers of the little pioneer band". The local council was in full support of the venture with Councillor Cameron giving a speech on the railway station congratulating the system of open payment of players that had been adopted in preference to the veiled payment of the so-called amateurs.

Ebbw Vale couldn't defy the odds and lost 26–3. Their solitary try scorer that day was William Evans, the club secretary whose idea it was to switch "in the face of bogus amateurism in the Monmouthshire [rugby union] League".

Back in South Wales, Merthyr didn't fare much better in their home match against Oldham, losing 25–6 with the visitors running in seven tries. However, the professional venture was a complete success. The *Merthyr Express* ran a match advertisement on 7 September and a week later reported that "the takings amounted to over £150, and after the match the Merthyr men were paid over the table."

Professional rugby in Wales ran for just a handful of years at this point. The Merthyr club disbanded in January 1911 due to constant financial losses and a reported lack of assistance from the Northern

3

Union while Ebbw Vale lasted until the end of the 1911–12 season before going out of business.

Clubs from Aberdare, Barry, Treherbert and Mid-Rhondda all switched to Northern Union in 1908 but none of them lasted more than two seasons for the same reason as the initial two clubs and soon collapsed, with the exception of Mid-Rhondda, who turned their efforts to professional association football.

Other club attempts in Wales during the first 100 years of rugby league were few and far between. There was a team in Pontypridd, a different organisation to the rugby union club, who played from 1926 to 1927 at Taff Vale Park. Launched in the aftermath of the General Strike, and with the miners involved in industrial action, it is hard to think of a worse time to launch a new club. This side was even complemented by an amateur league that played until 1930. Glamorgan and Monmouthshire competed in the County Championship from 1927 to 1931.

In 1951–52, following a successful stint in the new Welsh League, Cardiff was elected to the Rugby Football League. However, after one disastrous season with low attendances, the club withdrew from the League.

The final team to have a go at the professional game before 1995 was the Cardiff City Blue Dragons, a club run by the same owners as the famous football club and also playing at Ninian Park. They ran for four full seasons, from 1981 to 1985, and this was probably the most ambitious and successful out of all the attempts to bring professional club rugby into Wales. While the other clubs had generally failed due to lack of finances, lack of support from the governing body and travel hardships, Cardiff City had none of these problems. Their difficulty was keeping their attendances when the results started to go awry. The team needed to win promotion so that the game's top sides would have come to play in Cardiff. The knowledgeable Welsh public, used to watching the top players, has never found second division rugby league fare an attraction. After City chairman Bob Grogan died the other directors pulled the plug. For their final season the team moved to Bridgend, and struggled to field a competitive side.

The Blue Dragons were co-founded by former Wales and Great Britain dual-code international David Watkins, a man who scored a club record 2,907 points for Salford, which included 1,241 goals in

4

more than 450 games over 13 years. Watkins joined Salford from Newport in 1967 for £15,000, then a club record. He toured Australia and New Zealand with the rugby union Lions in 1966, with rugby league's Lions in 1974, went to Australia with Wales for the 1975 World Cup and was then player-coach and captain of Great Britain on the 1977 tour of Australia. His credentials were beyond repute.

Watkins and his colleagues then went on a recruitment mission to sign up some of Wales' best rugby union talent. These players included Tommy David, Steve Fenwick, Paul Ringer and Brynmor Williams, a man who was later to commentate on Celtic Crusaders rugby league games for television channel S4C.

Williams remembers his time at the Blue Dragons: "When I played for Cardiff City Blue Dragons in the 1980s, we attracted [good crowds] to the first few games," he says. "However we lost a lot of games so we lost the crowds which was just one area where the club failed. You have to be doing well to attract people on a regular basis. If you can, rugby league will flourish in Wales."

Williams, who is now a group director with Thomas-Carroll Insurance Brokers, played rugby union for Cardiff, Swansea, Newport and the Barbarians. He won three Welsh and three Lions caps before signing for the Blue Dragons in 1982.

"I was very friendly with some of their players – David Watkins, Tommy David and Paul Ringer," says Williams. "I was attracted to what they were doing and I've always liked watching rugby league. It's highly entertaining and I thought, at 31 years old, I'd like to have a go at playing it before it was too late. David kindly came in with an offer and I thought it was right for me and I don't regret it.

"I played at scrum-half and I found the game quite difficult at first. I did one of those 'rolling touch-finders' in my first game. I picked up the ball from the scrum and kicked it long into touch. I had a few funny looks from the boys because I'd just lost us possession before the first tackle. I soon learned my lesson though and things like that soon disappeared. Once I'd got a few games under my belt I was fine and able to act with my rugby league hat on.

"I was lucky enough to win one rugby league cap for Wales, and play against Australia in 1982, who on that tour were one of the greatest ever rugby sides, league or union, of all time. I scored a try which was a little icing on the cake for me although we were hammered. However, it was a great experience and I was proud to play rugby league for my country and nobody can ever take that away from me."

Internationally, Wales were the first side to ever host an international match under Northern Union rules when, on New Year's Day 1908, Wales beat New Zealand 9–8 in Aberdare in the heart of the Welsh valleys on a ground which is now a training pitch to many of the current Welsh international rugby league sides at different age groups. Both Wales and New Zealand had a lot in common 100 years ago. The game of rugby was the national sport in both countries, and both had caused controversy by inviting players to legitimately turn professional and play this new version of the game.

New Zealand were also newcomers to the professional game but no matches were played in their country until July 1908, a month after the tourists arrived back home. The tour was inspired by the 1905 union All Blacks who dominated and impressed on a European tour. In Wales however, they came a cropper as they lost 3–0 in front of 47,000 at Cardiff Arms Park after New Zealand controversially had a try disallowed. Wales had succeeded where the other home nations had failed and were unofficial champions of the rugby union world at the time. However there was unrest in the visitors' camp. The players had witnessed the Northern Union game and had seen that there was money to be made by playing rugby. Nine New Zealand rugby union internationals were selected for the 1907–08 Northern Union tour, four of whom had toured in 1905.

Wales versus New Zealand was game 29 in a gruelling 49-match, 10 month tour for the professional All Blacks, who were famously nicknamed the 'All Golds' by their local press due to their acceptance of money for playing rugby. The tourists had visited Wales two months earlier and defeated Merthyr Tydfil 27–9 in front of what was reported to be the largest crowd to have witnessed a rugby match in the town.

For the historic international on that New Years Day, reports of the crowd ranged from 12,000 to 20,000, but one thing was certain – it was large. Despite the obvious prejudices and backlashes from Welsh Rugby Union quarters, the game had taken off in the heads of the Welsh valleys with many enjoying the new version of the sport and seemingly pleased that players could legitimately earn a crust from playing rugby. The fact that many people from the valleys remembered the Welsh Rugby Union's historic defeat of the amateur All Blacks under three years earlier would have also helped to boost the gate.

It was a hard-fought game for the Welsh in freezing conditions at the Athletic Ground in Aberdare, as they scraped home 9–8 after being 8–3 down at half-time. Dai Jones (one of six Dais in the Welsh team) scored the winning try for the Welsh just minutes before the end to put them a point in front.

The local press loved the spectacle. Reporters from the *Rhondda Leader*, *South Wales Echo* and *Western Mail* were all present with the *Western Mail* calling the match "a red-letter day in the history of Welsh sport" and also adding that the spectators were "quite thrilled... when they saw the scarlet-clad warriors attacking in the old sweet way."

New Zealand returned to Wales exactly a month later to beat Ebbw Vale 3–2 before going on to win a test series against the Northern Union (England) by two games to one. Wales went on to beat England 35–18 on 20 April 1908 in Tonypandy while another of Wales's biggest achievement in the early years was beating Australia 14–13 in Merthyr on 16 January 1909 with a team made up of entirely Welsh-based players. A month later, the Merthyr club followed that up by beating the Australians 15–13.

The centenary of the first ever international was chosen not to be celebrated by the Rugby Football League in 2007 when the New Zealand touring side came to these shores and Wales Rugby League's executive chairman Mark Rowley was understandably a little disgruntled: "I approached the RFL to see if we could play the centenary game in Wales," Rowley said. "But they wanted to play it in Warrington and we had to abide by that decision. It's a shame though as Wales against New Zealand was the first ever international match anywhere in the world. We faced them and beat them before they played and beat England twice later in the year. At that time the Welsh rugby union and league sides were the best in the world. Celtic Crusaders celebrated the centenary of club rugby league when they played Oldham and Keighley in league matches last year, it's just a shame that the national side didn't have the chance do the same against New Zealand."

Wales carried on playing on a regular basis with some success. The regular flow of players from South Wales to play rugby league in the north usually gave them a good base for a team, even at times when rugby league was hardly played in the country itself. From 1908 to 1984 they played 118 matches, 58 of them against England, 30 against France, 10 against Australia, six against New Zealand, five against the Other Nationalities side and single games against a Northern RL XIII in 1937, an Empire XIII in 1951 and France B in 1955. Wales also played six matches against club sides on a tour of Australia and New Zealand in 1975.

Wales won 36 of these matches and drew twice (both against England) and on the way won a hat-trick of European Championships in 1935–36, 1936–37 and 1937–38. However Wales's biggest year for rugby league before the 1990s was 1975 when the team, revived after a gap of five years, played in a year-long World Championship with home and away matches against England, France, Australia and New Zealand. In total, Wales played 16 matches that year and included legends such as David Watkins, Eddie Cunningham, Jim Mills and Clive Sullivan in the side.

Sullivan, who is mentioned in the same breath as other immortals like Billy Boston, Jim Sullivan, Gus Risman, Lewis Jones and Trevor Foster, is the only Welshman to have ever captained a World Cup winning side in any football code, with the exception of truncated versions of a game, (and with respect to all of Wales's sportsmen and women, this doesn't look like it's going to change anytime soon) when he led Great Britain to Rugby League World Cup success in 1972.

Clive is a rugby league legend. Cardiff-born (in Splott to be exact), he signed for Hull FC as an 18-year-old in 1961 and later did the unthinkable by transferring to Hull Kingston Rovers. In 1972 he was appointed captain of Great Britain and scored a try in all four of their World Cup games that year, the most famous being a length-of-the-field run against Australia in the Final. With Wales he won 15 caps between 1968 and 1979. In his 17 Great Britain appearances he scored 13 tries and captained the side on nine occasions. In all games, club and international, he scored 406 tries in 639 appearances, a record bettered by only two other Welshmen and only half-a-dozen players of any nationality. He will always rank as one of the greatest finishers in rugby league and was awarded the MBE for services to rugby league. When Sullivan died in 1985 aged just 42, the city of Hull held him in such high regard that the main road to the Humber Bridge was named Clive Sullivan Way.

When Wales played in the Australian leg of the World Cup in 1975, Clive led Wales in four of the matches, scoring a try in the 12–7 defeat of England in Brisbane. That result meant a third-placed finish for Wales and ultimately denied England a World Cup win.

Welsh captain for all eight of their World Cup matches was David Watkins. "We had a very good team in 1975," Watkins says. "And while the tournament was a little elongated being played over a whole year, it was a great experience to play in a World Cup for Wales, which is something that no set of Welsh rugby players had ever done before. While we didn't win the tournament we certainly made our presence known with a number of good performances, including wins over England, France and New Zealand."

Following a mammoth 1975, no Welsh international matches were played the following year. Wales won games against England and France in 1977 and 1978 respectively, but their 29–7 victory against the French in Widnes would be their last win for almost 14 years. Wales played 11 more games from 1978 to 1984, losing them all, before the national side was wound up at the same time as the Blue Dragons.

Wales bowed out of the international game on 14 October 1984 with a 28–9 defeat against England in Ebbw Vale in front of just 2,111 fans, the lowest crowd to ever watch a Wales game at this point in time. The national side wouldn't return until 1991 but when it – and professional rugby league – did return to Wales, it created shockwaves around the nation.

Wales versus England 10 April 1935 at Liverpool. Standing: Lewthwaite,
Mountain, Griffiths, Orchard, G. Davies, Day, Edwards, Pugh, I. Davies, Rees,
Talbot; front: Watkins, Jenkins, Scourfield. (Courtesy Robert Gate)

Wales versus England 16 September 1953 at St Helens. Standing: Daniels,
Parsons, Winslade, Gwyther, Phillips, Bevan, Goldswain; front: The trainer,
Williams, Price, Evans, Gullick, Banks, Harris. (Courtesy Robert Gate)

2. League returns

Professional rugby league finally came back to Wales in August 1990 when Widnes faced Wigan in the Charity Shield at the Vetch Field, the then home of Swansea City Football Club.

The Charity Shield was an excellent idea, albeit a complete replication of football's version, pitting the league champions against the Challenge Cup winners. However, unlike the more successful round-ball equivalent, it was short-lived running from 1985 until 1992 and making a comeback in 1995 before being scrapped at the advent of Super League.

It was about this time that I'd started to take an interest in rugby league. I'd known of the Blue Dragons six or seven years before, but had no knowledge at all about the differences between the league and union games. I had been taken to a union match on 26 December 1981. Cardiff faced Pontypridd and won 20–0 and for me the most memorable part of the match was the Double Decker chocolate bar that I ate at half-time.

As a 10 year old, the whole matchday experience didn't enthuse me and I didn't go back. I read about the Blue Dragons in the *South Wales Echo* and how they moved to Bridgend. Imagine my surprise then when I realised there was a still a rugby [union] team in Cardiff. It was a confusing time, especially when I asked my sports teacher at Cowbridge Comprehensive School what the difference was between rugby union and rugby league.

"Well what game do we play?" was his answer.

"Rugby union?" I questioned.

"That's all you need to know," he replied, and the conversation was closed.

As this games teacher's son now plays rugby union for Cardiff Blues and Wales, one can understand why his remarks were so negative about the 13-a-side game.

For a while I forgot about rugby league. I wasn't a rugby union fan either, football was my game and very loosely at that, having being a Cardiff City supporter during the terrible 1980s. I knew about the best moments in rugby union. I celebrated with the rest of them when Wales achieved third place in the inaugural Rugby World Cup (sic) in 1987. I once marvelled at a long-range penalty in the Five Nations that

I believe was kicked by Gavin Hastings. And most importantly of all, I knew of Jonathan Davies.

Born on Wednesday 24 October 1962 in Trimsaran, Carmarthenshire, Davies initially played for Neath RFC and after just 35 games for the club, he was selected to play for Wales in 1985 at home to England. Aged 22, he scored a try and a drop-goal and was named man-of-the-match in a 24-15 victory.

He eventually moved to Llanelli, who had previously rejected him, and played an important part in Wales's 1988 Triple Crown (which very nearly became a Grand Slam) success in 1988.

However, the rest of the year would be failure for Davies and Wales. The problems in the Welsh game were cruelly exposed on the 1988 tour to New Zealand. Davies captained the side in four games on tour and stood out as the class player. Wales lost 52–2 and 54–9 although Davies did scored a 90 metre try in the latter game. Wales scraped a win in Western Samoa before losing 15–9 to Romania in Cardiff. Davies was blamed by the media for this defeat as the journalists conveniently forgot his heroics in the Five Nations just half a year earlier, when Wales were just a point away from a Grand Slam. A big money offer, reputedly £225,000 came from Widnes, Davies was happy to accept and one of Wales's greatest rugby sons went north.

Allan Bateman, who signed for Warrington from Neath explained the whole situation in his autobiography, *There and Back Again*: "The tour to New Zealand in 1988 led to the coaches being sacked and players leaving for rugby league: Adrian Hadley joined Salford; John Devereux and Paul Moriarty signed for Widnes, soon to be followed by Jonathan Davies; Rowland Phillips went to Warrington and David Young was tempted by Leeds after being unable to find a job in Wales. Other internationals joined them: Jonathan Griffiths, Mark Jones, David Bishop and I left, and Terry Holmes, Stuart Evans, Roy Ackerman and Gary Pearce had followed the path north in the middle of the 1980s. Players were driven by the money factor but not exclusively. There was a concern that the game in Wales was decaying and that unrealistic demands were being placed on players."

One player that decided not to sign a rugby league contract was Neil Jenkins. The fly-half played 87 times for the Welsh union side scoring a record 1,049 points, but things may have been a lot different had he signed for Warrington after having a trial in 1993.

It was Allan Bateman that spotted Jenkins turning out for Warrington's reserves: "He scored two tries and landed goals from everywhere," Bateman said. "There was a crowd of more than 1,000 there at Wilderspool, but the secret never came out. Had it done then the history of Welsh rugby would have been vastly different." If Jenkins's trial with Warrington had become public knowledge, he would have been banned from rugby union for playing with rugby league professional players under union's rules at that time about amateurism.

So in August 1990 Davies was coming back to Wales, but with Widnes. It was Davies's move that ignited my interest in rugby league and I first had the chance of seeing him and Widnes in action when BBC1's *Sportsnight* showed highlights of Widnes' 30-18 win over Canberra Raiders in the World Club Challenge on Wednesday 4 October 1989. Davies scored a try, kicked three goals and was almost decapitated by Laurie Daley in a challenge that earned the Australian 10 minutes in the sin bin. I was hooked and, after buying the official BBC Video of the match, I was delighted to hear that Widnes, with Davies, Devereux and Moriarty in tow, would be facing Wigan just 30 miles from my house.

And what a day that was for the Welsh. The game wasn't a classic, but the script was. Davies scored three tries and a goal as Widnes, Premiership winners in 1990, retained the Charity Shield for the third year in succession. Looking back, one can hypothesise that it was this game, and Widnes's performance that re-introduced the game of rugby league back to Wales. It's ironic that it was Widnes who were one of the clubs who were refused a Super League place in 2008 thanks to the success of Welsh club Celtic Crusaders.

Davies had a marvellous game at the Vetch Field that day and could have had a couple more points, but twice hit the post when going for a drop-goal. All three tries were classics – skipper Tony Myler set up the first for him as he used Martin Offiah as a decoy to score in the corner. The second, after 52 minutes, was when he picked up a Shaun Edwards grubber kick to run 80 metres to the line, while his hat-trick was achieved by bursting through the slack Wigan defence from 30 metres. Bridgend-born Devereux scored a try after being set up by Andy Currier.

The day was a great success and Davies, who was used in all the pre-match publicity in South Wales, was once again a hero just a couple of years after supposedly walking out on his country.

Better was to come for the Welsh. The success of this game, played in front of 11,178 spectators, most of whom were from Wales, coupled with a number of Welsh players turning professional, meant that a Welsh international rugby league side was to be formed for the first time in seven years.

The touring Papua New Guinea side was the perfect first opposition for Wales, who hadn't had much to shout about in any form of rugby for a couple of years. The Papuans, nicknamed The Kumuls after a bird native to their country, were embarking on only their third ever tour of Great Britain. They had only ever played two full international test matches, so this was a team that Wales should have been able to beat to boost the morale of rugby league in the area even more.

Win they did, and win handsomely. The match, played on 27 October 1991, was shown live on Sky Sports, the fledgling channel's first ever international rugby league match and, despite the loss of sound for about 10 minutes during the second half, the transmission from Swansea was a great success. As the dulcet tones of *We'll keep a welcome in the hillside* played over montages of Davies and his colleagues, there was no doubt that this was going to be a match, and a broadcast, to remember.

"It's great for the boys to come home and represent their country in whatever code it is," Davies told Sky Sports. "We're still Welshmen at heart, it'll be a fantastic buzz for us and I hope that all the public get behind us."

In Swansea's 15th international match, but the first at the Vetch Field, Wales, coached by Clive Griffiths and managed by Jim Mills, ran riot scoring 13 tries to record their highest ever score at the time. I originally had a ticket for the terrace behind the goal, but eventually ended up in the centre of the rickety old grandstand using a ticket given to me by referee Bill Harrigan. The Australian was lost and couldn't find the official players' entrance which is unsurprising as it was located in an alleyway in the middle of a block of terraced housing. He had a ticket spare and I was the lucky recipient.

Wales were 46–0 up at the interval and had already beaten their previous record win, 41–7 over France in Llanelli in 1935. The large

14

crowd of 11,442 saw Wales take just two minutes to open the scoring from a Davies penalty. Jonathan ended up with a record 24 points from his two tries and eight goals, Phil Ford was a hat-trick hero and the official man-of-the-match, but it was the emotional Dai Bishop whom Sky Sports named as their star man.

'Bish', now a pundit with Real Radio in Wales, was a scrum-half in union, making his first-class debut for Pontypool in 1981, but soon after that, he broke his neck. Despite being told he would never play again, he was back for Pontypool within a year and won his only cap for the Welsh union side against Australia in 1984, scoring Wales's only try as they went down 28–9.

Constantly rejected by the Welsh rugby union side, Bishop was lured to Hull Kingston Rovers in 1989. After wiping away the tears during the national anthem in Swansea that Sunday night, he scored a second-half try after a gap was opened for him by Phil Ford, and he ran 30 metres to the line.

"It was a fabulous night," he said in the post-match interview. "Everybody did so well and I'm proud to be a Welshman... With our performance tonight, we've showed that we have the strength to go on from here. There's a great camaraderie in the squad and we want to carry on from here and face the best."

Wales did carry on and played France at the same venue on 22 March 1992. The French had just suffered a double defeat to Great Britain, so were at a low ebb. Devereux, who had played for Great Britain in both of those matches, was first on the board for Wales after only four minutes but, unlike the Kumuls before them, France were not overwhelmed and Wales were made to work for their 35–6 win.

John Devereux, Allan Bateman, Barry Williams, Phil Ford, Rowland Phillips and Jonathan Davies were the try scorers with Davies kicking five goals and a drop-goal, but it was the future Cardiff Blues boss Dai Young who was man-of-the-match.

Young had been snapped up by Leeds from Cardiff RUFC in 1990, spending a year there before going to Salford for a further five seasons. "The France game wasn't as easy as against Papua New Guinea," he commented. "And whether we took it a bit lightly or not, I don't know. It wasn't one of our better performances but we came through it. We were far too strong for PNG and perhaps taking on

France next gave us the kick in the backside that we needed and we went onto bigger and better things after that.

"It was just great to come back and play for Wales. When we went to rugby league, one of the most difficult decisions was that we would never play for Wales again as there wasn't a Welsh Rugby League side at that time so when the side was formed for the PNG game, everyone was really excited about it especially as a lot of us had played rugby union together in the past. We had a good time off the field, were very competitive on it and we all looked forward to playing internationals every year."

Wales's reward for their two wins was a home test against England, their first in eight years, on 27 November 1992 on a freezing cold night in Swansea after a day of pouring rain. The slippery surface made it a tough encounter for both sides. Wales went into the game missing Jonathan Davies who was recovering from a groin operation, and his lack of inspiration was noticeable. In addition, Cardiff-born Gerald Cordle was taken off with a fractured jaw soon after kick off.

After Lee Crooks got England off the mark with a penalty, they were to strike a double whammy with the crafty scrum-half Mike Ford instigating tries for Ellery Hanley, one of only two survivors from the last time that England faced Wales, and Stuart Spruce. With 15 minutes gone Wales were 12–0 down.

Allan Bateman sparked the fightback with a thumping tackle on Spruce which saw the England full-back spill the ball with Jonathan Griffiths on hand to take maximum advantage. Massive Hull prop Mark Jones crashed past four or five England players to score in the left corner and Kevin Ellis added a quick drop-goal to bring Wales back to 12–11. However, they were the last points that Wales would score in the game, because they went down 36–11 with Martin Offiah grabbing two of the English tries.

The next game for Wales was a match in France on 13 December which was a thriller. However, lack of television coverage meant that no one in Wales was able to see it. Wales won 19–18.

Wales built an impressive 19–4 lead with eight minutes of the first half left with Allan Bateman, Rob Ackerman and John Devereux scoring tries. Gary Pearce converted them all and then crucially added a drop-goal in the 32nd minute. Future French coach Gilles Dumas inspired the fightback, scoring a try just before the interval and setting up two more. However, Wales maintained their commitment and composure to survive the final minutes of the game.

Wales had to wait 10 months for their next fixture but a game against the touring New Zealand side was worth the wait. New Zealand arrived in Wales with a shaky recent record. They'd won one and lost one against Great Britain on the Lions tour in 1992 and had lost two and drawn one in the three-test series against Australia in June.

Now on 3 October 1993, they arrived in Wales as favourites but struggled for their 24–19 win. The match, as with all Wales's home matches at this time, was covered by Sky Sports in their usual Sunday evening slot, but for some strange reason the game was played at the Vetch Field was played in the afternoon and then broadcast "as live" a couple of hours later.

A disallowed try in the dying minutes was all that stopped Wales from pulling off a win. Wales went over for just two tries, both from Gerald Cordle. Jonathan Davies added five goals and Jonathan Griffiths, in the unfamiliar loose-forward role, kicked a drop-goal.

With just 11 minutes remaining, John Devereux took advantage of a hoisted bomb to send Wales into raptures with what they thought was the winning try. Agonisingly it was ruled out for offside. Devereux remembers the incident well: "It was an up-and-under [towards] their sticks which I caught and scored," he said. "I felt the ruling was a little harsh as it was Adrian Hadley that was offside and not myself. The decision was a very tight one and in all of our opinions it was what definitely turned the game.

"The defeat was disappointing as we'd acquitted ourselves so well. New Zealand were close to being the second best international side in the world at the time and we really proved we could hold our own against them. Clive Griffiths always goes on about that try saying if only it had been allowed then we may have beaten them."

But Wales had done enough to justify their inclusion in the 1995 World Cup, their first appearance in such an event for 20 years. On 24 January 1994, the Rugby Football League announced that England and Wales would compete separately in the tournament. And rightly so in my opinion. The other teams were to be Australia, New Zealand, France, Papua New Guinea, South Africa, Western Samoa, Fiji and Tonga.

17

Wales celebrated their inclusion with a restrained performance at Cardiff City's Ninian Park as they scraped home 13–12 against France on 4 March 1994. France looked like they were going to win the game, they were the better side throughout much of the match. Tries from Patrick Entat and Jean-Marc Garcia gave them a 12–7 lead as the game went into injury time.

Then came the only major piece of excitement in the 80 minutes. Wales were given a penalty just 10 metres from the line and following a quick tap, debutant Richard Webster, who had been on the field for fewer than five minutes, stormed past four Frenchmen to touch down and put Wales just a point behind with the kick to come. Ninian Park was silent as Jonathan Davies stepped up for the conversion, and what turned out to be the last kick of the game was the most crucial.

After taking on New Zealand the year before, Australia were visitors to Wales in 1994. While the Dragons had given the Kiwis a good game, the same couldn't be said when they met the Kangaroos. Yet again on 30 October, a wet day dawned at Ninian Park for a Welsh international match.

The game, that marked Iestyn Harris's international debut after Jonathan Davies failed a fitness test, was over by half-time as Australia racked up a 30–0 lead. It was disappointing not to see Davies in action after he had starred for Great Britain at Wembley the week before, scoring one of the tries of the century as Great Britain celebrated an 8–4 win. This was especially satisfying as Australia had a man advantage after skipper Shaun Edwards was sent off in the 25th minute for a tackle on Bradley Clyde that prevented what should have been the first try of the game. Allan Bateman, who also played at Wembley, failed a fitness test too, leaving Wales devoid of their two best players.

Although this game was only a week after the Wembley encounter, Australia had already played Sheffield Eagles who had felt the backlash of the smarting Kangaroos as they went down 80–2 at the Don Valley Stadium.

If anything, Australia looked a little tired in the second half, which wasn't surprising given the amount of travelling and their hectic match schedule. Daio Powell went over for Wales's only try, but the score finished 46–4. Iestyn Harris remembers his debut well. "It was daunting," he said. "I didn't expect to get the opportunity at that time and I'm grateful to Clive Griffiths for giving it to me. It was a tough old game facing the all conquering Kangaroos but we gave a good account of ourselves. The score didn't reflect the game in that instance but for my first international I really enjoyed it and it set me on the start of a journey that I had for my career."

However, the best was yet to come for Wales as they went into 1995 with the reintroduced European Championship and World Cup waiting for them as well as a two-match tour to the USA – 1995 was to be a memorable year in many ways. This was not just because of the many internationals that Wales would be playing but the fact that the rugby league world was about to change drastically.

The action started on 1 February when Wales hosted England at Ninian Park. England were hot favourites for the game and fielded stars such as Jason Robinson and Anthony Farrell, the latter eventually seeing the light in 2000 and pledging his allegiance instead to Wales.

Sneaking the game 18–16 thanks to a couple of late Jonathan Davies drop-goals, the Welsh fans had been waiting for this win for a long time following the disappointment of the loss in Swansea a few years earlier. The last time that Wales had beaten England was back in 1977 and no players, not even Phil Ford, had survived from that team.

The forwards that night were simply outstanding, and the English were well and truly beaten up front. But the individual performance of the match came from Kevin Ellis who scored two tries. The half-back had discovered a new lease of life at Workington Town where he had been loaned out from Warrington, and continued his outstanding club form with a non-stop effort. He led the Welsh backs around the park and proved too much for the England defence to handle.

Ellis was spotted by Warrington in 1990 after a scout from the Cheshire club had watched him play for Bridgend against Neath in the Welsh RU Challenge Cup Final. Despite a defeat for the Ravens that day, Ellis, who always been overlooked by the full Wales union side and had even been left out of the 'A' side for their forthcoming tour to Namibia, had impressed and signed a five-year contract.

After a number of excellent performances in a Welsh shirt, one can only question why he was ever left out of the Welsh union side especially considering their poor record at the time. But union's loss was league's gain and the half-back missed just two games in his tenure for the Dragons.

Ellis recalls his magnificent five years in a Welsh jersey: "I was over the moon to get selected for Wales, especially with the team that we were able to field at the time, people like John Devereux, Jonathan Davies, Paul Moriarty and the like. It's a real shame that we don't have them now but hopefully in a few years' time we'll have some new stars coming through.

"The England game was on a wet night and we had a good team out. I remember it being a very physical game and I was lucky enough to be on the end of a few inside balls to score a couple of tries. I think one was from Allan Bateman and Scott Gibbs was the other. To be on the winning side against England is fantastic and I really enjoyed the occasion. The atmosphere was immense, it was draining because it was such a physical game but there was such a good crowd who were making a lot of noise. They were over the moon and were a great help to us."

Dai Young also has fond memories of 1995: "Beating England was a big marker for us," he said. "Being converts to the game and always being surrounded by the English, it was great to put one over on them and it showed that we were a force to be reckoned with."

Wales's win meant that they were just a game away from being European Champions. England beat France 19–16 two weeks after their defeat in Cardiff meaning that the title was still anyone's game as the French hosted the final match on 5 March. Like the situation a couple of years back, Sky Sports once again did not show the game live despite there being cameras at the ground in Carcassonne.

The game was played in sticky conditions throughout and Wales struggled in the first half, going into the break on the wrong side of a 10–8 scoreline, Iestyn Harris scoring his first ever international try and Allan Bateman adding another. Jonathan Davies had missed both conversions in the first half and his in-play kicking was strangely unthreatening. He took the field after the break determined to run the ball more and a trademark dash of speed saw the defence disappear in his wake – Paul Atcheson was the support player on hand to finish the move and restore a lead Wales were never to surrender.

Wales had achieved their first goal for 1995. Importantly, the rugby league team had restored national pride, bringing a trophy back to take some of the pain away from the union side's wooden spoon in the Five Nations.

Following the European Championship, Wales planned a tour of Australia to gear up to the World Cup, but other events meant that this had to be cancelled.

Sport was rapidly becoming more reliant on money and television rights. The media world was changing from around the late 1980s, but this especially accelerated in the 1990s. Media magnate Rupert Murdoch's News Limited company launched Sky TV in February 1989 and Foxtel in Australia in January 1995 and with these networks came extensive sports coverage and more money for the sports teams who were involved. At the time, Sky didn't have any real competition for sport after the company merger with British Satellite Broadcasting in 1990 to form BSkyB, but in Australia, there were a host of other media competitors attempting to rival Foxtel such as television mogul Kerry Packer's Network Nine, Telstra, Optus, ABC, Channel Seven and Channel Ten.

BSkyB had become the big players in British television sport. They had just paid £304 million for a five-year deal to cover Premier League football from 1992. This came just after they sold 100,000 dishes on the back of their exclusive coverage of that year's Cricket World Cup. They were broadcasting the Premier League and rugby union in the winter. All they really had in the summer was cricket. Moving rugby league to summer seemed to be the perfect solution for them and would make viewing conditions better for the fans who attended matches. When this change, combined with huge funding for the game, was first announced by the Rugby Football League and BSkyB on 4 April 1995, it caused a lot of controversy. Rugby league, as the fans knew it, was changing. Initially there were plans to merge existing clubs in England to form super clubs for the new Super League and this was voted for by the professional clubs. Leeds's chief executive Alf Davies accused the RFL of holding a gun to the heads of clubs to force through the changes while the Australian Rugby League chairman, Ken Arthurson, accused his British counterpart Maurice Lindsay of betrayal and said that Super League would mean the end of the traditional Lions and Kangaroo tours. This was because the organisers of Super League planned to align the British and Australian seasons, with a play-off to decide the world champions at the end of the season, leaving no separate off-season to allow for the traditional type of tour.

On 21 April, it was announced that Great Britain would make a shortened tour to Australia and New Zealand in October 1996 to replace the proposed standard tour that would now not take place in June and July of that same year. This tour didn't go ahead in that form, nor did the club mergers, but the clubs still got their payments from BSkyB, which was to be £87 million shared out between the existing 32 clubs, although the clubs in Super League took the bulk of it, and two new ones over five years.

The same events were happening in Australia as Murdoch attempted to launch a Super League competition there. Mergers and cuts were proposed causing clubs and fans to be up in arms. Two high profile Welsh players were caught up in this with the Australian Rugby League offering Iestyn Harris £70,000 to sign for their competition in opposition to Rupert Murdoch's proposed Super League and declare himself ineligible for Wales or Great Britain who were aligned to their rivals. Fortunately, Super League was able to offer him a vastly improved contract which kept him with Warrington and Wales. Jonathan Davies, however, did sign a deal with the ARL set to run from the end of his Warrington contract in 1997. He declared in August that the World Cup would be his international swansong and he would play only club rugby league for the remainder of his career.

Rugby union knew that it had to do something for the code to survive at the top level because they realised that they were going to lose players both in Great Britain and down under. For 100 years, union had been strictly amateur, at least on the surface anyway. Now with football, cricket and rugby league becoming bigger and the players more highly paid all around the world, on 26 August 1995, following the success of the World Cup in South Africa, rugby union's international board declared that their game should be 'open' game thus removing all restrictions on payments or benefits to anyone in the game.

This decision had a big effect on the immediate future of rugby league in Wales. While in the last 10 years, many players had moved from rugby union to league to make a living, after this they could move back – their lifelong bans revoked. It also meant that there would be no economic incentive for players to switch codes in the future. On the positive side, players could play both codes without restrictions from the game's authorities, and decide which one they preferred.

Jonathan Davies had probably been the most famous move of his generation over to league, his move back was to be just as high profile. Signing for Cardiff RFC in October 1995, it seemed to many people that this was quite ironic. Just after Davies had moved to Widnes, he was hired as a commentator at the Arms Park National Stadium for a Welsh rugby union international. However he wasn't allowed to walk on the field, probably due to the fact that his professional, traitorous feet were no longer fit for the hallowed amateur turf. Now he was to make his living next door for Wales's richest union club. But before Davies, and some other Welsh players, moved back to union, they had a Rugby League World Cup to play.

The Australian tour had been replaced by a less glamorous one to the USA involving only Wales where two matches against the national side in Philadelphia were arranged. American Rugby League was still in its infancy. There had been attempts to launch the game there in the 1950s with a newly formed international side making an 18-game tour of Australia as well as playing a game against France. They were hoping to be included in that year's inaugural World Cup, but were refused entry. Once again international rugby league had missed an opportunity for expansion.

Following entry into the World Sevens in Sydney in 1992, the USA launched a domestic league and relaunched their international side. They played matches against Canada, Russia and Ireland 'A' over the next three years, but two full internationals against Wales were to be an entirely different prospect.

The Wales squad for the 1995 tour to the USA
(Courtesy Clive Griffiths)

Iestyn Harris, who had played in the last three Welsh matches after making his debut against Australia, came into his own against lesser opposition. Playing in both matches on the tour, he scored a hat-trick of tries and nine goals in the first game before scoring a try and two goals in the second. Wales registered two easy wins, 66–10 and 92–4.

"We nicknamed it 'Eddie Shoestring Tours' because the whole thing was on a shoestring, but we enjoyed each other's company so much it made up for it," Dai Young recalls.

Among the many players to make their international debuts in Philadelphia was Ian Watson. He was just 18 at the time and playing for Salford. In fact, when he went to the USA he hadn't even made his first team debut, thus being one of select few players to have turned out for his country before club at senior level.

By the end of 2008, he had made 22 appearances for Wales, just four behind record holder Jim Sullivan, and with four games due for the national side at the end of 2009, Watson has the perfect chance to equal the great man's record.

Watson went on to play for Workington on loan, but has mainly stayed around his native Greater Manchester area, turning out regularly for Swinton, Widnes, Rochdale, Oldham, Halifax and Leigh. However, Watson says that Wales were his one and only choice of international team to play for and loved his first two matches: "My mum's Welsh and all my family's from Wales," he said. "We always went to Holywell to visit for holidays so I've been brought up Welsh.

"I was really lucky to make my international debut in the USA. There were a lot of established players there like Dai Young, Rowland Phillips, Gerald Cordle and Martin Hall so it was very easy for me to settle in and they helped me both on and off the field. The professionalism was good, they were great people and they had good attitudes to training. Clive Griffiths brought pride in it and told us how lucky we were to wear the Welsh jersey so all of us youngsters were all very impressed.

"I always consider it a massive honour to play for Wales. It's a big thing for my family and me. I've had some great experiences playing for Wales in the World Cup against teams like Australia and New Zealand and playing in the Millennium Stadium. I'm proud to play for Wales. I'm not even thinking about breaking the appearance record, it's just an honour to play every time I pull on that red jersey."

Rowland Phillips, who had ironically made his rugby union international debut against USA, played in both matches in Philadelphia: "It was a good run out for us before the World Cup. The whole squad played in both games and there were unlimited substitutions," he said. "But the standard of opposition that we were facing wasn't that good. They were physical, not particularly organised, they took more of an American Football type of approach and thought it would just be running hard. They didn't understand the physicality of the defence because they got a little irate with us.

"The crowd was virtually nonexistent, as the games weren't promoted that well. They were played at a college field which had a running track around it. It wasn't like we were a visiting international side, it was like an obscure sport was visiting their shores, there wasn't much fuss. There were no formalities after the game, no official presentations, we just met up in a bar after the games, had a few beers and as many chicken wings as we could eat."

Phillips remembers some of the funniest moments from a tour that he says was marvellous for team morale: "We trained the day before the first game and the rain hammered down," he said. "Clive Griffiths turned round to place some more cones out and when he came back to the field, the entire squad had run under cover to shelter. I've never seen Clive so angry in all my life. There was also the time when we all went out to a Chinese restaurant and they gave out the fortune cookies at the end. We were all asking each other what the little messages said but Paul Moriarty hadn't realised that there was a message inside and had eaten the whole thing!"

The America trip was meant to be Phil Ford's international swansong. The full-back was coming to the end of an illustrious career that saw him play for Wigan, Bradford, Salford, Warrington and Leeds as well as winning 13 Great Britain caps. He became a hero to all British rugby league fans in 1988 when scoring a length of the field try for the Lions as they beat Australia for the first time in 10 years.

Ford was part of the 25-man travelling squad to the States but didn't get to play in either of the games due to a ligament injury. However he was given a more important role to play.

"I was the touch-judge," he said. "Only the referee was provided so each side had to provide a touch-judge and as I was injured, I was the man. Both games were easy wins for Wales so I didn't have too much to do, but during the second game a big fight broke out and us 'officials' had to take charge. So I rushed onto the pitch and knocked a few of the boys on the head with my flag saying 'You can't do that'. That was what this tour was like – a good laugh all round."

Wales had been given a warm-up for the World Cup but knew that group matches against Western Samoa and their old adversaries France would prove to be far stiffer tests.

All three matches in the group were to be played in Wales, giving the home side a big advantage. As mentioned earlier, this, like 2008, was a 10-team tournament, but unlike 2008 it was far better organised with the qualification system for the semi-finals being fairer and less biased in favour of the three leading teams.

There was one group of four teams and two groups of three. Group three – the Welsh group – was by far the toughest with all three matches to be played within the space of the week.

Kicking off at Ninian Park on a Monday evening, the organisers hadn't realised how popular the opening game between Wales and France was going to be. Pre-match ticket sales reached 2,000, yet the number of people who turned up on the night was immense, and there were queues at the wholly inadequate ticket office stretching some way down Sloper Road. The organisers bravely took the decision to delay kick-off by half an hour to allow as many fans as possible to enter the ground. Eventually 10,250, Wales's second highest crowd since their revival in 1991, packed into Cardiff City's stadium.

Wales were the only country to have all of their matches shown live on terrestrial television in this tournament with S4C covering the group matches and BBC covering the knockout stages. This was to be the Welsh language broadcaster's last foray into the 13-man code for more than 11 years. English language commentary was provided by BBC Radio Five Live.

The match itself belonged to Anthony Sullivan, son of the late Clive who had achieved so much in the game. Anthony scored a hat-trick in the game, his first tries since the Papua New Guinea game, as Wales ran out 28–6 winners.

Anthony originally had no aspirations to follow in his father's footsteps. Formerly an association footballer, he only turned to rugby after his father died of cancer in 1985: "Playing for Wales is so important for me as it was so important for my father," Anthony told

26

Sky Sports in 2000. "I know that my mother and all my family are very proud of me and I'm sure my father would have been too. I've never tried to fill his shoes but to be a player in my own right. If people remember my father when watching me play then that makes me more than happy. The things he achieved were tremendous."

If his previous games hadn't already placed Anthony Sullivan into the highest category, then this classic Monday night match certainly put his name into the elite.

His first try finished off a crisp passing move involving Paul Moriarty, Jonathan Davies, Iestyn Harris and Allan Bateman. His second was a true winger's try as he showed a superb change of pace to score in the corner after being set up by Harris, while his third was again a run down the wing after he was put through by Davies.

The group returned to Ninian Park on Thursday night but the difference between seeing Wales in action and the presence of two 'neutral' sides was clear. This time there are no queues outside the ground and the Bob Bank looked sparse as just 2,173 people welcomed the Western Samoans into the tournament as they scored try after try after try after try against a poor French side who were steamrollered 56–10. With Wales only scoring half that many a few days earlier, what hope was there for them against the Samoans that coming Sunday in Swansea?

Wales versus Western Samoa – just those words are enough to send a chill down every Welsh rugby union fan's spine. In 1991, the South Sea islanders beat their Welsh compatriots 16–13 in their opening match of that year's union World Cup – a result that would eventually prove crucial in seeing Western Samoa through to the knockout stages and Wales tumbling out. By 1994 Wales hadn't learnt their lesson as they went on tour to the southern hemisphere and lost again, 34–9. "It's lucky we're not playing the whole of Samoa," was the common joke in Wales at the time. In 1999 they did... and lost.

It was up to rugby league to put the record straight and this match achieved publicity and generated enthusiasm like no other before or since in Wales. A record Welsh international crowd in the modern era turned up at the Vetch Field to watch a classic match. The gates were locked with 15,385 inside the ground and hundreds more still outside, and there were appeals for fans to move forward on the terracing. A friend of mine made the long trip down from Sheffield like many not anticipating that the game would be a sell-out. He was scratching his head on how to get in then he saw a few medics entering the ground through the official entrance. A doctor himself, he quickly followed them in, showing his pager to the steward while making eye contact and nodding and looking like he was meant to be going into the ground. The steward fell for it and my friend quickly made his way to a terrace position once inside.

The atmosphere was charged before kick-off and Wales added fuel to the fire by forming a line and advancing on the Samoans as they performed their haka. Welsh hooker Martin Hall was so close to one of the Samoan's final punches, he almost got his head struck before the game, flinching as the fist came towards him.

This psyched up the crowd even more, not that they needed it. Sitting in that horrible old stand that was used as an away seating area at Swansea City games, the first piece of major action was very close to me when Tea Ropati was sin binned for holding down man-of-the-match Scott Quinnell after he'd played the ball. Tempers started flaring straight away.

From the restart Harris went over and Wales had an early cushion. Vila Matauti responded for Samoa straight away, despite them still being down to 12 men and the game was well and truly on. Anthony Sullivan scored another splendid try as he got onto the end of a brave 60-metre grubber kick from Jonathan Davies. Among the big hits and penalties galore that highly enthused the crowd, Kevin Ellis added a third try in the second half and Wales were just about home and dry. The final score was 22–10.

Wales had earned their place in the semi-finals and faced a difficult trip to Old Trafford to play England. An estimated 10,000 Welsh fans – most of the Samoan crowd probably – made their way up to Manchester to compete against 20,000 Englishmen in a battle royal. Old Trafford was undergoing construction work at the time, but the ground and occasion were impressive. The atmosphere in the largest crowd to ever watch a Welsh international was louder, but not quite as electric as the week before, as the supporters realised Wales were realistically beaten by the better side.

Rowland Phillips was the only try scorer for Wales that day in a tight game that could have been closer than the 25–10 scoreline had it not been for two controversial Martin Offiah tries. If video referees had been used then at least one try probably wouldn't have been allowed. Kevin Ellis recalls: "I think the Western Samoa game took it out of us a bit," he admitted. "That was one of the hardest games that I've played in and I think I can also say that on behalf of the majority of the players at the time. We had a couple of days rest after the Samoa game and maybe we should have come up to Manchester a bit earlier. On the day, though, we gave them a hell of a game. There were two dubious tries from Martin Offiah – he bounced the ball on one of them instead of placing it down – and had those decisions gone our way, then who knows what might have happened?"

"It was a bit frustrating," Dai Young added. "But to be honest if our preparation had been a lot better, if we hadn't enjoyed ourselves quite as much off the field and if we'd taken our opportunities on the field, perhaps we could have created our own little bit of history."

"It's been a pleasure playing with the boys," Jonathan Davies commented after the game. "This was my last game in international football. It would have been nice to win but England were the better team on the day.

"Rugby league has given me everything. I've thoroughly enjoyed my time in the sport and I couldn't have wished to have played with a better bunch of lads. I'm just sad it had to come to an end here but there we are."

The BBC gave Wales the credit they deserved in more than one respect. Ray French named Iestyn Harris and Anthony Sullivan in his team of the tournament while it was also good, and surprising, to see BBC Wales recognise the side by awarding them team-of-the-year in their end-of-year televised ceremony. But to be honest, with no disrespect to the marvellous league boys, there wasn't much competition. The union side had again crashed out of their World Cup in the first round while there was no major club rugby union competition to speak of; the Welsh football side had recently lost to Moldova and Georgia; Glamorgan cricket was in the doldrums, Wrexham and Swansea City were hardly setting the football world alight while Cardiff City were having the worst season in their history, finishing 90th out of the 92 league clubs.

However, despite this success, it was the end of an era. Professionalism in rugby union meant that the rugby league team would lose a number of their stars over the next couple of years.

Clive Griffiths's pennants from the 1995 World Cup (Photo: Peter Lush)

The England semi-final was the final game not only for Davies, but also for Scott Gibbs, who was arguably Welsh rugby union's most successful returnee as he enjoyed seven successful years at Swansea RFC before playing in the Ospreys' first season in regional rugby union. Twice the player that he was before his rugby league days, Gibbs became famous for scoring a try at Wembley in the final minutes that gave Wales a 32–31 win over England to deny them a Grand Slam.

Adrian Hadley, who missed the 1995 World Cup semi-final due to injury, also immediately returned to rugby union as player-coach at Sale Sharks where he would recruit fellow Welshmen Kevin Ellis and John Devereux.

Allan Bateman would play against England the year in rugby league after before going to Richmond rugby union club, but he, Ellis and Devereux weren't finished in rugby league yet with all three having major development roles in the sport in the early 21st century.

Gerald Cordle, Dai Young and Rob Ackerman retired from all rugby a year later, while Mark Jones would play twice more for Wales at league before rejoining union and playing twice more for their national side. Richard Webster also played twice for the Wales rugby league side in 1996 before becoming a hero at Bath RFC as he led them to European Cup glory in 1998. Rowland Phillips would carry on for another three years and was Wales's only ever-present between 1991 and 1998. He also returned to Welsh rugby union, but as a coach.

Wales now needed some new heroes as the times were certainly a-changing. It was the end of an era, but rugby league in Wales refused to die and a new dawn was about to break.

3. South Wales and Super League

The first season of summer rugby league in Great Britain saw many changes in the game, including the launch of a domestic club in South Wales. Even though this was written into the original plans for Super League and its lower divisions back in early 1995, the club took a long time to become established and, unlike Celtic Crusaders 10 years later, the launch of the club that was to be known simply as South Wales RLFC was very quiet. So quiet in fact that in the month the first fixture was due to be played, there was still no announcement of the name of the club. The April edition of *Open Rugby* magazine said: "At the time of writing, 20 March, the RFL were unable to confirm the name of the new Welsh club, or tell us their colours or any of their players. But they did confirm that the South Wales club would be making their debut at home in Aberavon against Hull KR on 31 March."

Mike Nicholas spoke in the same edition of the magazine and was also interviewed by Sky Sports: "There will be rugby union players from the top flight Heineken League," he said. "There will be players from the Sydney Metropolitan Cup and some BARLA signings.

"There will be no flash-in-the-pan stunts, although we have the facility to fast-track into Super League if we are a success. I wouldn't have come back down home to Wales after 25 years in the north if I didn't relish the job of delivering our game to Wales.

"There is a window of opportunity after the sparkling performance by the Welsh national team in the World Cup. If we do not grasp it now then the flame could be extinguished and league in Wales go out of existence as players grab the financial chances and softer option of playing union.

"We know how big a job it is. [Journalist] Dave Hadfield described it as the Everest of the rugby league game and we're already finding it something like that. However we're undeterred. We really want to establish the game here and obtain our rightful place in Welsh sport at club level."

So a club with no name, no ground, no announced signings, no nickname, no kit, no souvenir shop and no mascot somehow kicked off as planned, in Aberavon on 31 March 1996. A very wet west Wales didn't deter 1,879 fans from attending the game with interest. Hull Kingston Rovers were a big name to everyone, except it seemed to the tannoy announcer that day who throughout the match called them "Hull Kings Rovers". One can only suspect that he was given an abbreviation of the name on his cue sheet and wasn't corrected. In a match refereed by Steve Ganson and with Hull KR giving a debut to a Papua New Guinean youngster by the name of Stanley Gene, a 70–8 defeat for South Wales meant that "Hull Kings Rovers" were talked about on the tannoy a lot that day. With the now soaking wet Humberside fans laughing in their squelching boots, the new club had learnt a painful lesson.

The new side wore the Welsh international kit for their first few games until a plain red strip with the traditional three feathers logo was designed to distinguish them from the national side. Looking back, the 16-page programme priced £2.50 seems a little expensive, especially when 12 years later Celtic Crusaders were charging the same price for a publication double the size. Nevertheless, the programme for the Hull KR game was informative and detailed all of the new club's signings with pen pictures. Among these were Australians Matt Benjamin and Andrew Lippiatt, although the former never played for the club and the latter only made five appearances.

Great Britain international Andy Currier was the club's only ever-present, and their joint top try scorer with 14 tries from 22 games. Caerphilly-born Sean Marshall was their other star man while Ioan Bebb from Aberystwyth was the top points scorer with 118, from seven tries and 45 goals.

Currier was a star signing for South Wales. Still the eighth-highest try scorer in the history of Widnes Vikings, he also played for Featherstone Rovers, Warrington and Balmain Tigers in his long and distinguished career that saw him turn out twice for the Lions. He went back to Widnes for further season in 1997 following his season in Wales. For Marshall, this was his only season in league. He had previously played for Cross Keys, Swansea and Newbridge, but was snapped up by Caerphilly after 1996. Bebb had been more active in league before the South Wales season. A former Wales student international who had played in the 1992 Student World Cup in Australia, he had previously turned out for the Cardiff Sea Eagles in the old Welsh League in the early 1990s. While he was famous for playing all three football codes, having played for Wolverhampton Wanderers in association football, he also hit the headlines in 2000 after his career while playing for Cross Keys. He was punched so hard by Bridgend RFC's Chris Stephens in a Welsh-Scottish League match that he was left with a detached retina and a 25 per cent loss in vision. Despite an operation to save his sight, Bebb had to go through the courts to get justice for himself after the WRU felt that 10 minutes in the sin bin was sufficient punishment for Stephens. Bebb was eventually awarded a paltry £2,000 in compensation from Stephens who also had to perform 200 hours of community service.

But four years before the dramas at Blackwood Court, Bebb and the rest of the South Wales team were performing heroics on the pitch to try to earn their club a Super League place. While this wasn't technically being competed for on the field, just like in 2008 with Celtic Crusaders, Super League Europe was keen to expand its competition into another country as soon as possible and were willing to accept an application from the fledgling side.

The hammering by Hull KR was followed by a hard-fought 24–22 win at Prescot Panthers before an even more impressive win 22–18 win over Bramley at the Morfa Stadium in Swansea, the highlights of which were shown on Sky Sports. The presenter Bill Arthur, forever a fan of the game in Wales, reported on this match for Sky, and was also the man who announced that South Wales would be playing in Super League in 1997 following a meeting of the Rugby League Council on 3 July 1996 when it was agreed that Super League would be extended to 13 teams.

By that time, South Wales were doing fairly well. They had beaten Leigh 23–20 – the first of six consecutive losses by Leigh to Welsh sides with South Wales completing the double over them before four consecutive defeats to Celtic Crusaders a decade later – Chorley 58–0, Carlisle 37–18 and Prescot again 50–18. The Carlisle win was a major success story for the club, not just the margin of the victory against an established side, but because it was played as a curtain raiser to a

Super League match between Sheffield Eagles and St Helens, a 43–32 victory for Saints in front of 6,708 fans at Cardiff Arms Park.

In June 1996 *Open Rugby* magazine had said that there would be "no chance of them being turned down" for a Super League place and they were right. South Wales's coach Clive Griffiths, the natural choice for this position after doing so well with the national side throughout the decade, spoke with delight to Sky Sports: "It means that we bring rugby league of the highest calibre down here to South Wales," he said. "It's a great shot in the arm for Welsh sport and I think it's a great shot in the arm for rugby league in general."

Cardiff Arms Park was to be the venue for the new Super League side and, with players signed and ready to go, such as Paul Moriarty, who had moved back from Halifax and signed a two-year contract, South Wales, who had finished the season with a healthy 12 wins from 22 matches, were ready for Super League in 1997.

So what went wrong? Why did South Wales not take part in Super League in 1997 as agreed? In fact, why did they not take part in rugby league again? The atmosphere at the grounds was good and the club presented an enjoyable day out as many away fans remarked. *Open Rugby* magazine writer Dave Hadfield described Super League's about-turn as "one of the most depressing afternoons in the time I have been writing about rugby league" and "it all ended when the council members did their sums" when it was announced that due to costs, South Wales would now not play in Super League but would instead be promoted to Division One. Basically the Super League clubs realised that they would have to take a cut in money to let South Wales in and refused to let them in. One can only wonder why the announcement was made in the first place before the clubs had given their approval – such was the shambolic situation in rugby league at the time. Hadfield went on to say that "I don't know whether South Wales and their backers are going to pull the plug completely or whether they will try to limp along for a season or two in the First Division. Either way, there is no future in it. The code in Wales has been effectively killed off."

For the record, South Wales finished sixth out of 12 teams in the Second Division. Although the aim of the club was to establish a presence for the game, after the Hull KR match, only one more crowd topped 1,000. The last six home games were played at Cardiff RFC's ground, which was now available for rugby league following union becoming 'open' the previous year. The club's owners felt that playing in the First Division would not work. Rugby fans in South Wales watched Super League on television, and knew they would not be watching the top players and teams. Mike Nicholas and his colleagues looked back on a year's work, and a big financial commitment, which had come to nothing.

Amid all this drama at club level, the international game continued and 1996 started with a trip to Fiji for Wales to compete in the Super League World Nines. The tournament, which was held in Suva from 22 to 24 February, was momentous in a number of ways, one being that this marked the very first time that a video referee was used for a game of rugby league.

The tournament was ambitious and would have been extremely successful had rain not washed out the entire day on 23 February. Sixteen countries entered sides with Australia, Western Samoa, Scotland and USA in Pool A, England, Tonga, Italy and Morocco in Pool B, New Zealand, Ireland, France and Japan in Pool C and Papua New Guinea, Wales, Fiji and the Cook Islands in Pool D. All the teams in each pool would play each other once with the top two in each group supposedly qualifying for the quarter-finals. However, thanks to the rain on the second day the competition was changed.

Rowland Phillips was in the Welsh squad and he remembers his three days in the South Pacific: "It was a very good trip," he said. "We won the competition for the teams who finished second place in each group, but I remember that it rained so badly that they had to abandon one of the days, so they changed the format of the qualification. It was meant to be the top two who went through but as we'd lost to Papua New Guinea and finished in second place in the group, we didn't qualify as they declared only the top team would go through to the knockout stages."

Wales had a good start to the tournament with a 10–8 win over the Cook Islands before losing 14–12 to Papua New Guinea in the second match and beating Fiji 10–6 in the third. Two sensational tries from Jason Critchley gave Wales a 16–6 win over Tonga in the Bowl semi-final for second-placed teams and the opportunity to face Western Samoa for the second time in six months.

"We played Samoa in the Bowl Final and beat them 12–8 after extra time," Phillips remembers. "A lot of that was because of the rain and we adjusted to the conditions a lot easier than the Samoans. Allan Bateman, who was playing for Cronulla Sharks at the time, came over to join us and while everyone else was trudging through boggy conditions, he looked so comfortable. It was probably because he comes from Maesteg and he's used to it!"

The Trophy final was one of the best games in the tournament. Willie Poching gave Western Samoa the lead before Mark Perrett levelled things for Wales at 4–4. Paul Atcheson added another before Poching's second took the game into extra time where Ian Watson grabbed the winner after excellent work from Allan Bateman.

In the post-tournament press conference, Welsh coach Clive Griffiths demanded greater recognition for the national side in the full test arena. Griffiths said: "We were very unlucky to lose to Papua in the earlier round, and but for that last-minute try we could have been competing with the big boys in the main competition. I believe Wales should now be given the opportunity of playing full Test matches against the Pacific Nations, and perhaps even a tour of Australia."

In the main competition, a disappointing England came fourth after slipping to a 15–14 defeat against Papua New Guinea in the final seconds of their semi-final. Australia were surprisingly beaten by the eventual winners, New Zealand who beat PNG 26–10 in the Final and, when facing Australia in the third-place play-off, England were again heading for victory before the Kangaroos forced the game into extra-time and a tired England allowed Robbie Beckett to score the winning try for a 14–10 win.

Wales' next fixtures were to be in June in the newly named "European Super League Championships". England were to face France in Gateshead on 12 June, Wales would then travel to Paris to take on France on 19 June before the final match in Cardiff on 26 June – Wales versus England. These fixtures were announced in good time and publicised in the South Wales match programmes so a number of people, booked and paid for flights over to Paris for the mid-week game. However, by 12 May when Chorley Chieftans were the visitors to South Wales, the date and venue of the France versus Wales match had changed, with Wales now travelling to Carcassonne on 5 June. This decision left the supporters out of pocket. However, this was a small problem compared to the Great Britain fans who were really disadvantaged when the 1996 Lions tour to Australia was relocated to New Zealand and the Pacific Islands. More than 3,000 supporters originally booked for Australia. Only 300 eventually went to New Zealand.

Wales also had a player drain to contend with, as mentioned in the previous chapter, after a number of Welsh internationals returned to the union game following the introduction of professionalism. New Welsh captain Dai Young, one of the players who had remained in league, had also announced that he was to go back to union in 1997 after signing a big-money deal with Cardiff RFC: "Originally I had no thoughts to go back to union," he said. "But when the game went professional they wanted to get as many Welsh internationals as possible back into their game. I was only 28 then and I felt that I could have played league for another couple of years, but it's a faster game, certainly in my position, and if I was going to have an extended professional rugby career I had to come back to union. I had two years left at Salford, but Cardiff offered me four and a job with the club that was to give me long term security after my playing days were over." He did, however, play in the 1996 European Championships.

"It was a difficult game against France but we had a couple of training sessions and played with a lot of heart and team spirit. Gelling people in and out wasn't too difficult because in 1995 we had the Wigan crowd like Kelvin Skerrett and Neil Cowie coming in. We always made people welcome as they'd opted to play for Wales when they could have played for England, and they were all good enough to play for England, so it was never any problem fitting people into the game plan."

Wales were missing stars like Scott Gibbs and John Devereux who, while still in rugby league, were injured and unable to travel. However, Sky Sports made the journey to cover Wales live in France for the first time and they weren't disappointed as Wales, with new star Iestyn Harris, the man tipped to be the new Jonathan Davies as he slipped into the former Welsh captain's place as both stand-off and goalkicker, ran the show. Wales were 34–14 winners over what was effectively a Paris St Germain side with 13 of the French players coming from the new Super League club.

Harris scored three tries and five goals on that balmy French summer night, but it was France who struck first blood when Eric Vergniol pounced on a Patrick Entat grubber kick following an error by Gerald Cordle in the in-goal area. A Harris solo effort levelled things, with his first successful kick giving Wales a lead they weren't to lose. Paul Atcheson after receiving the ball from Jason Critchley scored the second try, while Richard Webster increased the lead before the interval. Harris produced two more solo efforts in the second half with Gareth Davies scoring his fifth Welsh try to round off the win and record Wales' highest ever points total on French soil: "I'm really happy, it was a good result, just what we wanted," Iestyn Harris commented after the game. "We came here to get the win which we got and we can now look forward to the England game. We had a few new players and a few late changes but we know that anybody who puts on the Welsh shirt gives 110 per cent."

England had to get past France before the Welsh decider but this was merely a formality as they dominated from start to finish, winning 73–6. So it was to be a difficult job for Wales at Cardiff Arms Park against a tough England side who were captained by Andy Farrell for the first time. With Dai Young and Anthony Sullivan out of the side injured, Allan Bateman agreed to fly halfway round the world for the one match. His Sydney-based club Cronulla Sharks allowed him to travel because Australia were playing New Zealand and there was a break in the Australian domestic programme.

Bateman spoke about the match in his autobiography: "The Australian game had adapted a number of different rules and it was difficult to adjust back to the old way," he said. "We lost [the game] and I'd wondered if it had all been worth it. It meant an exhausting flight, taking off from the North of Queensland, I had to pay the cost of my own flight [later reimbursed by the British rugby league authorities] and there was no match fee."

Wales fought hard but eventually lost out 26–12. Chris Morley gave Wales the lead in a try created by man-of-the-tournament Iestyn Harris after the stand-off ran half the length of the field. Chris Joynt levelled things for England and Bobby Goulding gave them the lead just after Welsh skipper Paul Moriarty was carried off injured. Jason Critchley replied immediately for Wales but late tries from Shaun Edwards and Steve Prescott gave England the title.

A crowd of 5,425 was a success considering that the match clashed with an England versus Germany Euro 96 football semi-final that was being shown live on television at the same time. With the football going into extra time, the atmosphere was electric in the bar at the Arms Park following the rugby with the support divided between England and Germany. Those present can still remember former Welsh international Phil Ford jumping up with delight when Gareth Southgate missed the penalty that sent Germany through.

Despite two years of thrilling matches in the European Championship, Super League decided not to continue the tournament in 1997, giving Wales no matches at all that year. However, the Welsh side was scheduled to play two lucrative home internationals in 1998. A game against England in July was to be followed by another at home to New Zealand in October. Unfortunately, only the England game took place after New Zealand cut their proposed six-game tour to just three, all against Great Britain, which they won 2–0 with only a 23–23 draw at Watford in the third test saving the Lions' blushes.

Super League announced in 1998 that it would be extending their 1999 competition to 14 clubs with one team being promoted from Division One while another would be a brand-new side from an area that didn't currently have a professional club. Five bids entered the fold, one from Northampton, one from Glasgow, one from Gateshead and, surprisingly, two from Wales. This, in hindsight, can be seen as a mistake as surely the Welsh would have had more chance of obtaining a Super League franchise had they entered a unified bid. As it was, franchises from Cardiff and Swansea entered the fray with the team from the capital looking early favourites. In May 1998 it was reported that Cardiff RFC were backing the bid with their millions and had verbal agreements from four Canberra Raiders players (three Australians and one New Zealander) that they would join Cardiff should it get the go-ahead.

All five of the franchise bidders were given a one off 'on the road' Super League match in 1998 to demonstrate their readiness, with Gateshead having the distinct advantage of being given two.

Wales had a weekend of Super League fixtures starting with Castleford Tigers against Warrington Wolves on the Saturday at Cardiff Arms Park where 4,437 witnessed a classic. With the score at 16-16 with six minutes remaining, Warrington's Lee Briers attempted a drop goal but the ball hit the post, bounced into Mike Wainwright's arms who set up Gary Chambers for a try. However the video referee showed that there was a knock-on before Briers received the ball and this was disallowed. From the scrum, Castleford worked their way downfield, Brad Davis scored a drop goal then a converted Danny Orr try from kick-off gave the Tigers a 23–16 win.

The match in Swansea the next day was a complete anticlimax in comparison. Wigan versus St Helens was not the classic that everyone predicted and the 8,572 people in the ground would have wanted, Warriors fans excepted of course as they ran away with a 36–2 win. However, the on-the-road experiment was a complete success and it's a great shame that this was not to be repeated on a regular basis.

This two week on-the-road extravaganza would also include the England versus Wales match at Widnes with England to be known as Emerging England once they could not guarantee that all of their Super League stars would be playing. With Scotland, Ireland and France taking part in a tournament later in the year, it was most disappointing that Wales weren't also to be included in that, but this game against the English, whatever they were choosing to call their team, was most welcome.

Kelvin Skerrett from Halifax was named as Welsh skipper with Anthony Sullivan and Rowland Phillips being the only survivors from Wales's 68–0 win over Papua New Guinea in 1991. Paul Moriarty, now back in union with Swansea, had been named in the initial 22-man squad, but was eventually refused permission to play. Five exciting young players made their debut for Wales on Sunday 19 July. They were Damien Gibson, Lee Briers, Dean Busby, Karle Hammond and Martin Pearson.

Wales, who were sponsored by Brannigan's pub in Cardiff where a framed Welsh shirt from the game was on display until the pub's closure a handful of years later, went behind to an early Graham Holroyd penalty. However, Wales scored the first try straight from the kick-off after Paul Atcheson sold a dummy fooling Nathan McAvoy and combining with Iestyn Harris to send Daio Powell over. England struck back with Keith Senior putting Andy Hay over for a short-range try but Wales took a 12–8 lead on 15 minutes when Keiron Cunningham charged through.

Astonishingly there was no further score for 53 minutes as what had started as a classic fizzled out as a game where defences ruled. Wales held the English off until a crunching tackle from Darren Fleary on Paul Atcheson forced him to drop the ball and Sean Long set up Paul Davidson, who ran through two Welsh tackles for a try under the posts. Long hit a drop-goal six minutes before the final hooter to secure England's 15–12 victory.

Clive Griffiths was frustrated that the Welsh team would play no more games in 1998: "It looks as though we are now not going to play New Zealand," he said in the press conference after the match. "There is talk of a return game against England but it is all speculation. If we are serious about international rugby league then we need to play international games and our last game was two years ago."

With England beating Wales in the international, could they also win off the field in their franchise bids? With Northampton and Glasgow being ruled out by the experts early on, it looked to be a three-horse race between Gateshead, Cardiff and Swansea with many feeling that both Cardiff and Gateshead should have been given the nod to progress the development of the sport in their respective areas. The Gateshead Thunder club had the backing of a hugely supportive local council, an excellent ground in their International Stadium that had successfully hosted major matches in recent years, as well as enthusiastic local businesses. The proposed Cardiff Dragons club were to play at the Arms Park with the opportunity to use the brand new Millennium Stadium if needed. They were reported to have had the additional support of Cardiff Devils Ice Hockey club as well as money from former Wigan chairman Jack Robinson. They would take the existing Wales under-16 and under-19 sides under their wing with the hope that, in five years time, most of the side would be Welsh-born. For the record, the weaker bid from The Black Swans would have seen the Swansea-based club playing their matches at the Vetch Field.

Maurice Lindsay, the Super League managing director said at the time that "Cardiff have a good ground and a strong commercial environment while Swansea have wonderful support and tremendous backing from the council. We now have the chance to take the game forward. We just can't afford to ignore it. If we spurn this opportunity, particularly in South Wales, it will possibly be lost forever."

41

Super League chose Gateshead over the two Welsh sides, a decision that arguably can now be seen to have been a mistake after the Thunder lasted just one season in Super League. Despite a very healthy fifth-place finish, their finances were not strong enough to maintain the side and they merged with Hull FC. However a new Thunder club was reformed by the fans and finally saw success in 2008 when they won the National League Two title and are aiming to be back in Super League by 2012.

All this was quite ironic considering that both of the Welsh applications were rejected on the advice of consultants Deloitte Touche because their financial structures weren't strong enough. Hopes were high that at least one of the Welsh clubs would join Super League in 2000 with at least one Super League game to be staged in Wales in 1999. Neither happened.

"Wales was a terrible missed opportunity in the mid-1990s," Dave Hadfield remembers. "Their rugby union was in a state of confusion and the time was right for a concerted stab at it but the opportunity was missed. I thought that this would probably be the last opportunity but as it turns out we've had some more last opportunities after that, especially now with Celtic Crusaders."

Wales was now largely forgotten for the rest of the 20th century. A three-match tournament between Wales, Ireland and Scotland was given little publicity and this led to very low crowds throughout the entire competition. Wales kicked off the Lincoln Financial Group Triangular Challenge with a home game against Ireland, to be played at the Vetch Field in Swansea, home of many marvellous Welsh nights out coupled with large crowds in the early half of the decade.

But how things had changed. On arriving at the ground early to avoid the heavy traffic on the atrocious old link road that used to be the only major access route into Swansea, supporters wondered if they had picked the wrong day as no-one seemed to be around. Local pubs didn't know there was a game on, but there was a poster in the football club shop. "We'd have put posters up if people had given us some," local traders said. There didn't seem to be much in the local press before or after the game and the national rugby league media were all sunning themselves down-under watching Great Britain being humiliated in the Tri-Nations. Even Sky Sports, who had loyally followed Wales throughout the decade, had lost interest and decided not to give any airtime to the tournament.

As a result, just 812 people turned up on that Friday night in October, Wales's lowest ever international crowd and a record that will probably never be broken, to see a 24–17 loss to a strong Irish side who were building towards the 2000 World Cup. Missing key players such as Iestyn Harris, Keiron Cunningham and Anthony Sullivan, who were all on Lions duty, Clive Griffiths gave seven youngsters their international debuts, the most notable being St Helens' Hendy-born prop Gareth Price. He won the first of his 11 Welsh caps to date as well as Lenny Woodard, who alongside Price, played for Celtic Crusaders in their inaugural season in 2006.

When Richie Eyres was sent off just 10 minutes into the game, the odds were stacked against Wales. Debutant Steve Thomas, who almost signed for Celtic Crusaders in 2008 and would have done had it not been for a contract issue with Neath RFC, scored Wales's opening try with Damian Gibson and Martin Pearson also crossing. Pearson kicked two goals with Lee Briers adding a one-pointer.

"There were a lot more plusses than minuses in that game," Clive Griffiths commented after the match. "There was lot of pride and passion and lads like Steve Thomas, Gareth Price and Lenny Woodard will have only gained from it."

Wales needed a good performance against Scotland a week later in Glasgow to save their tournament and they didn't get it, losing 36–16 in a performance Griffiths described as his worst as Wales coach. Lee Briers, Neil Cowie and Martin Pearson scored tries with Briers kicking two goals. Ireland went on to beat Scotland 31–10 to win the tournament in a sad end to the decade for Wales in international rugby league. The World Cup would open the 21st century and this had to be a success in all quarters for rugby league to survive at professional level in Wales.

Grassroots rugby league in Wales

The 1992 Student World Cup Wales squad.
(Photo: Courtesy Clive Griffiths)

Cardiff Demons versus Valley Cougars
Welsh Rugby League Conference July 2004
(Photo: Peter Lush)

4. The 2000 World Cup

It is often said that the 2000 Rugby League World Cup was a failure on and off the field. The main pieces of evidence for this were that it finished with a loss of £700,000 primarily due to torrential autumn rainstorms, poor publicity, and the crisis on Britain's railways following the Hatfield rail crash on 17 October, just 11 days before the tournament started, that left four dead and 70 injured which also restricted fans travelling to matches.

Poor publicity was to some extent down due to criticism by Britain's sports media who were seemingly happy to pounce on anything to ridicule rugby league. Some were critical of the inclusion of a New Zealand Maori team alongside the full New Zealand squad. Many supporters too believe that this was a major error by the Rugby League International Federation, because of the Maori did not represent a nation state.

The tournament was covered by Sky Sports and the BBC and while Sky Sports embraced the coverage with a fair share of live matches plus for the duration of the tournament a one-hour "World Cup Centre" every evening presented enthusiastically by Chris Warren, the BBC's coverage to the naked eye looked to be a little critical of the tournament. Among the presenters there was the positive Jonathan Davies who seemed to be looking forward to every game over the coming month and on the other hand there was John Inverdale whose distaste for the 13-man game has been shown over the years and specifically his heated discussion live on a BBC Radio 5 programme where he publicly criticised the expansion of the game.

On one occasion, Davies and Inverdale were discussing the Lebanon side that had been included in the World Cup. Davies was saying positively that they could provide a good match for Wales because they contained a number of players who played in the NRL which gave Inverdale the opportunity to jump in saying they were all Australians. While they were all living in Australia at the time, it was not true to say that they were all Australians. For example, Lebanon's skipper Hazem El Masri, the world record holder for the most points scored in a NRL career by an individual player and also the holder of the most points scored in a NRL season by an individual record, was Lebanese born as were many others from the squad.

Following the 2000 World Cup, some of these players went back to the country of their birth and helped to form a domestic league in Lebanon. Their international side now plays regular matches and, in the years since the 2000 World Cup, have defeated France twice in international tournaments and famously knocked Wales out of the 2008 World Cup qualifiers on a dismal night for the Welsh in Widnes. Lebanon have since formed an 'A' side, known as Liban Espoirs (meaning 'hopefuls') and they have since toured Morocco, England, Wales, Cyprus and Serbia as well as facing United Arab Emirates in 2008 in the first ever game played by that nation.

Lebanon's inclusion in the World Cup, along with other fledgling nations, led to a few high scores which also added fuel to the fire for many of the southern-based anti-rugby league media. However, this is an argument that can also be easily refuted. While a score of 100 points was posted once in the tournament – Australia beating Russia 110–4 – this score wasn't nearly as high as some of the rugby union scores that have been recorded in recent years – Australia 142 Namibia 0 in 2003 and New Zealand 145 Japan 17 in 1995 being two of many notable large results in their version of the World Cup.

The RLIF must be applauded for bravely choosing to go with 16 teams for the 2000 World Cup, and there was some entertaining rugby. The 16 teams naturally split into four groups of four with the top two teams going through to the quarter-finals. While it could be argued that the eight favourites were the teams who qualified, they did not have it all their own way as some of the newer rugby league nations made a good fight of it.

Group 1 consisted of Australia, England, Fiji and Russia with Australia and England the obvious hot favourites to go through to the quarter-finals. The opening clash between England and Australia at Twickenham was almost certainly going to decide first and second place in the group table because both teams were highly expected to beat the minnows in the group. This game, like most others over the next month, was played in torrential rain and as they walked to the ground, trying not get drowned, many supporters wondered what on earth they were doing there. Some found that they were seated in the lower level of the stadium, which offered no protection at all. Fortunately the ground wasn't sold out and the supporters on that level were moved to the top of the stadium and into the dry. Australia sailed through the game to win 22–2 which just about rubber-stamped their tournament. They weren't to be challenged properly until the semi-finals.

Group 3 was far harder to predict. Arguably the most successful group of the tournament, this was played entirely in France with the hosts drawn against Papua New Guinea, Tonga and South Africa. Unlike their union counterparts, South Africa were – and still are – minnows of the 13-a-side game and were considered to be cannon fodder before the tournament even started. However, it was anyone's game between the other three nations, with France expected to be favourites to win the group.

Papua New Guinea immediately dismissed that idea. A nation who had been improving all the time, they shocked the hosts in a thrilling double-header on the opening day of the tournament at the Charlety Stadium in Paris winning 23–20. The teams tied at four tries each but an extra conversion and drop-goal sealed the match for the Kumuls. Tonga hammered South Africa 66–18 in the other match that day.

Some of the remaining games were nervy ones for the two qualifiers, France and PNG. France didn't have it all their own way when they beat Tonga 28–8 while PNG were 16–0 winners over South Africa and the lead changed hands a few times in their 30–22 win over the Tongans. It made for a competitive group and added to the excitement of a colourful and enjoyable tournament.

Group 4 was known as the group of death. It is now customary to have one of these groups at every international tournament and the 2000 World Cup version consisted of four relative unknown quantities: Scotland, Ireland, Samoa and the New Zealand Maori.

Instead of the Maori, many supporters wanted a team from nations such as the USA or Morocco to be included. Both had been building their rugby league competitions over the years and it would have been interesting to see what their inclusion in such a tournament would have done for the popularity of the sport in their countries. However, the Maori it was and they added to a thriller of a group with every result being unpredictable from the outset.

Ireland shocked everyone by winning the group. They beat Samoa 30–16 on the first day in Belfast and followed that with an 18–16 win over Scotland and a 30–16 victory against the Maori. Samoa also qualified, but were pushed to the limit by the other two teams.

47

The remaining group, numbered 2, was between Wales, New Zealand, Lebanon and the Cook Islands. Wales warmed up for their campaign by taking a trip to South Africa to play their first ever match against the Rhinos. The game was played at the Loftus Versefield stadium in Pretoria. A proposed venue for the 2010 FIFA World Cup, it was there in 1998 that the Welsh rugby union side suffered a 96–13 hammering against South Africa, and Clive Griffiths's men were eager for a little bit of revenge to restore some national pride.

South Africa had been making progress as a rugby league nation since the game was revived there in 1989. With a domestic league in place, they were producing players of their own like their captain Jamie Bloem. A product of local side Eastern Eagles, he was then playing for Halifax Blue Sox. Mark Johnson of Salford and Sean Rutgerson of Canberra Raiders also provided invaluable experience to the side that contained a few players who had turned out in rugby union's Super 12.

Wales had gone through some serious rebuilding. Nine years on from the reformation in 1991, only Anthony Sullivan remained in the side. Players like Iestyn Harris, Keiron Cunningham and Paul Atcheson now provided the experience as all the big name rugby union imports had now retired or gone back to the 15-a-side code.

The South Africa game gave eight Welsh players their full international debuts with Paul Sterling, Kris Tassell, Anthony Farrell, Mick Jenkins, Gareth Carvell, Hefin O'Hare, Dave Whittle and Justin Morgan all pulling on a red shirt for the first time.

Morgan, then at Canberra Raiders, is one player who has since served the Welsh set-up with distinction. The Pretoria match was the first of 10 caps for him in the space of 11 games, only missing a match against Australia in Bridgend in 2003, before retiring through injury aged just 28. Since then he has risen to prominence as a coach, first of Toulouse, guiding them to the Challenge Cup semi-final in 2005, then of Hull Kingston Rovers, leading them to Super League. At the time of writing he is one of the assistant coaches for Wales.

"My grandfather was Welsh-born," said Morgan. "He was born a Welshman and died a Welshman and was very proud of his heritage. He was the kind of person who was proud of his national anthem and had a red dragon Welsh flag up outside his house in Australia. It was a great honour for me to play for Wales for him and the family.

"The South Africa trip was outstanding, it was very exciting for me to play international rugby league for the first time anyway but to play it in a different environment and a new country made it even better especially as we were looking forward to the World Cup.

"I didn't have a bad game. I hurt my shoulder but it wasn't enough to keep me out of the World Cup which obviously I was pleased about.

"As I said before, the trip itself was amazing too. We went to Sun City and on safari, it was a perfect team-bonding trip before such an important tournament and was very enjoyable."

With 6,166 fans in the stadium, the atmosphere was good and the expert on the public address system helped the locals by explaining the intricacies of the game and how it differed from rugby union.

Wales got off to the worst possible start when in only the first minute, local lad Brian Best pounced on a grubber kick as Atcheson hesitated and the hosts were 4–0 up. Wales gained the advantage on the quarter hour and scored two quick tries, both from scrums. Jenkins, capping off a dream debut, scored the first to level the scores with Harris converting for a 6–4 lead with fellow debutant Sterling finishing off a fine passing move in the corner to extend the advantage. Jenkins went in under the sticks for his second and Wales's third. Dean Busby, on only his second Welsh appearance, scored Wales's fourth, which was given by referee Steve Ganson despite a suspicion of a forward pass. Harris converted for the fourth time and the Welsh side was 20 points up at the interval.

Harris added to his points early on in the second half as he scored Wales's fifth try, selling a beautiful dummy as he ran 40 metres to the line. Chris Smith, another man who was winning only his second Welsh cap, scored in the corner for a sixth while Billy Boston's grandson Wes Davies weaved his way under the sticks for a seventh. Best struck again for South Africa in the final minutes as Wales tired but the Dragons were home and dry with a 40–8 win.

World Cup preparations had certainly started well for Wales. Clive Griffiths claimed that the side had the potential to be as good as the 1995 line-up while Anthony Sullivan said that "It was ideal World Cup preparation for us. It finished off a great week of training and we are all looking forward to the start of the tournament against the Cook Islands now."

Wales versus the Cook Islands was to be played at Wrexham's Racecourse Ground on the day after the England versus Australia opener at Twickenham. The rain that had spoiled the previous day's events hadn't relented and with high winds adding to the already torrential weather conditions, many fans from south Wales probably made the wise decision of not making the 360-mile round trip to Wales's first ever international in North Wales. This in itself was surprising because Wrexham is just a stone's throw away from rugby league areas like Warrington and St Helens, and it's not surprising that the Crusaders have announced that they will play an 'on the road' game there in 2010.

The match was the second in Group 2 with New Zealand giving Lebanon a 64–0 thumping at Kingsholm Park in Gloucester earlier in the day with Richie Barnett, Tonie Carroll and Lesley Vainikolo each scoring a brace of tries. Wales knew that they would have to face New Zealand at the Millennium Stadium a week later but surely the Cook Islands would be a slightly easier prospect?

A crowd of 5,060 braved the weather and weren't disappointed as Wales fought through to a 38–6 win thanks to an outstanding second-half performance. Lee Briers gave Wales the lead with a fantastic try dancing through the Cook Islands' defensive line with utter enthusiasm and Harris adding the extras. The Cook Islands levelled things up on 20 minutes thanks to a Karl Temata try that was converted by Richard Piakura and kept Wales out until the interval with the sides going into the dressing rooms all square.

It was between Briers and Kris Tassell for man-of-the-match. Tassell was denied a try by the video referee in the 11th minute but the Queenslander, whose grandfather was born in Pontypridd, scored a second-half hat-trick to secure the points for Wales. The first was on 42 minutes after a fine run down the left wing with his second and third both in the last 10 minutes of the game. Jenkins scored yet again, after being set-up nicely by Harris. He was close to a second try, which would have made it four in two games, but after being denied by a solid defence, provided a score for Keiron Cunningham at dummy half.

"It took us a while to get together," Cunningham said. "But I think the Cook Islands tired a lot in the second half and we capitalised on everything. The conditions were terrible; it rained a lot all weekend. I was looking out of the hotel room and it did nothing but rain. We came down to the ground and found out that two inches of rain had fallen and that made it really tough out there."

"The Cook Islands game was probably one of the most physical games that I've been involved in," Lee Briers added. "A lot of the boys knew they'd been in a game after that one but it was good to go to Wrexham, get a win and kick-off our campaign."

Wales's win was comfortable, but they knew work was still needed for the Lebanon match four days later in Llanelli. Lebanon were having problems going into the match after reports that three of their players, George Katrib, Michael Coorey and Travis Touma, had to be treated for mild hypothermia after the defeat to New Zealand in a rain-swept game. The last two were fit enough to play in Llanelli, but Katrib had an additional knee cartilage problem and missed out. Wales went into the game with an unchanged starting line-up with the only change being Chris Morley coming onto the bench in place of Ian Watson.

It was my first and only visit to Llanelli's famous Stradey Park. The stadium, which was first used in 1879, was demolished in 2008 with the two local rugby union sides relocating to a new stadium in Pemberton, a few miles east of the city. The first ever union international game at the ground was between Wales and England in 1887 while in addition to this Rugby League World Cup match, the ground also staged a Rugby Union World Cup game in 1999 when Argentina beat Samoa 32–16.

It looked like the ground was going to be quite full when I arrived. An hour before kick-off the bars and restaurant were already packed. However, once inside the ground I realised that the crowd wasn't going to be as large as I thought. However, the 1,500 people that did make it tried to create a good atmosphere on another wet night.

Iestyn Harris, who at the time was contemplating a move to rugby union, could sense the lack of occasion there. Standing in the rain during the national anthem, he was spotted looking around at the empty seats and perhaps longing for a union international at the Millennium Stadium. "I think that was the case," Harris said. "I'd always wanted to have a go at playing international rugby union as it was something that my grandfather [Norman Harris, who played for Ebbw Vale, Pontypool and Newbridge before winning eight Welsh rugby league caps while playing for Oldham] never had the opportunity to do so I decided to give it a crack. I wouldn't change anything that I've done in my career." However, if he'd felt that off the pitch, Harris, the ultimate professional, didn't show it on the pitch and was man-of-the-match by a long chalk.

He scored a hard-fought try in the corner after only six minutes to give Wales the lead, scored a second not long after that and had a hand in the other three Welsh tries that were scored by Paul Sterling, Keiron Cunningham and Wes Davies.

However, Wales didn't have it all their own way. After going 18–0 up, Lebanon fought back and scored just before the interval through Michael Coorey with Hazem El Masri converting. In Clive Griffiths's words, he gave his side a bit of a kick up the backside in the dressing rooms at half-time because he felt that his players went to sleep in the last five or 10 minutes of the first half and gave the Lebanese what they described as "a scent of a chance of winning the game".

They started well in the second half as winger Samer El Masri picked up a loose ball to score in the corner to put them just eight points behind. Wes Davies's try made things a little more comfortable but two tries in the last three minutes from Hassen Saleh had the whole crowd on the edge of their seats and when the final hooter blew just after Hazem El Masri's kick had put the Lebanese just two points behind at 24–22, the Welsh fans in Stradey Park breathed a sigh of relief and – despite the torrential conditions – a World Cup classic had been witnessed.

So it was on to the brand new Millennium Stadium in Cardiff for the final match in the group against New Zealand. The Kiwis, who had seen off the Cook Islands 84–10 at the Madejski Stadium in Reading at the same time as Wales's victory over Lebanon, were the obvious hot favourites. Keiron Cunningham was looking forward to the match: "I've never played at the Millennium Stadium before, so this is going to be a whole new experience," he told the BBC at the time. "New Zealand are a great side and they are second favourites to win the World Cup. It will be good to play against them so we can really gauge just how good we are and how far we have come."

Since its opening in June 1999, Cardiff's now iconic landmark has become world famous and not just for rugby union and football, which has been its primary use. Motor sport and boxing have both been held there, as have many concerts, while a few episodes of *Doctor Who* have been filmed in the many corridors and stairways around the pitch. When, in 2005, the British public saw what they thought wasn't possible, a Dalek levitating up some stairs, that wasn't in a bunker in Utah as portrayed, but at the Millennium Stadium.

The first event to be held there was a rugby union match on 26 June 1999, when Wales beat South Africa 29–19 in a friendly before a crowd of 29,000. Football has played a major part at the stadium too, with the first game being Wales's 1–1 draw with Finland in a friendly in March 2000. Now, with a closed roof, rugby league was to be held there for the first time but, unlike the other two codes, Wales weren't to feature in the first match.

Sunday 5 November 2000 would produce fireworks as Cardiff saw one of the games of the tournament when Lebanon and the Cook Islands made history by taking part in the first ever rugby league game at the ground.

And it was a good crowd too. 17,612 can be considered a success for a tournament plagued by bad weather and transport problems. As the supporters trudged to the ground with their umbrellas up yet again, they were encouraged by the fact that the roof was on and at least everyone, fans and players alike, didn't have the rain to contend with when they got into the ground.

The roof has been one of the Millennium Stadium's greatest assets and it gave Lebanon and Cook Islands another piece of history with this being the first ever first-class rugby league match anywhere in the world to be staged indoors.

It was a superb fightback by Lebanon who were 22–10 down with four minutes to go after being 18–4 down at half-time as they repeated their heroics from three days before. When Steve Berryman was set up by Jason Temu with six minutes to go to make the score 22–10 to the Cook Islands, commentator Andrew Voss uttered the classic lines "They've won this game for sure from there. Berryman has scored the match winner."

The Cook Islands players certainly celebrated like they'd won the game but they weren't to predict a Lebanese fightback. Hassan Saleh stormed through two minutes later before Hazem El Masri produced his magic to score a converted try to level things.

Wales and New Zealand couldn't compete with such dramatics. The game was over as a contest by half-time as the Kiwis went in with a

30–6 lead with only a Lee Briers try – a classic 60-metre one-play score involving Iestyn Harris, Justin Morgan Hefin O'Hare and Anthony Sullivan – to make the large Welsh contingent cheer with delight.

For New Zealand, it was the Lesley Vainikolo show. Wales may have scored further tries from Paul Atcheson and Anthony Farrell, but 'The Volcano' ran things in Cardiff as he scored a brilliant hat-trick of tries, the third in the corner in the final minute as the Kiwis wrapped up a 58–18 win. "They closed the roof today," Sky commentator Bill Arthur said, "And then it fell in on Wales."

The Millennium Stadium would go on to host three Rugby League Challenge Cup Finals and two Millennium Magic weekends at which all 12 Super League clubs played over two days. But that was in the near future. For Wales in this World Cup, it was a trip to Widnes to face Papua New Guinea in the quarter-finals.

Before the tournament, Ray French had written that: "Three matches in eight days will be demanding for a squad that lacks genuine depth." This was now proving to be the case with preparations for the quarter-finals proving to be tough for the Welsh side who were now being plagued by injuries. Gareth Carvell, Hefin O'Hare, Dave Whittle and Barry Eaton were all out of the tournament thanks to knocks that they had picked up in the group stages, while Ian Watson was also out of the running for the Kumuls clash. While Keiron Cunningham, Dean Busby and Kris Tassell were fit again, Griffiths knew that has side needed one or two more quality players, so he drafted in Paul Moriarty and John Devereux.

"By the time the PNG game was on the horizon, we had a lot of injuries so Clive called Paul and me up," Devereux remembers. "I was playing for Bridgend in the Welsh Rugby Union Premiership at the time and we were doing quite well. I was in my second season there and won player-of-the-year so I was still playing rugby at quite a high standard.

"However, it had been a few years since I'd played rugby league so it was a bit difficult. The game had changed a lot since Super League started, the pace was faster, the hits were bigger, the defensive systems had changed so getting used to it all again was tough."

The sides exchanged penalties early on before Wales scored the first try after 19 minutes with an excellent Jason Critchley solo run which ended under the sticks after the centre had intercepted Adrian

Lam's pass. Lee Briers scored a second try in the corner before setting up Wes Davies for Wales's third. Harris converted all three to give Wales a 20–2 lead at the interval.

The Kumuls knew that something had to be done early if they were to compete and after only three minutes of the second half John Wilshire went over in the corner, but Atcheson had forced the future Salford player into touch and the try didn't count. However his effort on 67 minutes was allowed and his conversion made the final score 22–8 with Wales's solitary second half score coming from a second Harris penalty.

Wales's injury crisis gave Clive Griffiths a wake-up call over the state of rugby league in the country; not that he had really needed one. Following the PNG win, Griffiths spoke to the rugby league media and said that it was urgent that a Super League side should come to Wales. He wondered how long that rugby league would last in Wales if players carried on leaving the sport to go to rugby union, with Wales becoming more and more reliant on the parent and grandparent qualification rule for players.

"It was alright criticising us for bringing Paul [Moriarty] and Devs [John Devereux] back but we were down to Welsh students, that's the brutally honest truth," Griffiths said at the time. "I could have brought in someone like Gareth Stanley from Bradford Bulls, but he's a hooker and I don't need a hooker, I've got three of them already.

"We lost a great opportunity in 1995 to put Super League into Wales when there was a great amount of interest. We could have had an Auckland Warriors-type scenario [which would] provide our own players so that this team could survive beyond the players that we've got now. If the game doesn't want that, then bit by bit the team will be eroded and it will go into hibernation – and maybe this time permanent hibernation.

"There is no clash with rugby union now. The interest in Wales is there, there is no doubt about that. They are rugby daft and they know their rugby league, it's got a great history. There is no problem with rugby union and there are a lot of players who want to play this game. Paul Moriarty couldn't get up here quick enough."

The pundits gave Wales no chance to win in the semi-final against Australia who had been world champions for the last 25 years. Even Jonathan Davies spoke candidly about his nation's hopes: "I won't let sentiment get the better of me here. Wales have got no chance at all," Davies told the BBC at the time. "They will do well to restrict Australia to a 50-point winning margin in fact. It's a total mismatch and if it was a boxing contest, I doubt they would let it go ahead. I would love to be wrong, but I just can't see it happening sadly. I just hope Wales don't end up getting embarrassed."

A day of live Welsh sport on Sky Sports had already started well after Cardiff City Football Club had hammered Bristol Rovers 5–1 in an FA Cup first round game from Ninian Park. Could Wales carry on the success in another footballing code?

England had been embarrassed the day before in their semi-final against New Zealand. After Stephen Kearney had scored on three minutes, the floodgates had opened and the English were on the receiving-end of a record – until 2008 at least – 49–6 defeat. Wales weren't expected to fare any better. They had been beaten 25–10 by England at this stage five years before but, by comparison, this was Mount Everest.

It was no surprise to anyone that Australia won the game, but the story of that night is one that will go down in the memories of everyone who watched it. It's one of the only Welsh defeats that I'm able to watch again and have done so on a number of occasions.

Brett Kimmorley found a gap in the Welsh defence after four minutes for the first Australian try and Wendell Sailor doubled the lead with a try in the corner six minutes later.

It was 8–0 to Australia and a whitewash was predicted. However, Wales hadn't read the script and Ian Watson, returning from injury, scored under the sticks on 14 minutes after receiving a Farrell offload. Harris's kick put Wales just two points behind and three minutes later Lee Briers fed Kris Tassell who dived over in the corner to give Wales the lead. For the first, but not the only time that night, an excited Sky commentator Eddie Hemmings would be shouting "This is unbelievable!"

Harris's kick made the score 12–8 and Huddersfield's McAlpine Stadium was in raptures. The noise would increase even more five minutes later. Lee Briers, playing the game, nay the tournament of his life, picked up an Iestyn Harris bomb from underneath Darren Lockyer's nose. He outjumped the taller Brisbane Broncos full-back and ran unchallenged to the line. Harris's goal made the score 18–8.

By now Wales were playing possession rugby. If they kept hold of the ball, Australia couldn't score. From the first set after the kick-off, Briers landed a drop-goal on the fifth tackle: 19–8. The Australians were in disarray as Briers – once again from the fifth tackle of the first set after kick-off – kicked another one-pointer, this time from the halfway line to make the score 20–8.

Australia finally regained the ball and immediately scored, Brad Fittler running over and Ryan Girdler converting. However Wales almost extended their lead yet again as Anthony Sullivan came close to emulating his father's efforts in 1972 with a long-range World Cup try of his own. But Sullivan had slightly knocked on and was pulled back by the touch judge's decision.

Wales were 20–14 up at half-time and everyone at the McAlpine Stadium was walking around in a daze while having a drink or two to calm their nerves. Wales came out storming again in the second half and Briers went for a hat-trick of drop-goals. The ball went agonisingly wide, but soon there were two more points for Wales when Harris kicked a penalty after Robbie Kearns failed to play the ball properly.

However, by the hour mark, Australia were in the lead thanks to tries from Bryan Fletcher and Lockyer. Wales were tiring after putting their all into the first hour of the game and further tries from Fittler, Lockyer, Craig Gower and Ben Kennedy, the latter with 12 seconds left on the clock, gave Australia a 46–22 win and a place in the Final at Old Trafford against New Zealand – a game that they would win 44–12 but again weren't able to dominate until the last 20 minutes.

"I really enjoyed the 2000 Rugby League World Cup," Lee Briers said. "The Australia game was a team effort, everyone gave their all throughout the game, and the coaching team did a fantastic job getting us ready for it. We knew that we had to give more than 100 per cent, surprised a lot of people and it will go down in history how we almost beat Australia. But in the end it wasn't to be.

"I remember my own try quite well. Iestyn kicked a bomb through and I chased it just to see if I could tackle Lockyer first but I realised when I got there that I could catch it and I just ran for the line. It was one of my most memorable games and was the game of the tournament that year."

"It was fantastic to play against Australia," said Devereux. "We were given no chance. Briers had a great game and his performance helped us build a commanding lead until they finally pulled out the stops and prevented us from causing the biggest upset ever. It was a fantastic performance and occasion – everyone supporting us because we were beating the Aussies for almost an hour."

"The two World Cups that I played in were different for obvious reasons," Harris said. "For the 1995 World Cup, we were based in Cardiff for the majority of the time and it was my first experience of a tournament like that. It was quite a high profile time for Welsh Rugby League playing alongside the likes of Jonathan Davies and Scott Quinnell. In 2000 it was a bit different as the rugby union players had moved back and it was a completely new set of northern based players who had Welsh parents or grandparents. It was a bit more low profile and it didn't have the press or community interest like 1995. However it was an exciting five or six weeks and again a great experience."

The Australia defeat was the swansong for Sullivan, Devereux and Moriarty as Wales were left with none of the team that had kicked off their revival against Papua New Guinea nine years previously. Iestyn Harris was soon to have a spell in rugby union with Cardiff Blues and Wales were also to be without a coach as Clive Griffiths, having repeatedly failed to secure a coaching post in Super League, quit rugby league after 22 years in the game. He was already defence coach at Swansea RUFC by this time. He later joined future Wales rugby union coach Mike Ruddock at the Newport Gwent Dragons – again as defence coach – and was appointed to the Wales rugby union coaching team in 2001. He remained a part of the set up through to the 2003 Rugby Union World Cup and five Six Nations campaigns, including the 2005 Grand Slam where he was credited for his part in tightening Wales's defensive line, particularly in their tackling performance against England. In May 2006 he joined Doncaster RUFC as director of rugby on a three-year deal, leading them to third place in Division One before joining Worcester Warriors as head coach and assistant to director of rugby Mike Ruddock in 2007. Thankfully he was back in rugby league by 2008, coaching the successful Welsh students side in the World Cup in Australia.

For Wales to survive in rugby league they would have to go back to grassroots and build for the future. Fortunately these plans were already in place.

5. Building a base

In March 2003, longstanding Wales rugby league activist Danny Sheehy chaired a meeting of rugby league enthusiasts at Coychurch Road, the home of Bridgend Town Football Club. The idea was to launch a Welsh Rugby League Conference with six teams in the hope of one day turning potential amateur success into a professional organisation and to get the game in Wales back on track.

In the meeting, Sheehy described the events as historic. "This is Wales Rugby League and I am the chairman of Wales Rugby League," he said. "One day people may talk about these events as being as historic as those that took place almost 100 years ago in the George Hotel in Huddersfield."

Those words were prophetic from a man so renowned in the recent history of the amateur game in Wales. Sheehy had been involved in Welsh rugby league since 1982 after founding Aberavon RLC. In addition to that and founding the modern day Welsh Rugby League, he played for Bridgend Blue Dragons and has coached various Welsh sides including Aberavon Fighting Irish, Wales Students and Wales 'A'. It is because of Danny and people like him that there is rugby league to watch in Wales.

After playing friendlies in their first year, Aberavon played a few years in the London League and Southern Amateur Rugby League before entering a competition known as MASWARLA, or to give it its full name, the Midland and South West Amateur Rugby League Association. Aberavon played sides from places such as Plymouth, Bristol, Bath and Birmingham, but the competition wasn't well supported by the sport's governing bodies, the local media didn't really cover it and it folded after a few years.

However, this wasn't down to Aberavon as they were one of the strongest and most proactive teams in the competition and always the side who were willing to travel. Their best season was 1990–91 when they were unbeaten and managed a league and cup double. The first Welsh Amateur rugby league festival was held in Swansea in August 1991. In a 10-a-side tournament, a team called 'Griffins' won the final, beating Bryn Rangers 20-18.

Then the amateur game started to flourish domestically in Wales with a whole host of new clubs formed. In 1993, the game took a forward step when the Welsh Amateur Rugby League Association was renamed the Welsh Rugby League. This was a shift of emphasis which took into account the fact that rugby league in Wales didn't just mean Aberavon fulfilling their fixtures, but also extended to embrace the resurgent national side, the Past Players' Association and the hugely successful student scene at international and domestic level.

By 1994 there were 10 amateur clubs in existence, seven in South Wales and three in the north. Six of the former were in the Welsh Rugby League's own competition which kicked off in October of that year with a 10-a-side tournament in Aberavon that was won by Cardiff Sea Eagles. The three northern clubs competed in the BARLA North-West Counties League while the remaining side was from the Cardiff Institute of Higher Education who were dominating the UK's student game with alarming regularity.

A whole host of volunteers were involved. Danny Sheehy was now the finance executive of the Welsh Rugby League, Cardiff-based councillor Doug Francis was the chairman, Clive Millman, who had been involved with Bridgend Blue Dragons in the 1980s, was chief executive and, importantly, Kerry Sheehy, Danny's brother, was the new RFL-financed development officer.

There was even a little-known Wales 'A' side. A Welsh amateur team beat the touring Russian club side, Moscow Spartak at Swansea's St Helens rugby union ground in 1991. Their first ever international was in May 1994 when they were so close to beating England, but went down 14–10 at the Morfa Stadium in Swansea. This game may not have sent shockwaves around the country and did not receive the publicity that recent 'A' internationals have done, but did produce a new star. Jason Lee was promptly signed by Warrington and ended up playing seven times for the full Welsh national side, scoring four tries in the process.

When rugby league switched to summer and rugby union became open in 1995, allowing professionalism, this could have signalled the end for Welsh rugby league. However, by 1996 a new professional club was established, and attention was being paid to youth development. As part of the work around the failed Super League bids from Cardiff and Swansea, the Welsh Rugby League and their chairman at the time, Doug Francis, believed that it was necessary to form an Academy side to produce the players at grass-roots level. In order for rugby league to secure a permanent base in Wales, it was obvious that a bottom-up approach needed to be adopted. The RFL was approached to support this Academy side which they agreed to do, and following this, the Welsh Rugby League in association with the RFL renewed a partnership with Cardiff County Council to appoint a full-time development officer. With people of the calibre of Richard Hodges, Kerry Sheehy, Mark Isherwood, Stuart Singleton and Wayne Williams taking the role in the first few years, the transformation of Welsh rugby league was dramatic. From 1997 to 1999, over 30 junior schools and 15 secondary schools took part in a development programme and representative sides started to be formed at many different age groups and levels.

However, the main year-round focus from the base at the City Council offices in Cardiff Bay was new club side, Cardiff Demons. Mark Isherwood, who was then the Welsh Rugby League development officer, coached them and they were also temporarily backed by the then owners of Cardiff Devils Ice Hockey side, which apparently is where the Demons name came from. Based at Rumney RFC in the eastern suburbs of Cardiff, the team was made up of mainly first year UWIC (University of Wales Institute in Cardiff, which had previously been called the Cardiff Institute of Higher Education) players initially, because Isherwood thought it was logical that he should target players who were already playing rugby league.

The student game in Wales had been flourishing for a few years. In 1990, Swansea University were University Cup Finalists while in 1990 and 1991, Cardiff Institute of Higher Education swept all before them to become the top student team in the country. International success was achieved by the Welsh Students side in 1991 who beat England and Ireland to become the first British student champions.

Student rugby league was first played in 1967 at Leeds University. Over the next 20 years the student game flourished around the UK and also spread to other countries with the first World Cup being held in New Zealand in 1986. The hosts won the five-team competition with Great Britain, Australia, France and Papua New Guinea also competing.

The second World Cup was held three years later in York and included eight teams with Wales competing for the first time. Wales was drawn in a group with New Zealand, France and for the first time in any international rugby league competition, Holland. The first game

61

saw the Welsh team easily overcome the Dutch 48–10 before losing out to New Zealand 28–10 and France 19–4. Wales's third place group finish gave the team a play-off against Ireland for fifth place which was duly won 48–12.

Australia beat England 10–5 in the final at Wigan which started a domination of the world game at student level that would last for another 10 years. The 1992 World Cup moved to Australia and Wales finished fourth, having been denied third place by a length of the field try in the last minute in the play-off against New Zealand at Parramatta Stadium in Sydney. Wales only lost 14–12 and played superbly for the entire game.

It was a wonderful World Cup for the Welsh squad. In the 12 team tournament, Wales beat Fiji 20–18, Western Samoa 7–6 and Ireland 38–10 to qualify for the quarter-finals in style. Drawn against Fiji again, Wales won 57–20 which meant a semi-final against Australia which Wales lost 25–7.

Many of the 1992 World Cup squad went onto higher achievements. In rugby union Robert Appleyard gained full international honours in the 15-man game. Dai Williams and Gareth Davies went on to represent the full Welsh side in rugby league during the 1995 USA tour alongside Iestyn Harris. Gareth also played for Wales in the 1996 European Championships.

This World Cup saw the rise of the Pacific Islanders with Fiji, Samoa, Tonga and Papua New Guinea all entering sides and proving to be an instant hit. Tonga reached the Final after beating New Zealand 34–16 but went down 32–6 to the Australians.

The 1996 World Cup in England again saw an increase in the number of teams taking part. Japan entered the rugby league world stage for the first time, and the USA carried on the good work of their senior side in the 1995 Emerging Nations World Cup, by not only participating, but beating the Irish. With three groups of four, Wales were drawn in with Australia, Russia and South Africa. After losing all three games, Wales had more success in the consolation Plate competition, beating USA 42–18 then Ireland 20–12 to be ranked ninth in the tournament. Australia beat Samoa 38–16 in the Final.

So the foundations were there for a club side in Wales. As Cardiff Demons became successful, playing at under-18 Academy level against famous professional clubs from the north of England, word spread and there was a heavy influx of players from Merthyr, the Rhondda Valleys and Swansea.

A man who went on to play for Cardiff Demons for some years, Rhodri Thomas, was part of the initial squad and recalls: "Our rugby league knowledge was very limited, but what we could do was play fast exciting rugby which surprised a lot of the heartlanders," he recalled. "We finished fourth during that first season playing sides like Dewsbury, Doncaster and York and, in the second season, we reached the Academy Second Division Grand Final."

The 1998 Final was against Hunslet Hawks and Cardiff's side included future Welsh rugby league internationals Gareth Dean and Neil Davies as well as a man who has become more famous playing rugby union, Gethin Jenkins.

"Gethin and I were both playing [union] for Pontypridd when we decided to play some rugby league," Dean said. "We both had a good time playing for Cardiff Demons [academy side] and it put us both in the shop window. Gethin decided to go back to rugby union with Pontypridd and the Blues and fair play to him, he hasn't looked back as he's played many times for Wales and the Lions now. I was spotted by Wigan and I haven't looked back either. I've always enjoyed playing rugby league, I think my style of play is more suited to league than union and I've gone from being a flanker in union to prop or second row in league."

At one stage in the Final, Hunslet looked like they would walk it after going 28 points up at the interval without reply, but the Demons blasted their way back into the game in dramatic fashion to leave the Hawks hanging on desperately. The final score was 39-30 to Hunslet with substitute Damian Adams grabbing a second half hat-trick for the Demons, Stefan Santala and Nathan Hopkins also crossing.

Despite the defeat, Cardiff were promoted to Division One for 1999, but found life tougher at the higher level, losing all of their games, the last at home to Featherstone Rovers 80–6. After fulfilling just 14 out their 18 games in 2000, the club pulled out of the Academy League.

"The academy set up was fantastic and it was a shame that it stopped," Rhodri Thomas added. "I think the sponsors withdrew their backing after Cardiff lost out to Gateshead Thunder for that Super League franchise in 1999 and that didn't really help us."

In those four years, two other players made such an impression that they were given trial opportunities with professional clubs, Gareth King with Hunslet Hawks and Ian Macintyre with Hull Kingston Rovers. Aled James, later with Widnes, Sheffield Eagles and Celtic Crusaders, also started his rugby league career in this Academy side.

The next Student World Cup was in 1999 and was an ambitious and memorable 12-team tournament in six countries. Paris hosted Group A between France, Russia and Japan; Glasgow hosted Group B between England, South Africa and Scotland; Cardiff was home for Group C between Wales, New Zealand and Canada; while Belfast and Dublin shared Group D between Ireland, Australia and USA.

The games in the Welsh group were all played at Glamorgan Wanderers ground in Cardiff's western suburbs. Wales beat Canada 72–12 in the first game, New Zealand then beat Canada 88–0 before a dramatic and passionate clash when New Zealand beat Wales 46–10 to qualify for the semi-finals. They beat England 46–16 in the Final while Wales lost 26–16 to Ireland in the Bowl Semi-Finals before beating South Africa 26–24 to secure seventh place. All of the knockout stages were held in England.

Wales had representation in the Rugby League Challenge Cup for the first time in 14 years when UWIC were invited to take place in the 1998–99 competition. They lost 24–4 at Barrow Island in Cumbria but after retaining the British Student Rugby League (BUSA) Championship in 1999, they were again offered a first round spot for 1999-2000. However, because the RFL wanted a non-university Welsh side in the competition, Leeds Met University, who UWIC beat in the 1999 BUSA Final took the student place and Richard Hodges, the new rugby league development officer for Wales, contacted UWIC and asked if they could put a team on the park, but not under the name of UWIC or student Rugby League.

So Cardiff Demons and UWIC combined forces for a brief period. The Cardiff Demons name wasn't chosen for these matches as the players wanted to sever ties with the Academy club so for a brief period, the Cardiff Cougars were born and were drawn away to Durham in the first round. Rhodri Thomas, who played in all the matches in that Challenge Cup run, remembers the campaign starting with this trip in December 1999: "The first round was one hell of a game," he said. "We left Cardiff at 6am after literally driving around the city dragging players out of bed. There were 17 of us plus kit bags on a 16-seater mini bus all the way up to Durham. I think we got there about 45 minutes before kick-off, a quick warm-up and then it was one of those days when everything went right. I think we took Durham a bit unaware and won the game quite comfortably 36-6.

"The second round was played at UWIC Rugby League's home ground at Llandaff and was featured on BBC television's *Grandstand* with Ray French on the sidelines. Our 18–10 win was probably the shock of the round as Rochdale Mayfield were a very good side. We had some very good players at that time – I think we had six Great Britain student internationals and almost the entire squad had represented Wales at student level."

Cardiff's win over Rochdale Mayfield was heavily featured in local papers in both Cardiff and Rochdale with the *Rochdale Observer* producing the headline "Welshmen spoil Field's Dreams". Cardiff's reward for their efforts was an away trip to Keighley Cougars.

"The third round was a fantastic experience," Rhodri Thomas remembers. "This time the Student Rugby League handed some money to the university to let us stay in Leeds the night before. Cougar Park was the ground where we had won the BUSA final the year before and we all knew it was a nice facility, but the standard of play we came up against that day was outstanding. At that time Keighley were second in the Northern Ford Premiership and were challenging for Super League status. All I remember is that they scored on the fifth tackle about eight times and Jason Lee, their Welsh international, scored four tries. The Keighley crowd appreciated the effort we showed, but we were totally outclassed. It is a day that not one of the 17 [players] involved will ever forget, despite losing 90–0."

Following the success of the Challenge Cup run and the earlier demise of the Demons academy side, it was decided to reform at open-age level and enter a team from Cardiff in the new Rugby League Conference. This was a competition that had recently set British Rugby League alight. Formed by a group of pioneers including Julian Harrison, Bev Risman, Harry Jepson and Lionel Hurst in the south of England to take the amateur game into new areas by playing in the summer, the competition started with 10 teams in 1997. By the time Cardiff joined in 2001, they were one of 30, while in 2008, the competition that was won by Celtic Crusaders Colts included 88 teams in 13 divisions – one national, four premier and eight regional in a three-tiered set-up.

In early 2001 in the back room of UWIC's Llandaff gymnasium, Stuart Singleton, Mark Tattersall, Mark Lee and Pete Gooding met to discuss an opportunity for people in South Wales to continue to play rugby league at a senior, open-age level.

Stuart Singleton was the new Welsh Rugby League development officer. A former Welsh student international, he had signed forms for Gateshead Thunder before their 1999 Super League campaign. However, he broke his leg in a pre-season game, putting an end to his stint at Thunder and his professional career. So he returned to Wales after applying for the vacant development officer post.

Singleton remembers: "We decided to use the Cardiff Demons name for a number of reasons. They already had a high profile in the rugby league community and South Wales due to the work done previously, there were already a number of playing kits, albeit old, with the Cardiff Demons logo on it and there was already a jacquard at the embroidery shop so a lot of the initial set up costs had already been accounted for.

"Although the club was called Cardiff Demons, there was no relationship to the previous team. The initial name for the club had UWIC's name was in there somewhere because of the relationship with the club and UWIC at that stage, but the RFL asked us to drop it."

While the quartet didn't give themselves specific job titles to start with, Gooding was put in charge of junior development, Tattersall did more on the administration and media side of the club, Lee did all the matchday duties, team management and accessing money for the club, and Singleton worked more with the playing side.

Tattersall was certainly an influential man to have involved in rugby league in Wales because he was, at the time, sports editor on the *Western Mail.* While he wasn't directly involved in the earlier Academy club or in the Challenge Cup matches in 1999-2000, he had followed the games due to his position in the media when he had fairly regular contact with Singleton's predecessors, Richard Hodges and Mark Isherwood.

"I'd first met the others before at an amateur international against Ireland at Pontyclun," he remembers. "Mark Lee was captain and Stu was there to watch his brother Richard. Stu and I got chatting on the touchline, and then I got to know him when he subsequently got the development officer's job. My other memory of that day was a tree falling down near the pitch just before kick-off. I suppose you could say that we've pulled up a few trees since then with rugby league in South Wales.

"Although the initial meeting at UWIC represented the start of a lot of hard work and frustrations, it was quite exciting to be doing something about helping to establish rugby league here. UWIC were just about the top student side in those days, but students move on and we wanted to establish something that was rooted in South Wales and not at the university. We didn't know then whether it would succeed, but it was good to be doing something rather than just talking about it and bemoaning the missed chances in the past.

"A big part in our thinking was the various failed attempts to parachute in a Super League franchise in either Swansea or Cardiff. A lot of the resistance and prejudice had disappeared, but we felt strongly there was no real future in parachuting in an 'alien' Super League franchise, when the sport had no infrastructure or obvious fan base here to support it. That was my original aim: to start building that infrastructure."

Cardiff Demons' first season in the Rugby League Conference saw them finish with a 50 per cent record with four wins from eight games played. They were put in the South West Conference that included teams from Hemel Hempstead, Gloucestershire, Worcestershire and Oxford while cross-Conference games were also to be played against Leicester and St Albans.

The season was due to be 12 games, but four of Cardiff's opposition didn't get to the Welsh capital for one reason or another and their games were forfeited. While shortage of players or a bus breaking down were a couple of the reasons offered, the Demons' first game of the season against Gloucestershire Warriors on a sunny first weekend in May was in doubt throughout the week because foot-and-mouth disease had been diagnosed in farms the length and breadth of Britain. Gloucestershire was one of the worst areas affected with 76 outbreaks that year. It wasn't until the day of the match that Stuart Singleton made the official announcement that the game was off because the Warriors were unable to pull together a team to travel and the Demons, with no effort whatsoever, had earned their first competition points.

Their second season in 2002 was also reduced, this time to 10 games and Cardiff finished second with six wins and four defeats giving them a play-off place and an appearance on HTV Wales's show *Hot Pursuit*. Cardiff faced West London Sharks in their final match of the season going down 34–26 in the last play-off game despite leading 26–10 with 25 minutes left. This game was Stuart Singleton's and his brother Richard's final involvement with the club. Stuart left to take up a development role at London Skolars while Richard signed for Sheffield Eagles and later joined his brother in the capital.

Internationally, the Wales A side had been revived. From 1998-2001, the team played friendlies only, with a number of games against Scotland 'A' and England Lionhearts in grounds in Glasgow, Cardiff and Cheltenham. The final match was a 40–22 win over Scotland in Hull of all places which was featured on Sky Sports's *Boots 'n' All* programme. However, in 2002 a proper Home Nations tournament was organised with representative sides from England, Ireland, Scotland and Wales taking part. For the Celtic nations, this was simply the best talent that they could muster from outside the professional leagues, all of them home grown players. The English team comprised the best of their players competing in the Rugby League Conference and was called England Lionhearts.

Wales had an excellent start to the tournament, proving the critics wrong by beating Scotland 40–22 in Glasgow with Rhodri Thomas going over for a hat-trick of tries. Stuart Singleton, Pete Moore, Mark Dando and Sion Williams also crossed with Aled James kicking four goals and Richard Singleton two.

A bigger win was to follow against Ireland at Old Penarthians RFC, the home of Cardiff Demons at the time. The score was a clear 52–20. Two tries for Wes Palmer and one each for Gareth Morgan, Liam Doubler, Richard Singleton, Dave Jenkins, Pete Gooding, Matt Cannon and Pete Moore secured the victory, with Singleton kicking six goals, Doubler and Ben Kerr one each.

The scene was set for a decider at the Prince of Wales Stadium in Cheltenham on 15 September 2002. The England Lionhearts had beaten Scotland 58–8 following their opening round 32–10 win in

Ireland so, with home advantage, started out as strong favourites against the Welsh.

The trophy for the tournament is called the Cheltenham Regency Trophy after being donated by the town's council for the inaugural tournament. In addition to hosting an amateur friendly there two years before, Cheltenham had also staged a Great Britain versus New Zealand international way back in 1908. However, this game 94 years later was played in far less auspicious circumstances, after a Cheltenham Tigers rugby union match. The local gateman was close to refusing the Wales and England players entry into the ground when they arrived unless they each paid £5 because the rugby union game was still going on. After putting him firmly in his place about the importance of the 5.30pm fixture and the fact that the Tigers match was merely a curtain-raiser - the look on his face was priceless following that remark – the players and officials entered the ground through the players' entrance.

In the match itself, England led 12–4 at the break. Wales had enjoyed plenty of first-half possession, but kept losing the ball in English territory and only had a 28th-minute try from Gareth Honor to show for their efforts.

But the second half was a different story. The close-knit Welsh side, that featured several players from Cardiff Demons and UWIC supplemented by Welshmen who played for Conference clubs Hemel, Teesside and champions Coventry, were fired up by coach Wayne Williams's half-time talk and had levelled the scores within 10 minutes of the restart. Tries from Wes Palmer, Rhodri Thomas, Rich Pepperell and David Jenkins gave Wales a 22–12 lead with 17 minutes to play. Although England came back with a Dave Wattam try, Wales were not to be denied and when Matt Cannon went in at the corner, it was all over and a Richard Singleton penalty sealed a great night for Wales.

At the end of 2002, Cardiff were invited back into the Rugby League Challenge Cup. Welsh clubs had entered the competition in the 2000–01 and 2001–02 competitions but without success. At the end of 2000, a Welsh Students side was invited and drew Cumbrian side, Askam at home. A tricky tie on a wet pitch at UWIC, Llandaff in Cardiff on Sunday 3 December 2000, saw three conversions from Neil Atkinson that gave the Cumbrians a close 18–15 victory. Paul Jones, Tom Butler and Mike Bolton scored the three Askam tries. Welsh

Students replied with tries from Simon Scott, Richard Norton and Ben Stirling. Russ Thomas kicked one conversion while Neil Davies scored a drop-goal.

In 2001, a year later to the day, the Welsh entrants fell at the first hurdle again as the Royal Air Force hammered UWIC 40–13. Cardiff Demons were hoping to go one better in the 2002–03 season.

I was appointed team manager for this game and there couldn't have been a trickier tie as the draw sent us up to National Conference League Division One side, Shaw Cross Sharks who were right in the middle of their season. The game attracted a lot of interest in Yorkshire, so much so that it was agreed to switch the tie to Dewsbury Rams' stadium. The game was also to be transmitted live on BBC Radio Bradford while the newspapers were giving it plenty of coverage.

On the eve of the game we had a full squad. However, by 8am on Sunday morning, this had trickled down to only 14. Travelling with only one substitute meant that Cardiff were up against it right from the start and it was no surprise when the home side took an early lead through Joe Dickinson. By half-time, the Sharks had rattled in six more tries and we were 40–0 down.

The half-time talk from new coach Wayne Williams did wonders as after only 30 seconds of the second period, Dan Clements went over for Cardiff's first try while Matthew Dawe added another before the game was over. The final score was 56-12. Cardiff were well beaten but applauded off the field as their second half performance had won them plenty of friends at the Shaw Cross club and in the large crowd.

While 2003 won't be seen by much of the general public as a triumphant year for Welsh rugby league, for me it was a very memorable time. I took over as chairman of Cardiff Demons RLFC and by the end of the year had been appointed as press officer to the Welsh national side.

For Welsh rugby league as a whole, expansion certainly was the name of the game. The success of Cardiff Demons and the Wales 'A' side had highlighted the need for more teams to be formed in Wales. Already there was Swansea Bulls, who had played a number of friendlies in 2002, and Cynon Valley Cougars, who thanks to the work of people like Colin Neale and Andy Lindley, had already made some noises at junior levels, especially in the Abercynon, Pontypridd and Merthyr Tydfil areas.

Cardiff had applied for entry into the new National League Three, but eventually withdrew having decided that the level of competition would have been too much too soon. This decision was justified when looking at Hemel's record in the inaugural season. The Stags had beaten Cardiff every time that the two sides had met but went on to lose every game at this higher level.

Another decision that had to be made immediately was the choice of which region Cardiff would play in during 2003. For the last two years the Demons had been playing in England, but now there was to be some local competition. Six new sides had formed in Wales and a Welsh Conference had been created. After some intense deliberation it was decided that Cardiff should compete in England during the 2003 season, letting the new Welsh teams find their feet together.

In addition to Swansea and Cynon Valley, there were four more new sides: Rumney Rhinos, Torfaen Tigers, Aberavon Fighting Irish and Bridgend Blue Bulls. It was the Bulls who would set the benchmark for all the teams in Wales and it was their presence that seriously accelerated the development of the sport in the country. While these teams were all mainly drawing their players from local rugby union teams, players who were either eager to try a new sport or simply keep fit over the summer – in Bridgend it was a different story because it gave local rugby league heroes Allan Bateman, John Devereux and Kevin Ellis a chance to return to the sport.

Bateman was 38 at the time, Devereux 37 and Ellis 36. While none of them were of an age to be turning out regularly in Super League, they were all still performing at the highest level of Welsh rugby union, with Bateman winning his final Welsh union cap against Tonga just two years before, scoring a try in their 51–7 win. All three were very enthusiastic about returning to rugby league especially Ellis, who is still involved in the sport at time of writing.

"My Cardiff Blues contract had just come to an end in the summer of 2003," he said. "Niel Wood, the administrator of the Rugby League Conference, came down to Wales and had a chat with John, Allan and myself about setting up a club in the Welsh Conference. We started recruiting and spreading the word and it got up and running. I really enjoyed playing in the first few years of the Blue Bulls.

"We attracted high crowds, especially in the first season. I think it was due to the fact that we had high profile names in the side and we were especially thankful to all the shops and businesses around town for promoting the game. Everyone was so enthusiastic both on and off the field.

"We had a lot of boys turn out for us who were playing in the Welsh Rugby Union Premiership, such as Grant Epton and Karl Hocking. We also had players from a few other different rugby union clubs in the area and that helped to increase the crowds as well.

"We played at Coychurch Road, home of Bridgend Town Football Club and we were attracting regular crowds of between 600 and 800 people which were the highest crowds at this level of rugby league in Great Britain. We were very successful."

The Welsh Rugby League season launched a week after another momentous occasion for the country, when Cardiff's Millennium Stadium hosted the first of what was to be three Challenge Cup Finals in a row. Bradford Bulls beat Leeds Rhinos 22–20 in front of 71,212 people, all of whom seemed to thoroughly enjoy the occasion.

"The Millennium Stadium is the finest stadium in the British Isles," David Watkins told *Rugby League World* magazine at the time. "It has been fantastic to see a rugby league game being played here in front of a full house.

"The atmosphere was sensational, and those rugby union people I have spoken to cannot believe the power, the fitness, the strength and speed and the skills of the players on show. It was a tremendous spectacle and the drama was spellbinding. Welsh people love their rugby, and they know they are seeing quality and that game was real quality. I really enjoyed it and feel the Rugby League should look at bringing the Final back here next year."

Meanwhile, Bridgend Blue Bulls overcame all comers in the first regular season of the Welsh Conference. Ten wins out of 10 with 608 points scored and only 197 conceded culminated in an 84–1 win over Swansea in their final game. With media coverage in the *South Wales Echo*, *Glamorgan Gazette* and triumphantly on the BBC Sport website, this new competition had given Welsh rugby league the boost that it needed.

While Bridgend were gaining admirers in their final game at Coychurch Road, in the English South-West Conference Cardiff

Demons had also claimed a championship pennant by winning nine out of their 10 games. Unlike the Blue Bulls, they couldn't maintain a 100 per cent record and lost to new side Somerset Vikings 26–16 in Taunton in their final game.

So with the regular season over, the play-offs loomed large on the horizon. Niel Wood and his administrators had come up with the ingenious idea that in the eight Conferences around England and Wales, when it came to the play-offs, the two local leagues would team up with each other. The two champion sides would play-off in the first round with the winners going through to round 3 while the two second placed sides would also meet in round 1 with the winners of this tie facing the losers of the other match in the second round. It gets easier to understand if you carry on reading.

Bridgend had home advantage in the first game of the play-offs thanks to their superior record in the regular season and the scene was set for a tie that all local Welsh rugby league fans had been waiting for a game between Bridgend Blue Bulls and Cardiff Demons. Kevin Ellis reflects on that warm Thursday night in August 2003: "I remember the match against Cardiff Demons – the highlights were shown on Sky Sports," he said. "The Demons came down and really fronted up. It was quite a star-studded occasion. Lee Byrne was playing for us, Jonathan Davies was there watching, it was an amazing night."

A 38–14 win for Bridgend certainly didn't tell the whole story with Cardiff right in the game until the final 10 minutes when the Bulls scored two further tries. Writing for the *South Wales Echo*, Simon Davies was certainly impressed with what he saw.

"The crowd roared as breaks were made and tries were scored and gasped at the intensity from both sides," he wrote. "They marvelled at the skills and fitness of Welsh forwards like Cardiff's Wes Palmer and Bridgend's Karl Hocking, and the handling of Kevin Ellis, once of Warrington and now of Bridgend, and of young pretender Gareth Jones, the talented Demons stand-off from Carmarthenshire. And finally they were presented with a memorable rugby duel, a footrace for the try that decided the game. Small children played on a green and white bouncy castle 'Y Draig Goch' – the red dragon – perhaps to remind us all that we were really in Bridgend and not in Lancashire or Yorkshire."

Jonathan Davies was certainly impressed with what he saw: "I enjoyed seeing the game," he told the *South Wales Echo.* "It was very physical with lots of effort and I was pleasantly surprised with the great handling skills and commitment of both teams. Let us hope that events of this kind become a regular feature in the sporting calendar."

Bridgend went straight through to round three of the play-offs while Cardiff now had to travel to Aberavon Fighting Irish who had hammered Gloucestershire Warriors 58–30 in the first week. The game, played on Saturday 9 August 2003, was also the hottest weekend in British history with temperatures of 38 degrees Celsius being reached in certain parts of the country. The temperature reached more than 30 in Aberavon and with air conditioners on in cars which were being used as substitutes' benches on the side of the pitch, the Fighting Irish had a magnificent final quarter of the game that brought them 25 unanswered points – despite being down to 12 men – to win 47–21.

Aberavon's reward was a trip to Bridgend to decide the unofficial Welsh championship which Bridgend dominated from start to finish winning 42–8. A national semi-final against Ipswich Rhinos followed with the Blue Bulls winning comfortably 44–24. However, the Ipswich team was never outclassed, and their scrum-half Tane Trafford lost nothing in comparison with Kevin Ellis.

So Bridgend Blue Bulls were in the Final of the National Conference with Carlisle Centurions awaiting them. Meanwhile, the Rugby League Conference had organised a consolation tournament, known as the Shield, open to anyone who wasn't involved in the main play-offs. Torfaen Tigers enthusiastically stormed through to the Final with wins over Bristol Sonics 82–12, Oxford Cavaliers – again 82–12 – Somerset Vikings 50–18 and Gosport and Fareham Vikings 36–26. Bolton Le Moors awaited them in their Final.

There were dramas leading up to the games with both Bridgend and Torfaen expressing concerns that they wouldn't able to keep to the original date of Saturday 6 September because many of their players had contracts with rugby union clubs. Controversially, they requested a postponement of 24 hours and, even more controversially, the Rugby League Conference administrators, presumably after conferring with the other finalists accepted the change.

This is where the Rugby League Conference struck lucky. The postponement made for a bigger occasion because the two games would now sandwich a Super League tie between Warrington Wolves and Halifax at Wilderspool. The professional game was nowhere near a sell-out because this was an end-of-season clash with nothing to play for. But now added attractions were Warrington crowd favourites from the past, Kevin Ellis and Allan Bateman, playing for a final time at Wilderspool. Torfaen lost a hard-fought match 28–21, but Bridgend went home with their trophy and were National Conference champions thanks to a 33–26 win.

Torfaen's final was an exciting, if at times bad-tempered encounter. It looked like the Welsh side were going to take silverware in their first season as they cruised to a 20–12 half-time lead. However, a hat-trick for man of the match, hooker Craig Kay helped Bolton to their win.

Bridgend's win was a thriller from start to finish. Defences may have ruled for the first 20 minutes but after that the game opened up. John Williams claimed the first 10 points for the Welshmen, courtesy of two penalties and a converted try, but a fantastic tackle by Dean Haney forced Geraint Lewis to knock on from the restart and from the resultant scrum Dale Semple ghosted through the Welsh defence to lay on a perfect pass for Paul McGee to score the first of his two tries.

Very soon, Carlisle levelled the game at 10–10 and a see-saw game followed. A Mike Davies converted try made the score 16–10 at the interval, Dan Shore powered in at the corner to extend the lead from kick-off but Carlisle responded with three quick tries to go 26–22 up. However, Karl Hocking scored, but the missed conversion meant it was 26–26 with 10 minutes remaining before Ellis's long pass and Karl Hocking's judicious short one sent in Mike Davies to give the Bulls the lead again, one that they wouldn't let slip away.

Ellis was outstanding in the closing stages, his kick and chase put Carlisle on the back foot and his successful drop-goal added to the pressure as the clock wound down. Carlisle were caught offside wide out on their own '20' in the 76th minute and Williams' sixth successful goal sealed the win.

The game, which was transmitted live on BBC Radio Cumbria and made the sports pages of many of the national papers, was a massive boost to the publicity of rugby league in Wales. The Warrington crowd, who came early in numbers for their Super League encounter with

Halifax, witnessed a classic, and their passionate enthusiasm, principally for their former favourites, produced the perfect backdrop.

"The National Final at Warrington was amazing," Ellis remembers. "Allan Bateman and I loved going back to Wilderspool as we always enjoyed playing there. It was a wonderful atmosphere as usual and a very memorable day. It was a tough game, quite close in the end, and to play for Bridgend in a final at Warrington was, for me, a dream come true."

Wales 'A' retained the Cheltenham Regency Trophy in 2003 despite losing the first game in Ireland 32–28. Even though new clubs had entered the fray, the side was again dominated by players from Cardiff Demons with nine players in the 17 for the first game. Trips to places like Ireland had become a little controversial: players in the 'A' team had to pay for their own passage to away matches and if someone couldn't afford the trip then it wasn't possible for them to represent their country. Thankfully this would change within a few years.

Wayne Williams made a number of changes, both in manpower and positional, to the side for the Scotland game in Bridgend and these came to fruition as Wales recorded a 48–22 win. So, in the final game against England in Aberavon Wales needed a four-point win to retain their title because the Lionhearts had also won their first two games. For the third game in a row there were no Bridgend Blue Bulls players in the side. This was due to the fact that none of their players wanted or were able to play for their country. The club versus country argument had extended to 'A' international level, but thankfully this would change in the years to come and players from the Blue Bulls would become regulars for Wales 'A'.

England struck first in the sixth minute through Dave Wattam but Wales hit back in front of the home crowd through Aberavon Fighting Irish team mates Sean O'Brien and Darren Ryan to lead 10–4 after only 15 minutes.

England surprisingly went for the drop goal option through David Harries, to bring the Welsh' lead back to five points but, when O'Brien crossed again just before half time, the Dragons were up 14–5.

A more determined England side came out in the second half and instantly turned that determination into points. A try through Chris Keld in the corner followed by a lurking Tom Brown who dropped onto a loose ball in the Welsh in-goal area put the Lionhearts up 17–14, with the chance of an English victory back on the cards.

Swansea Bulls' Simon Bevan put Wales back in front when he crossed in the 67th minute, giving the Welsh a three-point advantage, but England came back again when David Harries kicked another one-pointer.

However, Wales had no intentions of letting the English get any closer. Cardiff prop, Wes Palmer powered over the line in the 75th minute, and winger Ben Kerr secured the championship when he scored right on time to make the final score 28–18 to Wales.

With Wales now producing players at the lower levels who could play some seriously good rugby league, the time was right for a proper revival of the international game at the highest level. The loss-making World Cup of 2000 had dented many nations' opportunities of hosting full internationals but that was about to change. In fact the next couple of years would lead to developments unheard of in the history of Welsh rugby league.

The Welsh players line up for the national anthems before the match against England at Wrexham in 2001. (Photo: Peter Lush)

Wales versus England at Wrexham in 2001 – a midfield battle.
(Photo: Peter Lush)

6. Rebuilding in Wales

The fall-out following the 2000 World Cup had ramifications throughout the world of rugby league. The tournament had expected to make a profit of between £2 and £10 million which would have been split between the Rugby League International Federation's member nations. Fiji had planned to build new headquarters to set up a much-needed academy while nations like Russia, Morocco, South Africa and the USA were banking on the essential development funding. However, this wasn't to be and the profits made just about covered the salary of a new international development officer.

The following year was the ultimate reboot for the Welsh national side. Long-term coach Clive Griffiths had departed for pastures new and Widnes coach Neil Kelly, who assisted Griffiths in the 2000 World Cup, had been appointed to the top role. It was a big disappointment that Wales were given just one game in 2001. But what a game it was – England at home, and another test in Wrexham, North Wales following the success of the Wales versus Cook Islands World Cup match at the Racecourse Ground the year before.

North Wales has unfortunately often been overlooked by many in Welsh Rugby League. The governing body has always been in South Wales, so perhaps unfairly there is a perception that they have sometimes been left out of things. However, a lot has changed in the last 20 years. The original North Wales Coasters club played between 1989 and 1997 in the North West Counties League, gaining promotion on two occasions and raising the profile of rugby league in Wales after being featured on S4C's magazine programme *Heno*.

The club regularly travelled the length and breadth of Wales to encourage the establishment of a rugby league network, playing in Holyhead, Ruthin, Wrexham and South Wales, with even a game at the Vetch Field before the Wales versus France international in 1992.

The club disbanded in 1997, not because of a shortage of players, but a lack of volunteers off the field. They reformed in 2001 to play in the Rugby League Conference determined not to repeat past mistakes and, after a period in Colwyn Bay, they have since renamed and become Rhyl Coasters. Now with former Welsh international and WRL president Mike Nicholas on board helping them from his Warrington base, they are producing quality players at all levels with Kriss Wilkes playing for the Great Britain under-18s in 2008 and 2009.

So, this international in North Wales in 2001 was necessary to further the advancement of the game in the area and it was a big success. However the first thing Wales had to do was to build a team.

Although Wales have never been afraid to call up players who qualify on the parent or grandparent rule, suspicious fans have periodically questioned their commitment to the red jersey, especially if they were not living in Wales. However one can never question the motives of one of the five Welsh debutants against England in 2001 – Mark Lennon.

Lennon, playing with Celtic Crusaders in 2009, qualified for Wales because his mother was born in Tredegar and brought up in Blackwood before moving to Australia after meeting Mark's dad. The half-back first decided that he wanted to play for Wales when he was only 14 sitting in the stands at Ninian Park not quite knowing who to support as he was watching Wales play Australia on the 1994 Kangaroo tour.

"We were on holiday to the UK as a family," Lennon explains. "And while visiting family in Blackwood and the Newport area we decided to go along to Ninian Park for the match. It was while watching the game that I decided that I wanted to play for Wales. I remember saying to my mum and dad that as I qualify for Wales, I want to play for them one day. I don't know why, it was just one of those things – I wanted to play for Wales."

While many other Welsh sportsmen (and some politicians), simply stand there while the National Anthem is played during a Welsh match or event, Mark Lennon didn't want to become another John Redwood, the former Conservative English minister for Wales, who clearly could not sing the anthem. So when he was first selected for the England clash, he made sure that he knew all the words.

"Although I don't speak Welsh, I know my national anthem by heart," he adds. "Mum taught it to me over the phone and by email when I told her I'd been selected for Wales. I'm very proud of my Welsh heritage and I knew that I just couldn't be standing there not knowing the anthem after seeing it being sung so well, so many times before by others. It's a very passionate anthem and it's always enjoyable to sing."

Wales versus England at Wrexham – Wales squashing an England attack.
(Photo: Peter Lush)

Other debutants that day were Gareth Dean, Gareth Price, Steffan Hughes and Keith Mason. For Hughes, it was his only Welsh cap after missing out through injury in both 1999 and 2000. Mason would make one further appearance, against New Zealand the following year, but the two Gareths would, like Lennon, go on to become regulars in the Welsh jersey.

Kelly was looking forward to the England clash that was to be played on a summer evening, one of the most perfect times of the year for an international game, Tuesday 31 July. England and Wales had been the losing semi-finalists from the 2000 World Cup and Kelly saw the match as an unofficial third-place play-off.

"We lost in the semi-finals against Australia, England lost to New Zealand in their semi-final, and there's probably a bit of unfinished business from that tournament," he told *Rugby League World* magazine at the time.

"That will be part of what we want to say when we meet up as a squad although any game between England and Wales is a big game anyway. The Welsh side has got such a great tradition and achieved so much over the last decade so it's a very exciting time for me. The World Cup gave me a good opportunity to get to know the players and the workings of the Welsh side. I enjoyed the whole experience and it whet my appetite for more."

81

It was a beautiful warm summer evening in Wrexham and the healthy crowd of 6,373 and one of Sky Sports' largest rugby audiences of that year witnessed a classic.

Wales were written off before the game had even started thanks to a few injury-forced withdrawals, including Iestyn Harris who, with Cardiff Blues on the horizon, wasn't given the swansong he deserved. However, to his credit, he turned up and was given the much-needed role of water carrier in this intense match. Keiron Cunningham did play, but nobody knew at the time that this would be his last match for Wales. It was expected that he would join Harris in Welsh rugby union but after "not wanting to play for Swansea in front of 1,500 on a wet November afternoon" he decided to stay with St Helens. With the exception of the New Zealand game in 2002 when he was injured, Cunningham was not selected for Wales again because he was too good; or in other words he was always picked for Great Britain in future years following the seemingly farcical decision by those in power to schedule Wales games at the same time as Lions tests.

But this game was played in the middle of summer and, just like in Wales's previous outing against Australia the year before it was Lee Briers who gave a man-of-the-match performance with a try, four goals and a drop-goal.

Wales scored three quick tries through Jason Lee, the first of two for him that night, Damien Gibson and Briers to go 16–0 up in 15 minutes. England hit back via tries from Jamie Peacock and Paul Sculthorpe, the first of his hat-trick, before Jason Lee scored his second to give Wales an eight-point lead at the interval.

At half-time, England coach David Waite shuffled his team around and this seemed to work as they scored four tries without reply in the first 25 minutes of the half. Wales replied with two further scores through Chris Morley and Paul Atcheson to cut the gap to five points but then Paul Wellens scored in the corner to give England an exciting 42–33 win.

"I'm thrilled and very grateful to a group of players whom we didn't have the right to expect a performance like that from," Kelly told the journalists after the game. "It was a hectic build-up and the last player we called up arrived at the team hotel at lunchtime on the day of the game. Jason Lee and Jason Critchley got very late call-ups and were very professional about it and played very well."

It was mooted that Wales would play a test against Australia later in the year, especially seeing as how they had done so well against them the year before. However, events across the Atlantic on 11 September put a lot of things into perspective, sport included such as events like Golf's Ryder Cup which was postponed for a year and its schedule was put back permanently as a result. Australia were due to travel over to the UK for a full Ashes tour including warm-up games but following the devastating attacks in New York and Washington DC where more than 3,000 people lost their lives, the Kangaroos wanted to cancel their tour completely. In the end they were persuaded to travel but played only a three-test series against Great Britain which they won 2–1.

The following year, Wales were still given just the one game. Despite the success of the England game, the match was strangely not rescheduled but Wales had the marvellous consolation of a home game against the touring New Zealand side at the Millennium Stadium in Cardiff – not that the stadium's authorities did anything to help promote the contest. The clash on 3 November 2002 was sandwiched between a couple of Welsh rugby union internationals and while the ticket office on St Mary Street in Cardiff was happily displaying large posters for these matches as well as other events at the stadium, the rugby league match was relegated to an A5 flyer on the desk. When asked them why they weren't promoting it as well the reply was "Well we're a rugby union ticket office!"

It hadn't helped matters that Cunningham had pulled out of the game after injuring his hand while training at home. The man who had taken over as Welsh skipper the year before had apparently been looking forward to the clash and was a central part of the Welsh Rugby League's promotion of the match.

Neil Kelly, now Super League's Coach-of-the-Year after guiding Widnes Vikings to within one point of a play-off spot just a year after their promotion, was disappointed to hear of the news of Cunningham's withdrawal second-hand and was unable to contact his captain personally.

"I didn't see Keiron here today and I don't know what the English doctor will diagnose with regard to him playing for Great Britain next week," he said. "Your guess is as good as mine." Cunningham was fit for Great Britain's test match in Blackburn six days later, which they lost 30–16.

Kelly gave three men their Welsh debuts that Sunday afternoon, Adam Hughes, Robert Roberts and David Mills, son of the legendary Jim Mills who had won 13 full caps for Wales between 1975 and 1979.

"It was great to make my debut at such a stadium," David said. "It meant a lot to me and I know it meant a lot to my dad as well. It was a real experience and it was a big occasion. We got beaten on the day but I think I did alright and like I said, it was just good to play at the Millennium Stadium as it's a special place. It's the only time that I played there for Wales but I did return for Millennium Magic weekends, and people may have criticised them but they were good for the fans and everyone gets a buzz in playing in such a big occasion."

New Zealand were far too strong for Wales that day in a Millennium Stadium that was bereft of any real atmosphere. The attendance was 8,746, very similar to a Welsh rugby union international in Wrexham the day before but, with the stadium only an eighth full, the noise echoed around. However, the League authorities did have the sensible idea of putting everyone on one side of the ground and in the lower tier there was the best atmosphere.

The first half was a close and exciting contest with the Kiwis just 18–10 up at the interval. New Zealand led from start to finish but did have a few scares when Wales were within two points at one stage thanks to a Hefin O'Hare try and three Lee Briers goals, but tries either side of half-time to Lance Hohaia and Stacey Jones ensured the Kiwis would run away with the match. They were 50–10 up before Kris Tassell and Paul Atcheson scored Welsh tries in the last 10 minutes as the visitors tired. The final score was Wales 22 New Zealand 50.

As previously mentioned, 2003 was a productive year for rugby league in Wales, and there was significant progress for the national side as well as the newly formed Rugby League European Federation (RLEF) which gave the international game a boost by reintroducing the European Nations Cup for the first time in seven years.

While previous tournaments had only involved England, France, Other Nationalities and Wales, this tournament introduced three new sides to the fold, Scotland, Ireland and Russia. The RLEF also introduced a very welcome rule that at least four players from each nation must be playing in their domestic leagues in a boost to assist development. However, while Wales didn't really disrespect this rule, they did bend the spirit of it a little by bringing back Kevin Ellis and Allan Bateman who were now playing for Welsh Champions Bridgend Blue Bulls. This was a move that greatly assisted with publicity though, of which I was now in charge after the previous press officer Gareth Jones had handed over the reigns.

Wales were drawn in a group with Russia and England, and this is where, in my opinion, the RLEF made the second of two major mistakes. The first mistake was to play the tournament in the autumn where it directly clashed with rugby union's World Cup. Wales, who were now utilising the kicking skills of former league star Iestyn Harris, qualified for the quarter-finals of this tournament where they were beaten 28–17 by England, and the Australian-based tournament was receiving maximum coverage in Wales. The last European Championship rugby league tournament had taken place in the summer of 1996 and, despite a clash with football's version, was a success. This time, with no television coverage except for the Final, it was going to be an uphill battle to promote it.

In 2008, Richard de la Riviere's number 1 proposal in his *Rugby League World* article on 50 ways to improve rugby league was "Play all international tournaments in June". He said that "In the UK, rugby league is presented as a summer sport but, paradoxically, internationals – the pinnacle of any sport – are played on wet, winter evenings on muddy pitches in Wigan and Huddersfield which makes little sense. In rugby league, internationals have a tagged-on-to-the-end-of-the-season feel about them. Play them in the middle of the year and the middle of the summer."

The other mistake was to call the England side, England 'A'. While clearly this tournament clashed with the Great Britain versus Australia tests meaning the majority of decent England players would be turning out for the Lions, calling the team England 'A' devalued it and the tournament, and as Scotland, Wales and Ireland players also qualified for Great Britain, surely their teams would also be 'A' sides? This was a mistake that the Rugby League authorities learned from and thankfully did not make again.

Wales's first game was against Russia in Aberavon. It was the Russians' first visit to Wales, but not their first to the United Kingdom.

The USSR national side was first formed in 1991 to play a representative match against an English team made up of players from English lower league teams Fulham and York. They played their first full international in France in October 1991 losing 26–6 and toured South Africa the next year, winning both internationals against the home side.

In 1995 they played in the Emerging Nations World Cup and beat the USA 28–26. They were promoted to the full World Cup in 2000 and, while they lost all three games, they won many friends, especially when they faced Australia. They may have lost 110–4, but the biggest cheer of the game was reserved for their try, scored in the corner by Matthew Donovan, one of only six players in their squad who wasn't born in Russia. This score spawned a legendary comment that deserves to go down in sporting history when Sky commentator Andrew Voss turned to fellow pundit Tony Rea and said "Break out the Vodka Tony because it's great to be a Russian!"

Russia's ambitions were rewarded in 2001 when their two top club sides Kazan Arrows and Lokomotiv Moscow because the first Russian teams to compete in the Rugby League Challenge Cup. Since then they have entered sides in the competition every year.

In 2002 Moscow hosted its first ever rugby league international. The match, shown in full on Russian national television, was the first league international to be played on artificial turf in front of American football posts. Their opponents, the USA, were outclassed 54–10 in front of a passionate 25,000 crowd.

Now, a year later, the Russians and the Welsh were playing their first competitive match since the 2000 World Cup. The game was given a good deal of publicity by some of the local papers, including a double-page spread in the Evening Pink *Sports Echo* the day before the game, despite clashes with the rugby union World Cup as well as a major football international between who else, but Wales and Russia. The Russians were given a heroes' welcome in Wales and their officials were greeted by the Lord Mayor of Neath Port Talbot at the local Civic Centre on the morning of the game.

However, the Welsh public was not impressed by what seemed to be such a low profile game and only 1,082 people turned up to the Talbot Athletic Ground. Those who did were given a rugby league exhibition by the Welsh who fielded Bridgend Blue Bulls's Lenny

Woodard and Torfaen Tigers's Damien Hudd as their development players, the latter making his international debut, alongside Ellis and Bateman.

And it was Woodard who led the way with a hat-trick of tries as Wales went over the line 14 times for a confidence-boosting 74–4 win. Adam Hughes also scored three times, Bateman and Ellis christened their return to the international game with a try each while other scores came from Rob Roberts, Ian Watson, Gareth Price and another debutant, Jordan James.

There were two James boys winning their first Welsh caps that day, both coming from similar rugby league backgrounds. Jordan, born and brought up in Bath, qualified for Wales through his Welsh grandfather and started playing rugby league in the Marines and then in the Conference for Gloucestershire Warriors in 1998. He was spotted by Sheffield Eagles and it was after a good season for them in National League One that he was selected by Neil Kelly.

The other James, first name Aled, was born in Caerphilly in the Welsh valleys and started playing his rugby league for Cardiff Demons. From there he was picked for Great Britain Students for the student Ashes tour of Australia in 2003, was British man-of-the-match in both tests and, after being recommended to Widnes Vikings, he made the move north.

"It was an exciting time for me," Aled James said. "Within a week of being recommended to Widnes, I had a trial for them and was playing in their under-21s. I scored a try and the following week Neil [Kelly] told me that I would playing for the first team in the centre against Paul Newlove, who was quite a big name at the time."

Aled had a good game against the Russians, but he and the Welsh team knew that they would have a stiffer test against the might of Australia who were over in the UK again, just two years after their last tour. This time around the political climate was more stable and the Kangaroos agreed to a longer tour with a game against Wales on the cards. The game was to be played a week after the Russian match, at Bridgend RFC, now the home of new ill-fated regional rugby union side Celtic Warriors who were the major promoters of the international. I was phoned up by the Warriors asking if I wanted to buy hospitality, and was encouraged that it was people from Wales promoting the occasion.

Aled, surprised to get the call for the Russian game, was even more astounded to hear that he was in the squad for the Australian game which was being shown live on Sky Sports. For Wales it was a role reversal compared to the previous week when they had been favourites, and in front more than 3,000 fans at the Brewery Field, Wales went down 74–4 with Kris Tassell scoring their only try.

"I wasn't expected the Welsh call up at all," Aled remembers, "And when it did happen I went quite white, especially when I found out that I would be facing Australia in my second game. I was very nervous for that one especially as I was walking out alongside Darren Lockyer, Shane Webcke and all these big-name players – it was quite a shock to the system. Even though we'd got beaten well that day, I really enjoyed it. I made a few tackles and tried my hardest but they were an amazing team, it was a really good experience."

The team would have to pick themselves up for the European Nations Cup group decider against England. Fans travelling north on the motorway to Leeds were getting increasingly annoyed that both BBC Radio Five Live and talkSport Radio weren't even mentioning the game and instead were concentrating on England's rugby union team who were taking on Wales in the World Cup that day. The fixture wasn't even mentioned in passing and on listening to the radio on the way back, the score wasn't mentioned either. Due to this obvious lack of publicity, few locals were tempted to the game.

If they had turned up on that cold afternoon in Headingley, they wouldn't have been entertained anyway, so perhaps it was a blessing in disguise. England won 22–4 with Mark Lennon scoring the lone Welsh try and the English went on to the Final in Warrington a week later. The final was the only tie of the tournament to be shown live on Sky Sports and again the lack of publicity was clear. England hammered France to take the title, but BBC Radio Five didn't announce that. When I phoned them up about it they seemed utterly confused as they didn't seem to realise that the game was even taking place.

More had to be done for the same tournament in 2004 if it was to be a success. However, once again Sky only wanted to show the Final which gave the publicity department another uphill battle to get the fans into the grounds.

The 2004 domestic season had once again gone very well for rugby league in Wales, with newspaper coverage at an all-time high – the game was being played throughout the summer months which gave it little competition from football and rugby union. Wales had failed to qualify for football's European Championships while the rugby union side were touring Argentina and South Africa and although the games were prominently discussed in the local media, the Welsh side had had a poor year and no one was expecting much from them. The time was right for rugby league.

The Welsh Conference, now boosted by Cardiff Demons' admission, was going from strength to strength. Attendances were on the rise with the pinnacle being more than 1,500 fans attending Bridgend Blue Bulls versus Aberavon Fighting Irish at Maesteg's Old Parish ground a few miles north of Bridgend. With the winners of the match qualifying for the first official Welsh Grand Final, everything was at stake and, to the delight of the home fans, the Blue Bulls romped home 48–8 on a hot July afternoon.

Aberavon had a second chance to qualify and didn't waste it, beating Torfaen Tigers 27–22 in a classic see-saw game at their Little Warren ground. The teams shared eight tries and it was just a 74th-minute try from Andy Llewellyn that put the West Wales side through.

However the staging of the Final at Aberavon's home ground was controversial. "The game may not happen," Gary Baker wrote in the *Western Mail* as Bridgend kicked up a fuss saying that the game should be played on neutral territory. However the staging of the Final was open to bids from all of the Welsh Conference clubs and before they had even qualified for the Final, Aberavon were judged to have put in the best bid.

The Grand Final was the second of a double header as the Welsh Conference staged a Shield competition for the first time with fourth-placed Newport Titans taking on fifth-placed Cardiff Demons in that final. The game was the first of two classics as a 79th-minute try from man-of-the-match Gareth Jones gave the Demons a 38–35 win. The scoring in the main final wasn't as high, but just as close with Dai Owen's 70th-minute try securing a 26–21 win for Bridgend. The matches were covered by *Wales on Sunday* who sent their leading rugby writer Simon Roberts and gave the event a full page.

The two winning sides went onto their respective British national tournaments with Bridgend Blue Bulls defending the Harry Jepson Trophy that they had won in Warrington the year before. However,

Cardiff Demons versus Thorne Moor Marauders
Rugby League Conference Shield Final 2004

Cardiff fight off a Marauders' attack (Photo: Peter Lush)

Cardiff celebrate their 29–20 victory. Note the then club chairman
to the right of the Shield. (Photo: Peter Lush)

this time they only reached the quarter-finals because, in an historic evening at Coychurch Road, they were beaten for the first time in their 28 game history by a well-drilled West London Sharks side, 30–18.

Instead, it was Cardiff Demons who achieved UK success in 2004. After seeing off Telford Raiders 46–6 in the quarter-finals, they pulled off a shock in the semi-final, beating St Albans Centurions 66–14 to qualify for the Shield Final against Yorkshire side Thorne Moor Marauders. The Demons were 22–0 up at half-time in the Final at St Albans thanks to tries from Gareth Jones, Idris Evans, Neil Thomas and Mark Bow. Graham Hughes's try after 51 minutes made the score 26–0, but Thorne fought back through four Shaun Carver tries to put them just seven points behind. He could have had a fifth with a minute to go, but dropped the ball as he was tackled by Pete Moore. The Sheffield Eagles bound Moore also added a drop-goal for Cardiff and Gareth Jones added a last-minute penalty to complete a 29–20 win.

On the international front, the Wales 'A' side completed a hat-trick of titles in 2004 and, just like in 2002, produced a clean sweep of results against their British rivals.

In the first match, Wales easily overcame an under-strength, but spirited, Ireland side at the Cardiff Athletics Stadium. The match was part of a very successful weekend of rugby league in Wales to celebrate the second Millennium Stadium-based Challenge Cup Final. Friday night had already seen a bumper crowd watch a rugby league classic at Cardiff Demons' brand-new first-class Taffs Well ground where the home side narrowly lost 27–26 to Aberavon Fighting Irish thanks to a last-minute Dean Scully penalty goal. Scully, to his credit, played again less than 16 hours after walking off the pitch in Taffs Well, to lead Wales to glory. He was man-of-the-match for Wales scoring a hat-trick of tries and kicking eight goals as his team romped to a 56–12 victory over an Irish Wolfhounds side that was missing many players due to involvement in another rugby league tournament being run at the same time – the Victory Cup – that was taking place in Russia. Fellow future Crusaders star Richard Johnson scored two tries as did James Strover and Darren Ryan with Joel Keen completing the rout.

The second game saw a tougher battle in Scotland, Wales winning 34–26 with Dai Hawkins scoring a hat-trick of tries, Owen Jones scoring two and Pete Moore one.

The championship was secured in Coventry with Wales beating England for the third year in succession. The game was won early on after Wales went 28–0 up in as many minutes with tries from Damien Hudd, Mark Burke, Mark Wheeler, Simon Bevan and Dean Scully. England fought back to be just 28–14 down at the interval, but Wales were on the scoreboard first in the second half after Scully beat off three defenders for his second after 46 minutes. Three converted English tries in the last 15 minutes weren't enough and Wales 'A' hung on for the title.

The full Welsh side, again competing in the European Nations Cup, had a new coach after Neil Kelly stood down in an announcement made in June 2004: "I have three daughters and we've not had the chance of a family holiday for some time," Kelly said in his statement. "It's a decision I didn't want to make but I've made it for my family. I can't juggle everything."

Unfortunately for Kelly, within three weeks he had more time to spend with his family after being sacked as Widnes coach following a disastrous run of results in Super League. Widnes eventually avoided relegation that year by the skin of their teeth following Castleford's defeat to Wakefield on a dramatic and memorable last day of the season. However, they couldn't avoid the drop in 2005 and at the time of writing have yet to return to Super League.

Leeds Rhinos' assistant coach Stuart Wilkinson was quickly appointed by the RFL as Kelly's successor. He was to be assisted by Wales 'A' coach Wayne O'Kell with Aberavon Fighting Irish coach Chris O'Callaghan appointed as team manager. On their recommendations, six Welsh Conference players were included in the original 23-man squad who were training hard for their first game at home to Ireland in Aberavon.

Wilkinson fielded five debutants against Ireland – Dave Clarke, Bryn Powell, Nathan Strong, Neil Davies and Barry Pugh – and the home side's inexperience showed as the Irish went 22–0 up in the first hour of the game. Jordan James finally got Wales onto the board, scoring under the sticks with Mark Lennon converting and from the next set of six, Lennon, who flew in from Sydney especially to play for his country, broke through himself and converted his own try to bring the score back to 22–12. Ireland, sensing Wales were rejuvenated, played possession rugby for the rest of the game and Pat Weisner kicked

92

three drop-goals in the last 10 minutes to give Ireland a 25–12 win. The game was Kevin Ellis's last for his country.

Wales had to travel to Scotland to save their campaign. The game was played the day after Australia's clash with New Zealand in the new Tri-Nations tournament in London. The Tri-Nations was staged by these sides along with Great Britain for three years from 2004 to 2006 and was considered to be a great success. The matches were competitive, well attended and as such brought a lot of money back into the game to compensate for the financial failings of the 2000 World Cup. This match at Queens Park Rangers FC's Loftus Road was the second of the tournament following the Antipodean sides' 16–16 draw a week earlier in Auckland. Having found an economical way to attend both this match in London and Wales' match in Scotland the day after, I travelled to London by coach, watched Australia win 32–12 (and giving Tonie Carroll the appropriate level of abuse for switching nations – he played for New Zealand in the 2000 World Cup and had now decided he was Australian) before catching the midnight coach to Glasgow thankfully sleeping for the entire journey.

For Wales, it was a more competitive game than the last outing but again they failed to win. Needing a 14-point victory to stay in the competition, Wales didn't ever look like getting close and the battle was made harder after Andy McPhail opened the scoring for Scotland. Just minutes later, Wales took the lead for the only time in the game with an Ian Watson try converted by Mark Lennon. Wales went into the interval 18–6 down, fought back to 22–22 after tries from Steve Thomas, Aled James and Bryn Powell, but in the end lost 30–22.

After catching the bus to Edinburgh and sending my match report through to the Welsh media via an internet café, I caught the plane back to Cardiff, taking in what the Welsh team manager Chris O'Callaghan had told me: "We're hoping to start a professional rugby league side in Wales for 2006," he had said. "And if this happens, I'd like you to be the press officer."

That was all the information I had at the time. While they didn't have a name back in October 2004, the foundations of Celtic Crusaders Rugby League Club were already in place and 2005 was set to be a very interesting year in the development of rugby league in Wales as the country took a step further towards Super League.

International action: Jordan James looks to offload for Wales
against France in November 2005
(Photo: Ian Lovell)

The Wales 'A' team has been
consistently successful. In this
match they won the Four Nations
championship again by beating
England in a close game.
(Courtesy Ian Golden)

7. 2005: Development and decisions

Professional rugby league in Europe was to change in 2006. New French club, Catalans Dragons, had controversially been admitted straight into Super League which left an odd number of professional clubs in the game's National League structure ideally requiring a new club to resolve the issue.

In March 2005, it was announced that a Welsh club was favourite to fill that gap with Coventry Bears and Bramley Buffaloes, both up-and-coming clubs in the amateur game, also in contention.

The timing for Wales couldn't have been better. In 2003, the Welsh Rugby Union formed five new regional super clubs to play at the top level against Scottish and Irish clubs as well as in the sport's European Cup. The idea was for these regions to be formed through mergers of existing clubs and the higher standard of rugby union that they would play would lead to a stronger Welsh national rugby union side.

The idea was fantastic in principle, especially as the Welsh rugby union side went on to Grand Slam Six Nations success less than two years later. The regions were set up – Cardiff Blues, Neath Swansea Ospreys, Llanelli Scarlets, Newport Gwent Dragons and a very unusual amalgamation between Pontypridd RFC and Bridgend RFC known as Celtic Warriors. With Bridgend having won the final Welsh Premier League title in 2002–03 and Pontypridd also consistently powerful, the Warriors were considered to be one of the strongest of the Welsh sides. The new club's name was finally chosen after Celtic Crusaders and Valley Ravens were rejected although the latter name seemed the most sensible of the three as Bridgend's nickname was Ravens and Valley would have embraced the rugby-loving public of the Rhondda Cynon Taff area that the region encompassed.

The Celtic Warriors, as expected, did very well. They finished fourth in the Celtic League, behind Llanelli, Ulster and Newport, and were the best-performing Welsh club in the European Cup. However, attendances were not so great because the local public failed to embrace the new franchise. Financial problems also forced Pontypridd to sell their half of the club to the Welsh Rugby Union and after attendances dropped further following this acquisition, Bridgend RFC owner Leighton Samuel accepted an offer from the WRU to fund and run the club as a whole. They then wound it up on 1 June 2004.

Leighton Samuel had been a prominent businessman in the area since 1988, which is when he founded his company Décor Frame PLC, now known simply as Dekor PLC. In 1999, he purchased Bridgend RFC, saving them from relegation and insolvency, guaranteeing debts of more than £1,000,000 and saving a few directors from losing their houses on the way.

Within two years, he'd transformed the club on and off the field. In 2001–02, the club qualified for European Cup for the first time and in 2002–03 they won their first and only Welsh Premiership. Following the year of the Warriors, he continued his association with Bridgend RFC in the Welsh Premiership until the end of the 2004–05 season when they finished third and reached the semi-finals of the Welsh Cup. Bridgend RFC then went out of business, but fans and club directors reformed it immediately and renamed it Bridgend Ravens. The new club rented the ground from Leighton Samuel and slotted into place in the Welsh Premiership with such ease that outsiders wouldn't have known that anything had happened. The old club was eventually wound up over a year later after the WRU made an out-of-court settlement to Leighton Samuel and his Dekor Frame business as compensation for closing down the Warriors club.

Samuel owned the ground but no club and this provided an opportunity for rugby league to step in. Niel Wood had been overseeing the Conference clubs in Wales since the turn of the century and he, along with Aberavon Fighting Irish coach Chris O'Callaghan and Wales Rugby League president Mike Nicholas, met with Samuel and the businessman was convinced to give rugby league a go – not that he needed much convincing. Samuel had made previous attempts to bring rugby league franchises who were in financial difficulties to Wales, including London Broncos, so it was only natural that if presented with a decent business plan for a potentially successful Welsh club, he would be on board.

The club's application to enter National League Two was accepted by the Rugby Football League on 22 June 2005 and O'Callaghan was appointed chief executive. He played rugby league for MASWARLA club Aberavon Steelers in the early 1980s and had trials with a few professional clubs, but was unsuccessful so stayed in rugby union playing more than 250 first class games with Aberavon, Bridgend and Neath. When appointed by Samuel, he was already the chief executive at Aberavon RFC and the Spanish rugby union side's forwards coach. He continued with the latter role while at the Crusaders.

"The club have set out clear ambitions to be the Welsh franchise for 2008 to 2009 when Super League is extended to 14 teams." O'Callaghan told *Rugby League World* magazine at the time. "But we've decided to come through on a bottom up approach in order that it can ensure that the roots for its survival, future prosperity and successes are firmly laid down. This is not just on the playing side but for supporters and sponsors alike.

"In the first season, we are looking to have a recognised squad of 25 players with the intention of recruiting a minimum of 18 players or 80 percent plus who have Welsh qualification. Most of these will come from the Welsh Conference, Wales under-19 or the Welsh Students whilst others will be players returning from current NL2, NL1 or even Super League clubs.

"League now dovetails perfectly into a niche market which complements union and allows the game of rugby football to become a continuous 52-week business. This was the main impetus behind the new club. However the new club would have been impossible without the formation of Cardiff Demons which led to the Welsh Conference starting in 2003."

RFL executive chairman Richard Lewis was also delighted at the progression that Welsh Rugby League had made: "The admission of the Celtic Crusaders is recognition of the progress that the sport is making in Wales," he said in a press statement. "The Crusaders come into professional rugby league playing out of the excellent Brewery Field Stadium in Bridgend and having lodged a robust business plan with the RFL."

Celtic Crusaders celebrated their achievement by holding a Super League game at the Brewery Field. London Broncos' Griffin Park ground which they rented from Brentford FC was being reseeded so they needed a stadium to host their Super League game against Hull FC on 2 July. Bridgend seemed the obvious choice. At £18 for adults in the grandstand and £13 on the terrace, prices seemed very steep but 3,775 people – equivalent if not better than some of the Broncos' home crowds – were entertained with a 24–24 draw.

Not that the Broncos were strangers to South Wales. This game was their third 'home' Super League game in Wales in six seasons. On

4 June 2000 they visited Rodney Parade, Newport where they were beaten 28–18 by Warrington Wolves while on 8 June 2003, Chris O'Callaghan was instrumental in bringing their match against Widnes Vikings to Talbot Athletic Ground in Aberavon, where they won 40–18. Each of these games were in Wales for the same reason as 2005, ground reseeding, but with 4,174 people in Newport, their third biggest 'home' crowd of 2000 and 3,124 in Aberavon, they were both successes and it showed that Wales was ripe for Super League.

London-based rugby league journalist David Ballheimer recalls: "Of course, we [Broncos] were the first team to play Super League matches at Bridgend, Aberavon, the Millennium Stadium and Newport. There aren't many fans who attended all of them, but I think I am the only journalist who worked at all four. Given that we have already had home games in four Welsh stadiums, does that make us more Welsh than Celtic Crusaders?"

If one major development in the Welsh game wasn't enough, another came later that month when Valley Cougars coach Mark Rowley was appointed the new chairman of Wales Rugby League following the resignation of long-standing supremo Danny Sheehy. Rowley, a former Pontypridd RFC and Wales Rugby Union international had been the Cougars' coach since their senior team was formed in 2003 and it was his appointment then that helped to revolutionise other areas of the Welsh game. At that time Rowley owned a sports shop, and could use his expertise to produce and sell Welsh rugby league merchandise. He made it far easier for players to play for Wales at grassroots levels: "When I took over, the one thing that I saw straight away was that we didn't have our own sponsors," Rowley said. "Everything financially at the time was controlled by the RFL from Conference to international level and we saw little of the money that was brought in.

"So we sought our own sponsors and people like 1 to 1 Vehicle Solutions, Picton Jones, Costley and Partners, Crouch the Jewellers and Eurovehicles to name just a few, had put a lot of money into Welsh Rugby League. This has helped to pay for the international game. In the past, amateur away trips have been paid for by the teams or players involved. With this sponsorship, we have funded all ages from under-13 to amateur and professional. Our aim was for every player to be funded by Wales Rugby League as they shouldn't have to pay to represent their country."

The Welsh game continued to develop successfully. After an absence of six years, the Student World Cup was held again, this time in Australia. There was to have been a competition in France in 2002, but the hosts pulled out due to reported funding problems and that tournament was unfortunately cancelled.

Eight teams were selected to take part in the 2005 event and I travelled with the Welsh side as media officer for both Wales and Scotland, who were in Group A along with Australia and New Zealand, while my fellow British journalist Chris Leak covered Group B's games that contained England, Ireland, France and a Pacific Islands select. It would be the third time in five years that the Welsh Students would face an Australian side having played against a John Dixon-coached Queensland Universities side in 2001 and the full Australian Student outfit in 2004. Both games were in Treorchy in the Rhondda Valleys with the Australian side winning each time.

The Australians made a good job of hosting the tournament which boded well for the senior World Cup that was to be held there three years later. All except two of the group matches were played at the Nathan University campus in Brisbane, with England versus France and Australia versus New Zealand taking place at the city's famous Suncorp Stadium, the former taking place before a weekend clash between Brisbane Broncos and Canterbury Bulldogs and the latter being the first game of the day at State of Origin 3.

Future Crusaders stars Dean Scully and Geraint Davies both played for Wales in a tough fortnight: "Representing your country at any sport is an honour. But to play in a World Cup, and pit yourself against the best, on the other side of the world, was an experience that I will never forget," Davies recalls. "In 2005 we were grouped in what was nicknamed the pool of death. Australia and New Zealand were in our group as well as our co-Celts Scotland. As you can imagine, the results didn't go our way against the two giants but to play against the Green and Golds and to face the haka was simply awesome.

"We were fortunate to be the best of the Celtic Nations as we beat Scotland 31-16 in the group stages and Ireland 25-10 in the Plate semi-final which led us to the fifth place play-off where we lost to a big, aggressive Pacific Islanders team. It was at this game funnily enough, where I met my current coaches, John Dixon and Anthony Seibold who were looking at potential players for the Celtic Crusaders.

"The tournament turned out to be a great success. It was well planned out and Brisbane played an excellent host. I didn't think that I would revisit Brisbane but fate took me there again as our first Super League pre-season camp in late 2008 was in the same place – even on the same pitch. It's fair to say that I enjoyed the experience the second time around just as much as the first."

Dixon had just been appointed Crusaders coach on Niel Wood's advice after the RFL administrator had heard much about his successes. Dixon had grown up with rugby league. He played for Queensland-based clubs Dalby, Rockhampton and Toowoomba, including a game against the touring English World Cup side in 1975 for Toowoomba. Working as a teacher and eventually headmaster, he took to coaching when he retired from playing, taking charge of the Toowoomba Clydesdales. He also worked for 10 years at Brisbane Broncos from 1995 in various roles under Wayne Bennett. He had a great deal of experience and knowledge to offer Welsh rugby league.

John Dixon spoke to *Rugby League World* magazine just after joining the club and was looking forward to the whole experience: "Being part of the establishment of a new rugby club in an area with such a strong sporting tradition is very exciting for me," Dixon told the magazine. "Although we are a brand new franchise, what gives me confidence that Celtic Crusaders can be successful is the support and infrastructure that are already in place. We have a growing Conference League that will provide us with a sound player base, we have a very good home ground, we have an administration staff that is working tirelessly to make certain everything off the field is spot on and we have major support in place with Décor Frame PLC. My task as coach will be to produce a rugby league team that people all along the M4 and all throughout Wales will want to come and support".

Domestically in Wales in 2005 it was once again Bridgend Blue Bulls' season as they replicated their efforts of 2003 by winning both Welsh and British Conference titles. Finals day at the Brewery Field on 14 August opened with a classic Shield Final game between Valley Cougars and Newport Titans that ended 42–41 with the Gwent side this time ending up victorious. The match saw the lead change hands five times. In fact, Newport were leading 42–29 with four minutes go before converted tries from Richard Andrews and Adrian Owen set up a nervous final minute.

The main final was less of a spectacle as Bridgend dominated, beating Torfaen Tigers 56–16. It is interesting to note that all bar two of the Blue Bulls' try scorers that day went onto play for Celtic Crusaders. Paul Morgan led the way with a hat-trick, Grant Epton scored two while Neil Dixon, Lloyd O'Connor, Lenny Woodard, Hywel Davies, Matthew Wareham and Gareth David also crossed. Bridgend then beat South London Storm 34–18 in the national semi-finals which set up a final against Leeds Akkies, a game that would form just one part of a memorable rugby league weekend in Wales.

Saturday 28 August saw the Millennium Stadium host another Challenge Cup Final, with Leeds Rhinos and Hull FC the contenders for the famous trophy. The weekend began on the Friday at the Cardiff Athletics Stadium with finals from Year 8, 9, 10 and 11 of the Champions Schools tournaments, a series of national knockout competitions for schools sides from all over the United Kingdom. The Year 7 Final is traditionally played before the Challenge Cup Final and this was an eagerly awaited contest as local school, Brynteg of Bridgend was to take on a school with a very famous rugby league pedigree, Castleford High.

Also taking place on the Friday night was a game between the Wales and Lebanon 'A' sides at the Brewery Field. Looking back, it was a big mistake for the Welsh Rugby League to stage this game in Bridgend – the majority of rugby league fans were staying in Cardiff and if this game had taken place at Cardiff Arms Park for example, the crowd would probably have been a lot bigger. As it happens, a very small crowd jangled around the Brewery Field as Wales won 52–12 with Valley Cougars' Adrian Owen and Torfaen's Chris Williams each scoring a brace of tries.

On Saturday the action moved to the Millennium Stadium with a chance for the 12-year-old Welsh lads to prove themselves on the big stage. And prove themselves they did as Brynteg, coached by Kevin Eliis, built a 22–0 lead inside the first quarter to leave Castleford shell-shocked. Ben Evans was named as the Chev Walker Man-of-the-Match, as Brynteg's all-round display proved too much for the Yorkshire side.

William Thomas scooted over from close range to give Brynteg the lead, Jay Robbins dived on the end of Oliver Olds's grubber before

Evans touched down for his try. Thomas added a scorching 80-metre effort and Olds grabbed his own try to seal the result before half-time.

Adam Hargreaves got Castleford on the scoreboard just before the break, but Rhys Evans raced over for two tries after the restart and Daniel James's spectacular dash down the touchline rounded off a superb afternoon as Brynteg won 40–4.

It was quite an outstanding win for the Welsh school and probably one of the biggest and most-remembered Welsh wins in the 21st century by fans and officials of rugby league alike. It's good to see club sides like Bridgend win games and it's always pleasing to see any Welsh national side take a victory, but in 2005 these boys were just 12 years old. By the time this book is published they will be 16 or 17 and in Celtic Crusaders' development squads ready to move into the under-18 side. Players like this are the future of rugby league and hopefully some of them will compete in the 2013 World Cup for Wales. Should this happen, then Welsh fans will look back fondly to 2005 when fans from all over the world watched BBC1's highlights of the game and the lads parading the cup around the Millennium Stadium to the applause of fans from Wales and Yorkshire.

"This was probably one of my most memorable times as a coach and player," said Kevin Ellis. "I've played in Cup Finals and World Cups and had some exciting times with Bridgend Blue Bulls and Celtic Crusaders, but bringing these lads through to win such a prestigious trophy at the very start of their rugby league careers was an honour. For the Brynteg boys, it was their first ever year playing rugby league, but Castleford were probably playing right the way through primary school as well as turning out for clubs in their area. That's how big this win was and it sent shockwaves throughout the rugby league and union world.

"It was taken seriously by the local papers as well. I can remember that it was front page news in the *Glamorgan Gazette* and the same in the midweek sports section of the *South Wales Echo*. Everyone knew that Welsh Rugby League was building from grass roots level and I think this win is probably one of the most important from any Welsh side over the last few years."

After such a momentous opener, Leeds Rhinos and Hull FC continued the drama in one of the most exciting Challenge Cup Finals of modern times as Hull won 25–24 with Danny Brough's drop-goal on

102

the hour proving to be the difference between the two sides. Leeds were leading 24–19 with five minutes to go, but Paul Cooke, who would later do the unthinkable and sign for Hull Kingston Rovers, ran over with the winning try.

The 20,000 strong Hull contingent was ecstatic – their side had won the Cup and were heading for the Super League play-offs as well. However it wasn't to be a happy ending for them in 2005 when they crashed out of the finals after a 71–0 defeat to Bradford Bulls.

Cup Final weekend wasn't going to get any better for the city of Leeds. Their amateur side Leeds Akkies contested the British Conference Final against Bridgend Blue Bulls at the Brewery Field and, frankly, were never in contention for the crown. The Welsh side won by an impressive 60 points to 10 and even more impressive was the crowd of 1,168, swelled a little by a passionate bunch of fans from Leeds who had braved an extra day in the country.

For the record, the Bulls ran in 11 tries with Grant Epton and Gareth David leading the way with a brace apiece. Paul Morgan, Owen Strong, Lenny Woodard, Neil Dixon and Nathan Strong also crossed, as did stalwart Kevin Ellis who said that this win completed one of the best weekends of his rugby career: "As I said before, Saturday at the Millennium Stadium with Brynteg was fabulous," he said, "But the win at the Brewery Field more than topped it off. After a good few years in the sporting doldrums, these performances certainly showed that Wales meant business and I think we've carried on to prove that over the next few years."

Wales were to carry on proving that during the rest of the season. It was only August, and the year was far from over. Wales 'A' were going into their final match of the season against England Lionhearts needing only to avoid a 100-point defeat in order to win the title for the fourth year in succession.

It was a massive weekend for sport in Great Britain. The England cricket team were on the verge of winning back The Ashes for the first time in 18 years and many eyes were on The Oval as history was in the making.

However, a little bit of history was certainly being made at the Brewery Field. Rugby union's *Scrum V* television programme was visiting and filming the action which was shown on BBC2 Wales that very night. It's taken a lot for the hierarchy in Welsh sport to recognise rugby league, especially in the media and even more so in the BBC, so this visit was more than welcome. The fact that Celtic Crusaders were about to open their doors was obviously a big part of it, but one couldn't discount the hard work done by everyone in Wales Rugby League over the past few years.

Wales 'A' had had a first class season. Kicking off at the Brewery Field on 12 June against Scotland, the favourites won 70–8 with the Royal Navy's Jim Barnes and Cardiff Demons' Gareth Holtham each scoring a hat-trick of tries. Neil Dixon scored twice while Damien Hudd, Damien Smith, Sean O'Brien, Matt Entwhistle, Ross Palmer and Gareth Jones, who also kicked seven goals, also crossed. For good measure, the Welsh under-15 and under-19 teams also registered emphatic victories earlier in the day, beating their Scottish counterparts 64–4 and 36–12 respectively.

It was this win that would virtually set up the title for Wales. Scotland won their remaining games against Ireland and England ensuring that they were Wales's only major rivals for the title. The Irish had surprisingly beat England 26–8 in Halifax and Wales knew that they had a tough job in Dublin in their second game.

Ireland, who had never won the tournament, but had recorded a narrow victory over Wales the last time the nations met on their home soil in 2003, got off to a great start with a 15th minute try from Darren Sharp. But Wales soon equalised when Neil Dixon finished off a fine handling move. Dixon thought he had a second try just before the break only to see it ruled out controversially for crossing.

Locked at 6–6 at the break, the second half continued as an intense physical battle, but it was Welsh handling skill which was once more to prove instrumental in breaking the deadlock, with Ryan again involved in setting up a try, this time for Newport Titans' Mark Wheeler. But after Jim Barnes, a great find for the Welsh from the Royal Navy, was lost temporarily to the sin bin, Ireland piled on the pressure and were rewarded with an unconverted try after a blind-side run from McAnn on 60 minutes.

The return of Barnes, along with strong captaincy from Bridgend's Nathan Strong ensured that Wales were able to repel all further attacks and a breakaway try from Torfaen's Darren Smith 10 minutes from time put the Welshmen firmly back in control at 18–10.

104

Wales coach Kevin Weaver described the match as "a real bone-crunching encounter", adding: "I take my hat off to the Welsh players, they were up against some big powerful guys from Ireland but they met fire with fire," he said after the match. "To come away from Dublin with a victory is possibly my finest moment in Rugby League."

So bottom-of-the-table England were attempting to ruin the party for Wales in front of the BBC Wales cameras. The pressure off them, they ran riot, going 22–0 up in the first 24 minutes. Jim Barnes eventually got Wales on the board with a 29th minute try, England then responded with a short-range effort from Karl Leach, but Wales narrowed the gap to 18 points with a Damien Smith score in the corner to go in 26–8 down at the break.

England restored their advantage after 46 minutes when substitute John Dudley crashed over but the sin-binning six minutes later of winger Ryan Knights gave the Welshmen real heart. Within a minute, Wales scored their third try through Neil Davies and five minutes later Karl Thomas brought the score back to 30–20. Marcus Sainsbury ensured a grandstand finish when he latched on to Gareth Jones's pass to score under the posts. Welsh fans thought their dominance was complete when Lloyd O'Connor went over from short range to make the score 32–30 to Wales.

However, England kept on pressing and scored a try in injury time to give them the game, but obviously not the Cheltenham Regency Trophy that remained in Wales for the fourth year in a row.

Could the Welsh senior team complete an exceptional year for Welsh Rugby League? The side hadn't been at its best since the 2000 World Cup and Stuart Wilkinson had just quit as Welsh coach after one of the shortest tenures of any coaching role – only two games.

The Welsh Rugby League made initially what looked to be a good move in appointing former Welsh hooker and Hull Kingston Rovers coach Martin Hall to the vacant position. He was to be assisted by Anthony Farrell, another former Welsh international, who had just coached Halifax to the National League One semi-finals.

Hall had wanted the job since Neil Kelly resigned in mid-2004. In fact, he'd gone on record in 2004 saying "I'd love to have a crack at the job. It's been close to my heart and I would see it as a great privilege."

"Martin was our first choice. He's very proud of his heritage and he's well up for the challenge," Mark Rowley said at the time. "It's good to have Anthony as well because he's making good progress at Halifax."

For the third year in a row, Wales were competing in the European Nations Cup and, just like in 2004, were drawn against Celtic rivals Scotland and Ireland with the fixtures reversed from the previous year, meaning that the Scots were to visit Bridgend for the first match.

However, unlike previous years, England were to play no part in the tournament. Also, for the first time, Sky Sports did not show the Final, showing a lack of interest following England's non-participation. Calls from me and other press officers fell on deaf ears but our enthusiasm probably benefited future scheduling. In 2007, Sky succumbed to public pressure and broadcast all of the World Cup qualifiers held in the UK. It certainly was a disappointment for international rugby league at the time though, because French television was broadcasting the Final live leading to criticism that all Sky had needed to do was send commentators to the match or even commentate from a studio in London, as they have done on occasions for Catalan Dragons games. The BBC were also contacted but as this game clashed with a Welsh rugby union match with New Zealand, which Wales lost heavily, they had other priorities.

"One of the main reasons that we didn't get enough newspaper coverage of the European Nations Cup was that the tournament wasn't on television," Mark Rowley commented at the end of the tournament. "This is something that we need to change. We'll be speaking to television companies soon to arrange weekly highlights programmes on the Crusaders and the Welsh Conference. If we successfully achieve this then we will be taken a lot more seriously by the newspapers and we can build from that." This was the start of negotiations that would run for more than a year and would eventually lead to a successful television contract with S4C.

Georgia replaced England in the 2005 European Nations Cup and they were drawn in the "European Group" along with France, who cemented their position as tournament favourites with an 80–0 thrashing of Russia in the first game.

Wales versus Scotland was a tad closer. The final score was 22–14, but Wales were always just about in control of the very competitive

106

match. Two early Bryn Powell tries set the pace with Danny Brough replying to make the half-time score 8–6. A Gareth Morton penalty levelled the scores, but Wales once again opened up a two-try gap through tries from Adam Hughes and Jordan James. Another Brough try got Scotland back in the hunt, but Lee Briers sealed things as he crossed the line on the final hooter.

"The spirit of the side has been second to none this week," Briers said after the game. "We've only been together for a few days making this win all the more remarkable. We lapsed in concentration at times but got back into it when it counted. I think we're good enough to win this competition. We're now looking forward to getting stuck into Ireland in two weeks' time."

And get stuck in they did, because Wales won 31–10 against an Ireland side who had done well to beat the Scots in Glasgow a week before. In a win that Wales president Mike Nicholas said at the time was "the best he'd ever seen Wales play", Briers was man-of-the-match after excelling with his leadership and his boot as he scored three conversions, two penalties and a drop-goal. Anthony Blackwood, in his second game for Wales, scored two tries. Richard Johnson and Adam Hughes also scored while Ian Watson was credited with a penalty try.

Wales were off to Carcassonne to face the hosts in the Final and, for the first time since 2000, the team that walked out onto the field against France contained no debutants. Six players had made their first appearance against Scotland – Richard Johnson, Anthony Blackwood, Phil Joseph, Karl Hocking, Byron Smith and Jon Breakingbury with his one and only cap, while Paul Morgan had made his senior debut against Ireland.

However, despite the consistency of the Welsh line-up, the European Rugby League Federation's rules of player eligibility in the tournament had caused a little controversy in the Welsh camp. The rules were that each side had to field three players from their domestic leagues, and in Wales's case this meant fielding amateur players while the French were all professional. Team manager Chris O'Callaghan especially spoke out at the time saying that the rules of the tournament had to be looked at because France had been perfectly able to field 17 professionals.

It made for a tough game for Wales who were 16–0 down in the first 20 minutes and failed to recover. Adam Hughes was first on the board for Wales after 29 minutes, but they were eventually 26–6 down at half-time. To their credit though, Wales tied the second half at two tries apiece, Hughes going over again straight from kick-off and Lee Briers six minutes later. The final score was 38–16 and the Welsh fans who didn't go to France did actually manage to see highlights on BBC Wales after the French television company provided two giant broadcast tapes to the BBC's Llandaff studios which I duly delivered after midnight on the Sunday for a Monday broadcast.

Despite the defeat and initial negative reaction to it by O'Callaghan, Martin Hall and Lee Briers, Hall was positive about the future: "Hopefully we have started something this year that we can continue," Hall told *Rugby League Express* at the time. "We have laid the groundwork for future years and the players have shown pride in playing for Wales.

"The players, along with Anthony Farrell and the other coaches, Matt Calland and Kevin Ellis, have all enjoyed being involved. It would be an honour for me to be there in forthcoming years ahead of the World Cup."

It may have been three years away but preparations for the 2008 World Cup were already starting, as of course were preparations for Celtic Crusaders' first ever season, something that would bring a lot of excitement and talking points for rugby league fans not just in Wales but all over the world.

8. Launching Celtic Crusaders

In 2006 Celtic Crusaders were ready for business and for Welsh Rugby League's first assault on the British professional domestic game in 10 years.

However, there were major differences to previous ventures. From the outset, Celtic Crusaders, unlike South Wales and the Blue Dragons before them, had a goal – Super League for 2009. For previous clubs, it was a case of throwing their all into promotion battles while trying to survive in an area to which the sport was still relatively alien, despite a long and rich history.

The other major difference was that in the 10 years since the demise of South Wales RLFC, rugby league had been built from the bottom up in Wales. Professionalism in union and the loss of the South Wales club made it essential for the reset switch to be pressed. Some may say that 1995 was the most successful year in Welsh Rugby League history and, certainly in the public eye, that seemed to be the case. However in 2006, the Celtic Crusaders were born following another stream of triumphs in 2005.

Bridgend Blue Bulls had won back their Totalrl.com Conference title, the Wales 'A' side, despite losing to England for the very first time, retained their Home Nations title for the fourth year in a row and the full Wales side reached the final of the European Nations Cup.

Newspaper coverage in the country was also slowly rising with *Wales on Sunday* in particular embracing rugby league and often giving a full page to the previous day's action in the Welsh Conference. There was periodical television coverage with highlights of all the above competitions shown on BBC Wales, while there was also a weekly rugby league slot on Saturday afternoons on the Pontypridd-based community radio station GTFM.

Crusaders coach John Dixon arrived in the UK in the early autumn and watched a lot of Wales's European Nations Cup campaign: "The first game I watched was Ireland versus Wales in Dublin," he said. "This was a good introduction to Welsh Rugby League for me and I could see the passion that was there in the Welsh side. While I thoroughly enjoyed the contest – Lee Briers against Barrie McDermott being a particular highlight – I felt that the tournament didn't have a lot of credibility to it at the time and this game in particular was played in a ground that was too low key for an international. This was something that needed to be changed in the future."

Dixon hired two assistant coaches, Kevin Ellis and Anthony Seibold, both of whom were coming to the end of their playing careers. Ellis, approaching his 40s, was still playing local semi-professional rugby union for Maesteg in addition to his league with Bridgend Blue Bulls, while 31-year-old Seibold had turned out for Brisbane Broncos, London Broncos, Canberra Raiders and Hull Kingston Rovers during his career. He'd come over to Wales not to play, but simply to coach, although he said that as events took their toll throughout the 2006 season, this was to change: "I finished at Hull KR in 2004," Seibold remembers. "I'd just turned 30 and I knew that I wanted to play one more season back in Australia because I'd not been back for a couple of years. I organised to go to Brisbane Broncos and captain their feeder club Toowoomba Clydesdales so I spent the year there and I thought that would be my last playing year.

"I had in my mindset that this was my last pre-season, my last proper game, my last play-off game, and we had a good year that year – we made the play-offs and I got the Players' Player-of-the-Year award so it was a really good way to finish. I helped to bring along youngsters like Steve Michaels, Sam Thaiday and Greg Eastwood to name just a few, so it was a really good year, one of the most enjoyable that I've had when playing. So I said to John Dixon that I'd rather be at the Crusaders in just an off-field capacity but I suppose just because I was only one year out of the game, I got the bug early, played up Workington Town in the first National League Two game, played a few other games, then my body started to tell me that I couldn't do this week-in, week-out.

"I said to John that I wanted to give it away again and concentrate on the coaching side of things and then towards the back end of the year, we were down a few players with injuries. John turned to me and said 'I think that it's time for you to put the boots back on' and I said to him 'Mate, I've been waiting for you to ask'. I played the last three or four fixture games and play-off games and again I really enjoyed playing and competing. My body was struggling all week but it was a good way to finish as I'd played at all three levels in the UK, Super League, National League One and National League Two."

The first Celtic Crusaders training squad was announced in late November 2005 with nine players from Bridgend Blue Bulls and eight from Aberavon Fighting Irish in the line-up. Also included was Carl de Chenu from Sheffield Eagles, a full Irish international who had scored against Wales in Aberavon in 2004, Phil Cushion from Swinton Lions, and six Australians: Ryan Barton, Tony Duggan, Jace van Dijk, Damien Quinn, Luke Young and Michael Ryan. The club was ready to launch themselves upon the Welsh public, but was the Welsh public ready for Celtic Crusaders?

Damien Quinn had been working as a teacher at Brisbane's Carmel College: "I ummed and ahhed a bit before joining," he said. "But it was too good an opportunity to say no. I thought I've got a chance to go over there and make a bit of money and see the world. If it goes ok that's great, and if things don't work out I can come back to my job in Australia. The idea of Super League was a real carrot but seemed a long way off at the time. The on and off field staff was a definite factor too."

Tony Duggan, a 27-year-old who had played just once for Brisbane Broncos, also snapped up the chance to move to Wales: "I had been at Brisbane Broncos for seven years and was ready for a change," he said. "John Dixon got offered the head coach job. He asked me if I would be interested in coming over and being part of something new. Starting from scratch and building a new club to develop league in Wales really appealed to me. It is the type of thing I will look back at after I retire and be proud that I was involved in."

Fellow Australian Michael Ryan was appointed as the first ever club captain: "I found it a real privilege to have captained such a great bunch of guys," he remembers. "The way the club conducted itself both on and off the park provided immediate results which made my job extremely easy and enjoyable.

"It didn't take me long to decide to move to Wales. Having worked under John Dixon in Australia, being coached again by him and being part of a newly established club was a real draw card."

By the start of 2006, the Celtic Crusaders offices had been open for more than a year in preparation for the big kick-off date, launching many innovations that had started to take off with the Welsh public.

By the end of November, almost 100 people had signed up for Celtic Crusaders Gold Membership. For just £5 a week, paid by standing order, fans got a grandstand season ticket worth £110, lottery membership worth £104, both home and away replica shirts worth £79.90, VIP hospitality worth £90 in the President's room for one match and a 10 per cent discount on any item in the club shop.

The club also launched a sponsorship raffle where for £299 + VAT, local businesses would have the chance of being the club's major shirt sponsor. Even if they lost, their business would still get an executive package that was worth a lot more than £300. Causing much hilarity in the rugby league world, the winner of that raffle was Malcolm Walker, of MW Builders. He entered the draw while at Bridgend in 2005 when he attended the Super League game between London Broncos and Hull FC. Unfortunately, he lived 300 miles away and supported York City Knights.

"I thought at £299 it was definitely worth a punt," Walker said at the time. "I never thought I'd win but with the odds at 100-1 it was better than the [National] Lottery."

All 100 tickets for the sponsorship raffle were reported to have been sold. Getting the businesses to invest in Celtic Crusaders seemed to be going fairly well. Promoting a brand new club to the general public, though, was more challenging.

"It was really difficult," Anthony Seibold remembers. "When we hopped off the plane and came to Wales, we didn't know what kind of response Celtic Crusaders had in the community. When playing for Hull KR I knew that they were an essential part of the east Hull community so I didn't know if it would be like that or like at London where London Broncos were in the shadow of soccer clubs.

"When we arrived, we set up promotional days at places like McArthur Glen [a designer outlet retail park on the outskirts of Bridgend], but to be honest there was little recognition of the Celtic Crusaders brand or what they were about.

"There was certainly plenty of interest though. I remember one day we set up a stall down there and quite a few of us went to promote the club. There was Gerald McCarthy, Michael Ryan, Tony Duggan, Jace van Dijk, Damien Quinn, John Dixon, Kevin Ellis and myself. It was a freezing cold December day and we were trying to get the Crusaders name out there and sell a few lottery tickets. The general awareness of the public wasn't there at that stage, but remember that was back in December 2005 when we hadn't even kicked a ball. It was interesting anyway."

Celtic Crusaders first kicked a ball on Sunday 5 February 2006 when a development side – in other words a team that was bereft of Australian imports – ran out at the Brewery Field to take on the Academy team of Super League Harlequins. Like the Crusaders, the Quins were a new set-up, in name only, with the long-standing rugby union club having formed a partnership with the London Broncos meaning the league side now being based at The Stoop. Both sides had a point to prove.

Of the 19 who took to the field for the Crusaders that day, just three remained at the club in their first Super League season in 2009. Only one was in the first team, Geraint Davies, who on that day in 2006 played in the centre alongside Lee Williams, who has since made a name for himself in the Crusaders Colts side and like Geraint, has won a full Welsh cap. Chris Vitalini, who that day played in an unusual position for him, full-back, is the third player who was still on the Crusaders books in 2009.

Geraint Davies remembers a lot about the game: "We had better individual talent but their experience and knowledge of the game kept them in it until the end," he said. "Current Quins star Louie McCarthy-Scarsbrook played centre for them that day. It wasn't a bad performance by the Welsh players at all and it set up the start of something that has turned out to be very, very special."

The match, witnessed by just a few hundred people, was a classic 22–22 draw. Those who attended must have certainly spread the word because by the time the Crusaders were due to play at home again, more than 1,000 people came through the gates. This was, of course, helped by the Crusaders excellent form in their first three away games, coupled with a lot of marketing in local schools and businesses.

The Crusaders entered three competitions in 2006. The club began life in British rugby league at the bottom of the professional ladder, National League Two, which was applauded by many coaches and experts around the country, with people like Keighley Cougars coach Peter Roe, a long standing critic of expansion in places, speaking highly of the club in its first season: "There are a lot of similarities you can draw between rugby union down here and the working class rugby league in the north of England," Roe said at the time, after watching his Keighley side being heavily beaten in South Wales. "The Crusaders just need to lift their profile a little and attract more of the rugby public as they climb up the league. They've gone the right way by not being fast-tracked into Super League like the French. I'm a big admirer of John Dixon and what he's doing down here and I think the Crusaders are as good as anyone in this division."

The club was, of course, to compete in rugby league's most famous competition, the Challenge Cup, but was also taking part in one of the less significant ones, the Northern Rail Cup.

This competition has had its critics throughout the years, mainly because a lot of people see it as a series of glorified pre-season friendlies. At that time, all of National League One and Two, and those who wanted to enter from the non-professional National League Three competition, were split into regional groups of four who played each other home-and-away for a six-game mini-league. For the Crusaders, this meant fixtures against three clubs from the London area – London Skolars, who were in the same division, National League Two, and two sides from the league below, St Albans Centurions and Hemel Stags.

The Stags' Pennine Way ground hosted Crusaders' first ever competitive match. Although little known in Wales, the Stags have a long history. Formed in 1981, they are the second oldest rugby league club south of Sheffield.

It was a horrible wet day on 12 February 2006. Tony Duggan ran over for the game's and Crusaders' first ever competitive try in only the second minute and, while the home side fought back and were just six points down at the interval, the Crusaders eventually triumphed 50–10.

"It was pouring rain and freezing cold that day," Duggan remembers. "I had two lots of skins on under my jersey, but I could not stop shivering even while I was running around. That made me question if I had made the right decision, ha ha! It was at that game that I also realised that we were to have a small, but fanatical band of supporters who followed us all over England to give a familiar voice in foreign territory. We were and still are all grateful for their support."

Further large wins followed at London Skolars and St Albans Centurions, 40–6 and 70–0 respectively, and the bookies' installation of the team as favourites to win the group before they'd kicked a ball was coming to fruition.

Celtic Crusaders' debut season

Left: Tony Duggan scores in the club's first game – a 50–10 win at Hemel Hempstead in the Northern Rail Cup
(Photo: Ian Lovell)

Middle: Crusaders fans at the Hemel game
(Photo: Gareth Laugharne)

Ryan Barton in action against London Skolars in the Crusaders' first home game – a then club record 78–14 win
(Photo: Ian Lovell)

Welsh sport at the time was in one of those 'average' stages. The international football side had failed to qualify for the World Cup held in Germany. John Toshack's team, that had finished second bottom of a group that also contained England, Poland, Austria, Northern Ireland and Azerbaijan, only managed to beat Azerbaijan and draw with Northern Ireland.

The international rugby union team had won the Six Nations tournament in 2005, but an average autumn international series where they were hammered 41–3 by New Zealand, only beat Fiji 11–10 and were outclassed 33–16 by South Africa didn't give the locals much confidence of retaining their title. A 24–22 win over Australia was the only result that gave them any confidence.

When the Crusaders kicked off in their first competitive home game on 4 March, the public was probably ready to watch a successful team. It was clear that the WRU side were not going to retain their title, heavy away defeats in England, 47–13, and Ireland, 31–5, had seen to that. So the Crusaders, with three wins under their belts, were prepared for Welsh action as London Skolars were the first visitors to the Brewery Field.

The Crusaders received a lot of publicity before the match and as such more than 1,000 attended to witness the Crusaders do the double winning 78–14. Further wins over Hemel, 72–14, and St Albans, 62–0, occurred, and the Crusaders were into the knockout stages of the Northern Rail Cup as unbeaten group champions.

Between the London and Hemel home matches, the Crusaders played in the third round of the Challenge Cup. The draw had been made live on BBC Radio Leeds on Sunday 19 February following the team's win at the Skolars and everyone in the club house at New River Stadium crowded round a speaker on a mobile phone as the draw was transmitted live over the internet, because the BBC did not broadcast it nationally on the radio.

The draw saw the Skolars paired in a potentially difficult tie at home to Gateshead Thunder, but for the Crusaders the romance of the Cup was in full swing when it was announced that Russian champions Lokomotiv Moscow would visit the Brewery Field.

The Russian national side had faced Wales just over two years before. The Moscow side who arrived at the Brewery Field had the same coaching staff and three of the players from that match in 2003

– Igor Gavrilin, Victor Netchaev and Roman Outchinnikov. The Russians were an unknown quantity apart from the fact that they were incredibly dominant in their home competition having won a string of national titles and cups and regularly running in 100-point scorelines.

Tony Duggan gave the Crusaders the lead in only the second minute but the Russians got a try back six minutes later as Sergey Dobrynin forced his way over. However, that was the only time that they were really in a game as Duggan scored three more tries, Carl de Chenu scored a brace while tries from Lenny Woodard, Marcus Sainsbury, Lee Williams, Lloyd O'Connor and Luke Young, who also kicked 10 goals, completed the 64–4 win.

The subsequent draw wasn't kind to the Crusaders. The club desperately wanted to entertain a Super League team, but instead were paired with National League One outfit Rochdale Hornets. But, like the Moscow game, the fixture did attract a lot of media attention. As the match was played on a Saturday, BBC1 Wales showed highlights on their evening sports show, even if the presentation did start with words such as "the game that robbed rugby union of a generation of stars is having another attempt" and ended with "well so much for the rugby league" after Crusaders lost 32–8. Clearly there was still a lot of work to do to get recognition with some of the local media. The BBC complemented this presentation with live updates on both BBC Radio Wales and Radio Cymru (albeit from the same reporter), a rarity in the club's first three years.

Sky Sports showed highlights of the match on their *Boots 'n' All* programme. They had also showed highlights on the Moscow game on *Sky Sports News,* and the coverage of the Rochdale match was far more positive than the BBC, interviewing many of the Crusaders fans who had travelled to Rochdale in large numbers.

But now it was time for Crusaders to begin their bread and butter – National League Two. While they had already faced and beaten London Skolars, the men from the capital were still recognised as one of the weaker sides in the competition and everyone was waiting to see just how the Crusaders would get on against long-established northern outfits such as Featherstone Rovers and Workington Town.

It was a trip to Cumbria to play the latter that faced the Crusaders in their first league game. Town were many people's favourites to win the competition in 2006 and many expected the Crusaders to slip up.

The team line-up had evolved a lot over the first nine games as John Dixon tried and tested a lot of local rugby league players. In total 40 players were used that season, 24 of them were Welsh-born with 20 of them new to professional rugby league.

As well as giving trials to players from the likes of Bridgend Blue Bulls and Aberavon Fighting Irish, the club weren't afraid to give local rugby union players a try out. Michael Hook, brother of Welsh rugby union international James, was one of them, playing eight games, scoring a try and six goals, but he left the club mid-season to play rugby union in Cornwall. Another player who caused more of a stir was Shawn van Rensburg. South African by birth, but qualifying to play for Wales, the big forward added a lot of strength to the Crusaders pack and whenever he got the ball, the team made metres if nothing else. The former Bridgend Ravens and Newport Gwent Dragons player was unable to break into the Welsh Rugby Union side and, unfortunately for him, didn't make it into the 13-man international squad either. Making his debut against Workington, he made 12 consecutive appearances, most of them from the bench, before picking up an injury which ended his Crusaders career.

Crusaders won that first game 50–18, ending Town's 23-month unbeaten home record, and sent shockwaves throughout the rugby league world. Team manager Gerald McCarthy remembers the trip: "Going to Cumbria has always been tough," he said. "It was never our favourite place to go and we've only won there about 50 per cent of the time. It was eight hours on the bus, I think it takes longer to get to Cumbria than it does to Moscow. However the trip to Workington was one to remember.

"There was a hostile crowd there and because of the distances involved we didn't have a very large support. However we produced one of our best performances of the season and made everyone sit up and take notice.

"There was even a 26-man fight late on in the game; that was the kind of day it was. Jace van Dijk was sin-binned and the fourth official told me he'd been red carded so I was going off at him and the next thing I knew, someone threw a pie at me from the crowd. It was one thing after another. But we beat them in the fight as well. It was their way of saying 'now you're up here, this is who we are' but that back-fired on them as well."

Crusaders took the lead after only a minute. Town's Dean Vaughan knocked on in just the third tackle of the game giving the visitors early possession. Karl Hocking charged through the middle, setting up Jace van Dijk at dummy-half who laid off to Damien Quinn for a try in the corner. Quinn converted and it was 6–0 in fewer than 120 seconds.

Tony Duggan was once again the star with a hat-trick, while Luke Young, Michael Ryan, Grant Epton, Ryan Barton and Carl de Chenu also scored. The Crusaders had really made themselves known and the publicity in the Welsh media was accelerating as London Skolars fell 70–0 on Good Friday in the second league match of the season.

By the end of May, the Crusaders were doing well. With the rugby union season now at an end, some of the Crusaders squad who had been playing two matches in a weekend could fully concentrate on league, and the side had reached a healthy fifth place in the table with four wins, three defeats and a draw in eight matches.

But something big was happening at the Brewery Field, something bigger than any rugby match to be played there – Bryan Adams was paying a visit. His open-air concert at the Brewery Field was one of the best spectacles seen at the ground in many a year and the risk of an open-air venue proved fruitful as temperatures reached 30 degrees on that Friday, 2 June. There were 15,000 people inside the ground, all with Celtic Crusaders advertised on their Bryan Adams tickets. It was a success in all quarters, with the Bryan Adams Fan Club writing to stadium manager Mike Owen telling him that it was one of the best, if not the best, organised concert that they'd been to. The club had shown that it could successfully organise a big event and that could only bide well for a Super League application.

It had always been Chris O'Callaghan's aim to get Celtic Crusaders into Super League, it was something he mentioned back in 2004 before the club had even been formed. So for him, it was a shame that he didn't see out his goal. On the Monday following the Bryan Adams concert and the day after a magnificent 58–18 win over Keighley Cougars, O'Callaghan parted company with the club. He had been working long days and his health had suffered consequently. In addition to the Crusaders, he had his coaching role with the Spanish national rugby union side and he had decided to concentrate on that. Protagonists were claiming that this single event was a major set-back for Celtic Crusaders, but nothing was further from the truth. The chief executive post was left vacant until 2007 when Dave Thompson was appointed to the job. However, the popular team manager Gerald McCarthy was given extra responsibilities; was appointed to the new role of operations manager and successfully ran the club in the interim.

Looking at the crowd figures, Crusaders' owner Leighton Samuel, concerned at the smaller-than-expected attendances, took action and quickly halved admission prices. Immediately the attendances more than doubled. In fact, the next home game, against Sheffield Eagles, brought in almost treble the amount of fans that had attended for the Blackpool Panthers game the previous month. This single move was a masterstroke, helped build the Crusaders fan base, brought a lot more money into the club from souvenirs, food and drink sales and was a major boost to the club's Super League application.

Promotion of the club also lifted with tickets for all matches given away at local schools. This again was a success as many of the children turned up, bringing parents in tow. Everyone worked together to distribute these tickets with many of the players and officials taking time out to hand deliver them for a more personal service. I remember being on the rota one week, trying to find 10 schools and stopping on the way for a quick telephone interview for BBC Radio Manchester's *Rugby League Hour*. It was an exciting time.

The club was also boosted by a double Welsh international signing with Carcassonne's Gareth Dean and Sheffield's Aled James returning to Wales. James made his debut in the first game following O'Callaghan's departure, a 50–18 win at league leaders Swinton, while Dean also had a successful start, scoring in the 28–12 win at home to Sheffield Eagles. Both players had started their rugby league careers with Cardiff Demons.

The team carried on their good form winning every game in June and three out of five in July. In fact, seven wins in nine games lifted the Crusaders to third in the league, just five points behind Dewsbury Rams and with an outside chance of taking the National League Two title in the club's first season.

The final win in that run was a 52–0 demolition of Blackpool Panthers in searing heat at Bloomfield Road. This was momentous for a few reasons. Blackpool, third from bottom of the table at the time,

Keighley Cougars versus Celtic Crusaders
National League Two 14 May 2006

Top: A Crusaders' try in the 30–30 draw.

Crusaders repel a Keighley attack.
(Both photos: Peter Lush)

had achieved an excellent 38–36 win at Gateshead the week before. However, that was the last game that they would win for almost two years. Their defeat against the Crusaders started a 45-game losing streak that finally ended on 6 April 2008 when they beat Workington Town 24–20.

The Crusaders embarked on a losing streak of their own, but thankfully it was only three matches – at home to Dewsbury and Gateshead and away to Featherstone Rovers, the last match an old fashioned 11–10 thriller that was only settled by a Jamie Benn drop-goal six minutes from time.

In the meantime, the club celebrated its first international cap – Anthony Seibold – who scored a hat-trick of tries for Germany as they beat Estonia 38–24 in a Tri-Nations match in Tallinn. Seibold, who had been appointed director of rugby for the German national side for 2006, coached the team before their earlier win over Austria, but was unable to play in that game. The German national coach Uwe Jenson visited Wales for a week to observe the Celtic Crusaders' coaching.

With three games to go in the regular season, the Crusaders knew that the team needed to win all three to even have a chance of taking third place. First and second were now completely out of reach, but third would give the team an easier run in the play-offs, enabling them to miss week one and have a second chance of qualifying for the play-off final should they lose in week two.

Two successive wins, at home to Workington Town, then at Gateshead, set up a dramatic last-day-of-the-season match at home to Featherstone Rovers. The visitors were two points above the Crusaders in the league and currently in that valuable third place position. However, the Crusaders' points difference was far superior so any win would enable them to leapfrog over Featherstone in the table.

The Crusaders were 11–4 down with two minutes to go, and it looked as if they were dead and buried and would have to settle for fourth place, but the players dramatically pulled a win out of the hat. Tony Duggan set up Aled James to score a try with van Dijk's kick putting the Crusaders to within a point of their northern opponents.

Featherstone looked to have won the game when the final hooter sounded less than 60 seconds later. The Rovers fans started celebrating, but there was another twist to this dramatic tale. The referee had given Crusaders a penalty on their own 30-metre line.

Jace Van Dijk kicked into touch and the team used up their last ounce of energy as two kicks down the centre made it a foot race for the try line. Tony Duggan was the fastest and leapt on the ball to win the match and secure third place. Van Dijk didn't even attempt the conversion as the Crusaders fans roared with delight and the Rovers fans were devastated.

Gerald McCarthy summed up the win: "To go from one emotion to another in the space of two minutes is not something I'd like to do again. That was the greatest game of the season and our best win to date. We were dead and buried with two minutes to go and I'm so proud of the lads for pulling this one out of the hat. It was a success on and off the field today as we'd invited all of our sponsors to the game and also some potential new sponsors. Obviously they all loved what they saw, the atmosphere was electric today and this performance means that Celtic Crusaders are really going places. "

Next up was a trip to Sheffield Eagles in the play-offs, due to be covered by the BBC on their *Rugby League Raw* programme. BBC Wales television had been proactive in previewing and reporting on the Featherstone Rovers match with the late Bob Humphreys becoming an enthusiastic fan. He was the legendary sports presenter on BBC's *Wales Today* and loved coming to the Crusaders. He died in August 2008 and is much missed by all at the club.

Bob was influential in getting the Crusaders on BBC television, but he couldn't manage to capture the broadcast of *Rugby League Raw* for Wales. Made for the north of England, the BBC was adamant that it would only be shown in the north of England despite the Crusaders being on it. Nigel Walker, the head of sport for BBC Wales, said that they would have shown it had the Crusaders been on every show, but as they started in the second round of the play-offs and couldn't guarantee a final spot, he couldn't risk it. However, they did show highlights of the Eagles game, played on a Friday night, on their *Wales on Saturday* programme, which was presented more enthusiastically than earlier in the season, despite another Crusaders defeat.

Following the 26–16 loss in Sheffield, the Crusaders needed to beat Swinton Lions at the Brewery Field to join Sheffield in the final. Another dramatic match ensued and the team was 26–20 up with just two minutes to go before a Lee Marsh converted try took the game into extra time.

123

With players tiring and going down with cramp, the winner was always going to be the team who could stay on their feet long enough to score or make the fewest number of errors.

Andy Saywell was first over the line for Swinton, grounding under the sticks midway through the first period, but it was disallowed for off-side. From then on, both sides went for the single point. Luke Young's hopeful attempt from the halfway line went wide, Lee Marsh's kick from a similar position didn't even reach the line and Young missed another with 20 seconds to go. So the game went into Golden Point overtime and Swinton were the strongest. Their attack led to a chance for Chris Hough to drop-kick the winning point from 15 metres out 91 seconds after the restart. The Crusaders had lost 27-26 and Sheffield went on to beat Swinton in the final a week later. Promotion for the Crusaders would have to wait for another year. But, it was essential that the Crusaders achieved this goal in 2007 because the club needed to be in National League One in 2008 in order to apply for a Super League licence for 2009.

Anthony Seibold, who went back to Australia for a year at the end of the season, has fond memories of 2006 and recalls that the club was creating an interest in South Wales: "When we first started playing, we were playing in the Northern Rail Cup against teams like St Albans and Hemel Hempstead who were non-professional clubs and they didn't have much support, so the awareness of them here in South Wales and around Bridgend was nonexistent," he said. "When we were playing teams at the back end of the season like Dewsbury and Featherstone, it's interesting to see how our crowds increased.

"We created a bit of a stir within the rugby union community too, there were often coaches and players from union clubs coming down to watch us. I can remember Rob Howley from Cardiff Blues being here, Lee Byrne has been a regular fan, Simon Easterby came down for a game or two. It was the first year and we were effectively in the third tier of British rugby league. Our crowds were increasing all the time but it was good to see the mix of people who were there."

Celtic Crusaders had well and truly arrived and the club had made its mark both locally and nationally. And if 2006 was full of excitement, 2007 would move to a different level entirely. The season would be a thriller from start to finish and would commence with a visit from a very important team indeed.

9. Champions

Rugby league's centenary year in Wales fell in 2007. The first two rugby league – Northern Union – matches played by Welsh clubs were both on 7 September 1907 when Merthyr Tydfil hosted Oldham and Ebbw Vale travelled to Keighley. By sheer coincidence, the Crusaders were to face both of these sides in National League Two in 2007.

The pioneers of 1907 broke into a brand new game amid much excitement, 100 years later that same sense of excitement was being replicated with plenty of developments on and off the field.

The build up started in late November 2006 when it was announced that the Crusaders would take on Australian champions Brisbane Broncos in a pre-season friendly because the NRL side requested a match to allow them to prepare for their forthcoming World Club Challenge game against St Helens. And with the fixture planners being extra kind to the club, the Crusaders were to open their Northern Rail Cup season by hosting Widnes Vikings six days earlier. "Two World Champions in a Week" read the promotional material, and an exciting start to the season was guaranteed.

It was a tremendous coup for the Crusaders to clinch the Broncos friendly as John Dixon explains: "The Broncos were looking for opposition for a warm-up game. They knew that to have a better chance against St Helens, they needed to acclimatise. They were looking at a few options, one in England and one in France but we managed to talk them into facing us. I mentioned to Broncos coach Wayne Bennett that we weren't far from London so it would be easy for them to get to and also that the Crusaders and rugby league in Wales needed a boost and we would get that if they played us. Of course Wayne agreed and the game was on."

The 2007 season was officially launched with a press conference at the Brewery Field where the club announced 14 new names in the first team squad in a massive shake up that saw 15 players from the 2006 squad released. New sponsors were also announced in the form of Redrow Homes while the club also paraded new cheerleaders who would become an integral part of the pre-match entertainment schedule.

Another major change for 2007 was that many Crusaders' matches would be screened live on television thanks to not one, but two, television contracts. Sky Sports had lost their NRL coverage to new kids on the block Setanta Sports and wanted more rugby league to fill their schedules and, despite a strong challenge from Eurosport, they signed the rights to cover one live National League match a week.

Closer to home, S4C were keen to get in on the act. The Welsh language broadcaster had never shown a live domestic rugby league match and had not shown the sport at all since the 1995 World Cup. More than a year of talks finally culminated mid-season in 2007 when it was announced that S4C would show four live Crusaders matches from the Brewery Field. As S4C is a free-to-air national channel, this also benefited away clubs' fans who could not travel to Bridgend because they could also watch the action, albeit in Welsh which certainly caused a major talking point among the fans. "We can't understand a word that they're saying, but they're still easier to understand than Sky Sports' Eddie and Stevo" was one of the tongue-in-cheek comments made.

To quote *League Express*, S4C's "version of Eddie Hemmings" was Sara Elgan, a prolific Welsh language sports presenter who also happens to be married to the Yorkshire-born Irish rugby union international Simon Easterby – Llanelli Scarlets' captain. Commentating would be Lyn Davies and former dual-code international Brynmor Williams.

S4C followed up the four games in 2007 by showing five in 2008 and it was a great shame that they weren't allowed to broadcast Super League games in 2009 after their outstanding work in the first two years. Williams, however, enjoyed every minute of his commentary work: "I spoke to a few staunch rugby union people the day after the first game was transmitted," Williams said, "And they told me, 'I watched that game last night and it had a real edge to it. I really enjoyed it.'

"The first match we broadcast, which was against Barrow, was an outstanding spectacle. I was jumping up and down in the gantry, and punching the air when we scored. I was like that for two reasons – first is that I love the game of rugby league just like I enjoy rugby union and second is that the Crusaders are the only professional club in Wales and they were facing an English adversary.

"S4C and the other media are important in this, as is the success of the team. If people find the team entertaining and the Crusaders are successful then more people will come to the games all the time. The fact that rugby league is played in summer now is superb. The conditions support fast, open rugby backing its entertainment factor. It's better for ball-handling, better skills and it's going to attract the people in."

When he wasn't in the first team, the Welsh-speaking Geraint Davies found himself in another role, as co-presenter alongside Sara Elgan: "It was a change and a great experience," said Davies. "It was certainly something different for me.

"I was very nervous on my first show, the Barrow game, as it was something new. Just like playing the game, you get a buzz doing it. It's very enjoyable, but without the bumps and bruises.

Davies was spotted by Rhondda-based independent programme makers The Pop Factory during his first appearance and recorded a piece for their S4C Planed Plant children's programme, *Stamina*.

"Again that was enjoyable," he said. "I recorded a quick fact profile about myself, did a 'what is rugby league?' section and had a chat about the Crusaders. The media side of the job is a perk in my eyes. It has allowed me to broaden my horizons and experience other things away from rugby. I am a proud Welsh speaker and am always happy to give an interview in my native tongue."

S4C started to broadcast Crusaders matches in early summer, but the 2007 season began in the cold of February on a Friday night at home to Widnes Vikings. Originally scheduled for Saturday, the game was brought forward a day to allow maximum rest time for the players before they took on the Broncos. The Widnes fans weren't impressed in having to travel a fair distance on a Friday night. They were less impressed when most of them were caught up in a traffic jam following an accident on the A442 just outside Newport and were stuck until around 9pm. The game kicked off at 7.30pm. Once they arrived at the roundabout in Newport on the M4 they simply circled it and went back up north. However, there were stories of fans who made it to the ground just in time for the final whistle, celebrated their team winning 56–6, had a quick pint and went back to Widnes. They said they'd come so far that they didn't care that they'd missed the game but had to get to the ground to have a drink.

Snow caused the accident, the white stuff was falling all day around Bridgend, but somehow the Brewery Field escaped it. All day people were phoning the club, asking if the was game on and couldn't believe it when it actually took place.

Six days later was one of the biggest days in both the Crusaders and Welsh rugby league history when the Broncos came to town. The match, known as the Bulmers' Original Cider Challenge, after their lucrative sponsorship deal, gave Celtic Crusaders column inches in the local and national press that had previously been unheard of.

Leading the way were the *South Wales Echo* with almost a page a day dedicated to the match for the three days leading up to the game, with a different picture of Brisbane skipper Darren Lockyer on each occasion.

Yes, the media and general public as a whole now knew that the Celtic Crusaders were there. BBC, ITV and S4C gave live feeds from the ground before the game, as well as broadcasting pre-match items in the days before and showed highlights of the game the following night. The club's debut in Super League two years later didn't even reach that level of coverage.

Real Radio Wales had an hour long Celtic Crusaders special on the evening before the game with John Dixon and Gerald McCarthy as guests in the studio. John assured the supporters that Brisbane were bringing a full strength side and weren't going to field reserves in a friendly against a lower league team.

To say that the Crusaders performed a lot better than they did against Widnes Vikings the previous week is an understatement. The Broncos, with nine Australian internationals in the team, struggled for the first quarter of the game, looking a little jet-lagged after their long trip as the Crusaders, initially, were the better side.

But the Crusaders couldn't break through and the Broncos took an early lead through a Darren Lockyer try. Grant Epton weaved his way through the Broncos defence to level things and instantly the national media were asking "Who's this kid Epton then?" and "How did he make fools of them like that?" The Crusaders finally lost 32–6, but the game was an experience both the players and all in the 2,000-strong crowd would never forget. The reality check came three days later when it was back to Northern Rail Cup action. Only 301 were in attendance to see a 44–28 win over London Skolars. This was the win the club needed to kick-start the season. Ten wins in 12 games followed and the team was top of the National League Two table and into the quarter-finals of the Northern Rail Cup.

The side were seriously entertaining the crowd along the way too, with a host of new signings. An upheaval was certainly needed at the club. In 2006 the management had experimented with a number of players and had done well to reach third in the table. However, promotion was essential in 2007 as without it the club could not have applied for a Super League licence and it is doubtful that the Crusaders would have continued, at least in the current strong format.

Fifteen first team players were released – Carl de Chenu returned to his native Ireland to become a policeman, Dave Simm picked up a serious injury at the latter part of 2006 and returned to Scotland, Gareth Price returned north and signed for Widnes, Matt Hill and Ryan Barton both returned to Australia with Matt signing for Redcliffe Dolphins and Ryan going to Canberra Raiders, while fellow Australian Matt Jobson joined Toulouse Olympique. Michael Hook went to Cornish rugby union club, Redruth, Dean Scully, Karl Hocking, Lenny Woodard and Paul Morgan all went back into local Welsh rugby union while the whereabouts of the charismatic Shawn van Rensburg were unclear.

However, the three most high-profile departures were skipper Michael Ryan, Welsh international Aled James and player-assistant coach Anthony Seibold. Ryan returned to Australia for family reasons and even took a year off from playing the game. However, in 2008 he signed for Queensland Cup side Ipswich Jets playing under former Australian international Kevin Walters. He was sorry to leave the Crusaders, but was happy to have played a large role in the first season: "I found it a real privilege to have captained such a great bunch of guys," Ryan said. "The way the club conducted itself both on and off the park provided immediate results which made my job extremely easy and enjoyable.

"Having worked under John Dixon in Australia, being coached again by him and being part of a newly established club was a real drawcard and making the playoffs in our first year was the highlight for me.

"With Super League always within sight, I think the way the organisation hit the ground running on the playing front really provided a platform for what is about to become a really successful Super League franchise."

Aled James initially quit rugby league for a career move but things didn't go according to plan: "I was planning to join the police force," he said. "I'd never had a proper job outside rugby league so I resigned from the Crusaders and started playing rugby union for Glamorgan Wanderers. But while I was waiting for the police training course to start, I was given some part-time work with Wales Rugby League going into schools and training children. The job then became permanent so I've abandoned my plans of becoming a policeman for now. Of course I ended up being selected for the Crusaders again in 2008 so I wasn't gone for long."

Anthony Seibold's departure was in similar circumstances: "I had a job offer with the University of Southern Queensland that was too good to refuse," he said. "I wanted to get some teaching experience so I went back to Australia knowing that I had the option to return any time I wanted to. I was only away for a year too."

So, with 14 players and an assistant coach departing, 14 players and an assistant coach were recruited. The assistant coach was Frenchman Thibault Giroud. He is an unusual sportsman and it is surprising that he'd not really been spoken about at a high level before signing for the Crusaders. Born in France to Tongan parents in 1974, his first adventure in professional sport was in the USA when he trained with the American Football NFL Europe camp at Atlanta Falcons. He didn't make a full NFL appearance but after a stint in the Canadian League with Calgary Stampeders he returned to Europe, playing for the Barcelona, Amsterdam and Munich American football sides in NFL Europe.

Following an invitation from Prince Albert of Monaco, he joined the Monaco bobsleigh team for the Olympics before the French Olympic team came in for him. From 1998 to 2002, he competed in the best French bobsleigh team ever, as they became World Champions in

1999, European Champions in 2000 and was in their 2002 Olympic team in Salt Lake City.

In 2002, he started working full-time with Olympic silver medal sprinter Frankie Fredericks and achieved a personal best of 10.53 seconds in the 100 metres before signing for the North West Province Leopards in rugby union's Currie Cup in South Africa. In 2003 he was appointed as Saracens' conditioner, but also played for the rugby union club on the wing. He was conditioner with French club Pau from 2004 to 2005 before working with Harlequins Super League club in the same role in 2006.

When interviewed on the official Crusaders season launch day in January 2007, Giroud expressed his enthusiasm and explained why he'd committed himself to the Crusaders: "I was very amazed and very surprised how they want to perform and how they want to go up to Super League," he said. "They're very serious about it. I met with the owner [Leighton Samuel] and knew how enthusiastic he was. They really want to go forward."

The players that the Crusaders signed were equally diverse. From Australia, there were experienced forwards Terry Martin and Darren Mapp, who had played 96 and 66 NRL games respectively. Mark Dalle Cort, Rob Toshack and Josh Cale, Australians who hadn't quite broken into first grade, were also recruited from down under.

Four Englishmen were signed: Jamie I'Anson, a youngster from Leeds Rhinos Academy who became an instant hit at the Brewery Field; speedy winger Paul Ballard, who eventually ran in 40 tries in 49 appearances in his first two years for the club; Andy Boothroyd, a good hooker in his own right, but who was overshadowed by the fourth Englishman, Neil Budworth, another number nine who was recruited from Harlequins RL. Hailing from Wigan, Budworth started his career with amateur club Blackbrook and gained extensive experience with Wigan at reserve grade prior to joining London Broncos (who became Harlequins RL) for the 2003 season. He was voted the Broncos' Young Player of the Year in 2003 and Players' Player of the Year in 2004 when he was an ever-present with the club.

"Joining the Crusaders was a step back to eventually go forward," Budworth said. "I could see a lot of potential at the club and it was good to be a part of building rugby league in Wales. Yes it was a risk at the time, but it was one that I was willing to take. As it happened, the plan worked and we got to Super League but it took a lot of hard work throughout those two years."

Completing the acquisitions were young Welshmen Tom Burnell, Owen Lewis and Chris Vitalini who had been recruited from Welsh Conference sides, Cardiff Demons, Valley Cougars and Newport Titans respectively, Welsh international Anthony Blackwood had also been brought back from Halifax, but gaining the most media attention was Craig Richards, a signing from Llanelli rugby union club.

The son of the famous Wales and British Lions rugby union international, David Richards, Craig had become a very successful Wales rugby union international in the sevens version of the sport. With more than 60 caps to his name, he played for Wales in the 2002 Commonwealth Games while with Bridgend RFC. He had also played for Neath, Coventry and Newport and also spent time in Australia with Sydney club, Gordon Highlanders RFC.

Richards became an instant hit. His speed and pace on the wing were too much for his National League Two opponents and he scored 10 tries in his first five competitive games, including four in the 68–0 win over Blackpool Panthers. Suddenly he was top of the scoring charts in the division, ahead of fellow Crusader Tony Duggan.

Tipped to go straight into the Welsh international side for the World Cup qualifiers later in the year, it unfortunately wasn't to be. Richards was mysteriously dropped from the side despite his form and it was later revealed that he had tested positive for a metabolite of cocaine in May. Three months later, he was banned from all sports for two years and, in the opinion of many fans, Wales had lost the best international winger they'd never had.

On the field the team's good form came to a temporary end in May as they crashed to a 34–26 defeat in a high-profile game at home to Oldham Roughyeds in front of a Co-operative National League Two record crowd of 3,441 and thousands more who were watching the game live on Sky Sports, the club's first appearance on that channel.

The match also celebrated 100 years of rugby league in Wales – Oldham were the first visitors to the Principality back in September 1907 and Sky Sports made a special effort with the presentation of this game because of that. Normally a National League game would have just been presented from the ground on the sidelines and would just command a two hour slot, but Sky extended their coverage by an hour giving the game a full half-hour preview and there were also specially prepared pieces on the history and potential future of rugby league in Wales.

The show was presented from the Millennium Stadium due to quite a large event being held there that weekend – the first ever Millennium Magic, a complete round of six Super League games, including five local derbies, with three matches per day. The format had its critics, but was essentially a success as it showcased Super League in South Wales with many local fans attending the weekend.

Coverage in the local papers was first class throughout the weekend with all of Media Wales's publications, *South Wales Echo*, *Western Mail* and *Wales on Sunday* giving it double-page spreads with the Crusaders match getting the same treatment for once. Sky Sports coverage continued with live transmission of four out of the six games and highlights of the other two, while BBC provided online, radio and Super League Show coverage.

The weekend was a fantastic advert for rugby league with drama all the way. First up was Catalans Dragons versus Harlequins, the only non-derby game but a good one to start proceedings as Quins won a fantastic see-saw encounter 32–28. Their players were in no hurry to leave the pitch. Treating it like a cup final, they lapped up the applause and thanked the 20,000 or so fans who turned up to watch.

The atmosphere heated up considerably in game two – Hull FC versus Hull Kingston Rovers. With a long history of rivalry behind them, this match is sometimes referred to as the only real derby in rugby league as the two teams are from the same city. Their most famous meeting was in the 1980 Challenge Cup Final at Wembley where Rovers won 10–5.

Hull is the certainly one of the most passionate rugby league cities, even rivalling Sydney and its countless clubs and the passion spilled over into Cardiff in May 2007 with added controversy – Paul Cooke.

Can you imagine a player going from Liverpool to Everton then scoring the winner in a Cup Final, or worse, Cardiff City to Swansea City? Double that and you have Paul Cooke and 2007.

Just two weeks previously, BBC Radio Humberside sensationally announced that Cooke was to walk out on Hull FC to join Rovers due to a row over pay. Cooke was born in East Hull where Hull KR are based and supported the club as a youngster but went through the junior ranks at their rivals because they were the lone Super League club at the time.

With cries of "Cookey is a traitor" ringing in his ears, Paul was man-of-the-match despite having a dreadful start to the game, knocking on from kick-off after trying to catch the ball on the half-volley. In the end it was 14–10 to Rovers with Cooke kicking three goals. St Helens 34 Wigan 18 provided a less exciting end to a dramatic first day.

Day one provided the glamour while day two was down to the nitty gritty. The first two games weren't much to write home about as Huddersfield beat Wakefield 36–12 and Warrington hammered relegation- bound Salford 50–18. However, the final match was a classic and had one of the most dramatic finishes in rugby league history to rival the previous season's Celtic Crusaders win over Featherstone Rovers.

It was a high-scoring contest between Bradford Bulls and Leeds Rhinos where the Bulls had the upper hand for much of the game, but were never in total control. The Bulls were 38–30 ahead going into the last 15 minutes, but Brent Webb scored his third try of the game on 67 minutes which Kevin Sinfield converted to put the Rhinos within two points of their Yorkshire rivals.

Ten minutes later, Bradford thought they'd sealed the game with a Michael Platt try, but the video referee controversially ruled it out for a knock-on. Two minutes after that, another Bulls' try was disallowed by the video referee as Iestyn Harris's kick to the corner found Lesley Vainikolo, but James Evans was ruled to have knocked it on just before Vainikolo got the ball.

Then, in the final seconds, came one of the biggest talking points ever in rugby league. Referee Steve Ganson awarded a penalty for offside against Bradford's Matt Cook. The ball came loose from Leeds's Gareth Ellis, but Ganson ruled that the ball came off Iestyn Harris first.

Kevin Sinfield kicked the penalty, trying to salvage a draw, but the ball hit the post and rebounded for Jordan Tansey to score under the sticks. All replays showed that Tansey was offside, but the try was given and Sinfield landed the extras to give Leeds a 42–38 win.

It was a remarkable end to an outstanding weekend which was, despite some negative feedback from some critics, a success for Wales. There were almost 59,000 tickets sold over the two days and according to the extensive Millennium Magic review paper, 14 per cent of them were from Wales – around 8,000 people. This was not bad considering many were watching 'neutral' teams play and it certainly gave everyone great optimism for Super League in Wales. Travelling home on the train on the following day two people were saying "I'll come down to Celtic Crusaders if you get to Super League." It certainly proved that there is a major difference in the general public's perception of 'rugby league' and 'Super League' and this was shown by both the big increase in the Crusaders attendances in their first year in Super League and the media interest surrounding it.

Following Millennium Magic the Crusaders went through a mini lull, winning just one game in May, 26–4 victory at York, followed by defeats at Workington and Halifax, the latter in the Northern Rail Cup.

The next two games were against title challengers Featherstone Rovers and Barrow Raiders and wins were essential. Crusaders were 18–6 up at half-time against Rovers, but they fought back. However, a Rovers penalty miss with a few minutes to go, then a converted Luke Young try made the final score 36–28 to the Crusaders.

After the game, Crusaders coach John Dixon said: "That was a really good contest between two good football teams. We had the ascendancy at half-time but good teams don't lie down and they made a real contest of it in the second half. What really pleased me today is that we held on for the win. We were in a winning position, we were challenged and we answered the challenge."

The next week, in front of S4C's cameras for the first time, Crusaders bear Barrow 26–14 with the forwards, led by Darren Mapp, in control. However, all the good work that went into beating the two divisional giants was undermined by a disappointing 23–16 defeat at Hunslet the week after. This is a match often spoken about at the Brewery Field, and everyone says that the Crusaders should not have lost. While the report in *League Express* says that "victory wasn't confirmed until Darren Robinson slotted home a field goal two minutes from time", in reality it was a game in which the team looked second best for most of the time with only wingers Anthony Blackwood and Paul Ballard standing out.

That defeat left the Crusaders fourth in the table, five points behind leaders Featherstone, but with a game in hand. The season was not even half over, but with trips due to Featherstone and Barrow, the players knew that they couldn't afford any more slip ups.

2007: Action from Crusaders' promotion season

Crusaders' Dean Fitzgerald charges into the Blackpool defence in the National League 2 home match on 9 April 2007. (Photo: Ian Lovell)

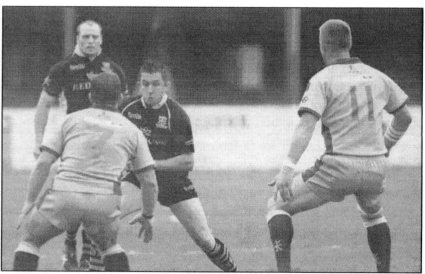

Grant Epton tries to run through the Barrow defence in the Crusaders' great 26–24 win at Craven Park in August 2007. (Photo: Ian Lovell)

Third-placed Workington Town were next up as they came to the Brewery Field to try to complete the double. A 26–12 win enabled the Crusaders to leapfrog over them. Then 30–16 and 50–6 home wins followed over York City Knights and London Skolars respectively before four tough away games on the trot.

The wins kept on coming – Crusaders edged past Swinton Lions 26–20 before winning easily 54–8 at Blackpool. This was followed by two hard-earned victories. The first was 32–12 at Featherstone, live on Sky Sports. This was one of the season's most important wins because had Rovers won, then the Crusaders would have been virtually out of the title race.

Next up was a trip to Barrow. The Raiders were also chasing the Crusaders towards the top of the table, and despite the latter's good run of form, the home side were strong favourites thanks to their equally good form and the Crusaders' uneven record in Cumbria.

At half-time the Crusaders were 26–16 ahead thanks to two tries from Tony Duggan and one each from Rob Toshack and Mark Dalle Cort. However, Barrow drew first blood in the second half after 45 minutes. Weisner set up Michael Basan to go over and Holt converted to put them just four points behind. They then pulled two more points back after 63 minutes after Holt kicked a penalty following a high tackle. Hywel Davies had a try ruled out when the referee ruled he received the ball from a knock-on, but that was the closest Crusaders came to scoring in the second period.

Barrow pressed right up to the end and had many chances to get a winning try but the Crusaders' strong defensive line kept out 10 minutes of pressure for a valuable three points.

"Barrow and Featherstone were our two main contenders for the title in 2007," John Dixon remembers. "But the real rivalry was between us and Featherstone. Being a new club, we don't have any traditional local rivals of course or a history of rivalry, so it sort of built up with Featherstone. 2006 was our first year in NL2 and of our existence of course and it was also their first year in NL2 after being relegated so we both had points to prove.

"The rivalry was a bit engineered from our end really. We were competing with a long-established club and one of the most famous names in rugby league and we promoted that for our own benefit. The clashes at end of 2006 were quite a tussle while 2007 was fierce again. In every contest against them, we never knew who was going to win. Barrow were an important part of the title campaigns in both years but it was really the rivalry between us and Featherstone that I really enjoyed."

Three home games followed the four games on the road. Hunslet were next up and there was no chance of a shock this time as the home players ran riot, winning 84–10. As John Paul Davies said on the ITV Wales news: "It's hard to believe that Hunslet were the last team to beat the Crusaders."

A 34–12 win over Keighley Cougars was followed by a dramatic 64–26 win over Gateshead Thunder during which 17 tries were scored and Thunder's Dylan Nash was sent off.

That win was the final game at home in 2007. Two away games remained, at Oldham and Gateshead, and the Crusaders needed to win both to take the title and the automatic promotion slot. The first of the two was arguably the toughest. Oldham still had an outside chance of taking the title themselves and for them a win was just as essential. Sky Sports had recognised the importance of the game and broadcast it live. Despite the game being moved to a Thursday and one large group of supporters not being able to attend because of a stag weekend in Manchester for the Saturday, which was to include this game, a good number of Crusaders fans made the journey to Greater Manchester.

The Crusaders were six points down at half-time and not playing at their best. Oldham's defence was resolute with substitute Matty Brooks and Welsh international Rob Roberts especially shining and the Crusaders did not do themselves any favours with some indiscipline, giving away four penalties, all of which Scottish international Gareth Morton had no problems in converting.

But in the second half, the players came out all guns blazing, scoring within a minute, knocking up 26 points and even denying Oldham a bonus point. The final score was 32–18 with the highlight being Tony Duggan's length-of-the-field run, beating all and sundry on his way to the line. It was arguably his best try for the club and his 37th of the season, equalling the previous year's total. The effort was also later recognised in *League Weekly* newspaper as the best televised try of 2007.

The Crusaders' National League Two attendance record was also broken thanks to Oldham introducing free admission for this game – believed to be only the second time in British professional rugby league that such a venture has taken place.

So it was onto Gateshead for the final game of the season. Only Featherstone Rovers could catch the Crusaders now and their last match was at Barrow the night before. They needed to win in the hope that the Crusaders would slip up at Gateshead 24 hours later. As it happened, Rovers were never in the game at Craven Park losing 30–4.

"The news came through when we were at our hotel in Gateshead," recalls Kevin Ellis. "We were ecstatic and there were high fives all round. We were all allowed one celebration drink before going to bed because we still wanted to win our final game against Gateshead. We owed it to all the fans who were coming to watch us."

And travel up they did, in vast numbers, by plane, train and automobile. The Crusaders fans getting to Gateshead was a real saga. I was in a minibus travelling to Bristol Airport to fly. It seemed like it would be an easy journey but for the Bristol Marathon that was taking place that day. Half the roads were closed off, none of the stewards, who were at the road closures knew any alternative routes and poor Gareth Laugharne's sat nav kept taking us to another road closure. We were afraid that we'd miss the plane at one point, but did make it and within an hour we were being met at Newcastle Airport by the infamous Gary Thunder who, along with the other Gateshead fans, were fantastic hosts that day. The plane journey back was a merry one. Fans had got used to singing on the coach following a few drinks after an away match, but singing on a plane? I don't think the other passengers knew what had hit them.

Thunder gave the Crusaders an early scare when Robin Peers gave them a third minute lead, but the visitors equalised straight from kick-off with a Paul Ballard try. From then on it was exhibition stuff.

Tony Duggan fed Rob Toshack for a second try after 13 minutes while Damien Quinn slid in under the posts two minutes later. Duggan surpassed his 2006 scoring record by notching his 38th try of 2007 on 19 minutes, running the ball in under the posts after fine work from Welsh international Gareth Dean.

Darren Mapp added a further try after 24 minutes with Neale Wyatt running over five minutes later. Neil Budworth created the next try,

139

offloading to Quinn who in turn set up Duggan for his second of the game. Jace Van Dijk's fifth goal of the half gave the Crusaders a 38–4 lead at the interval.

Thunder dominated the first five minutes of the second half following a Crusaders error from kick-off and they were rewarded when Michael Knowles went over after 45 minutes and converted his own try.

A 70-metre run from Quinn and van Dijk goal restored the balance five minutes later while Chris Beasley set up Grant Epton for a further score straight from kick-off.

Knowles went over for his second of the game, converting it himself once again after 64 minutes to make the score 48–16. Duggan touched down for his hat-trick and his 40th of the season five minutes later. Van Dijk converted before scoring a try of his own with six minutes left. Beasley, the only regular first team player not to have made the scoresheet that season, then took and scored his first ever conversion for the club to complete a successful year.

"This is a really good day for rugby league," John Dixon said at the time. "It's a great day for everyone associated with our club and for everyone involved in rugby league in Wales. This is the fruit of 12 months of hard work. The competition in National League One will be tougher. We think we've got the core here of a team that can compete really well."

Crusaders' operations manager Gerald McCarthy added: "This championship is a credit to all the hard work that everyone in the club has done but the biggest thanks of all go to Leighton Samuel for his commitment, support and belief that we would succeed. Without him none of this would have happened."

McCarthy also paid respect to John Dixon that day: "I think we've got the best coach in rugby league in Britain at the moment in John Dixon," McCarthy said. "His expertise, his knowledge of the game, his contacts in the game and the respect he has in the game is going to push us forward."

So for 2007 it was mission accomplished. The Crusaders were in National League One and able to apply for a Super League licence. Now the hard work was about to begin.

10. 2008: Promotion

Make no mistake, 2008 was a massive year for Welsh sport. For most Welsh people, the Welsh rugby union side's Grand Slam win will live long in their memories while one of the Welsh regional side, the Ospreys won rugby union's version of the Challenge Cup.

For other people, their memories of 2008 may differ depending on the sport that they follow. St Asaph-born Mark Webster started the year off with a bang after winning the BDO World Darts Championship in Surrey on 13 January.

In boxing, Joe Calzaghe beat both Bernard Hopkins and Roy Jones junior to retire undefeated as World Light Heavyweight Champion, only the third European boxer after Terry Marsh and Sven Ottke to retire as an undefeated world champion.

In football, for both whites and blues, there was something to celebrate. Swansea City were promoted to the Championship, the second tier of English football, as Champions but Cardiff City stole their thunder by reaching the FA Cup Final for only the third time in their history, narrowly losing 1-0 to Portsmouth.

And then there was the Beijing Olympics: Bridgend's own Nicole Cooke inspired the greatest British Olympic gold rush for 100 years. Her road race cycling victory was the first British gold of the Games and the first Welsh gold for 36 years.

Rower Tom James and cycling prodigy Geraint Thomas also struck gold while David Davies produced an inspirational two-hour open water swim to take silver in the 10,000m.

Tom Lucy's silver in the eight-man rowing boat ensured that these games were Wales's best Olympics since 1920 while swimmer David Roberts took four golds at the Paralympics.

After all that, there was still room for rugby league and Celtic Crusaders. When anyone looks back on Welsh rugby league, it can be put forward that 2008 was the most important year in the history of the sport. A Super League side was absolutely essential for the game in Wales. The sport in Wales had been building for well over 10 years in this modern era and now was its chance to seize the day.

The RFL had laid out the guidelines for those who wanted to apply for Super League status. Back in May 2005 their executive chairman Richard Lewis had announced that promotion and relegation would be scrapped by 2009 to drive the sport's professional development. In

2008 all 12 existing Super League clubs had to reapply for their status and new clubs could also apply to join them. The idea was to expand to 14 teams, but Lewis had said that there was no guarantee that this would happen if that many suitable applications were not received.

The licence applications would not be judged just by what was occurring on the field. There were 10 individual criteria on which the applications were assessed. These were:

Rugby activity: this was based on the team's first-team success, specifically top eight finishes in each of the last three years as well as development of juniors which included number of scholarships and performances of academy teams over the last three years (a possible two points).

Financial performance: whether clubs had a turnover of at least £4m per annum and were solvent (a possible two points).

Facilities: whether the capacity of the stadium was more than 12,000 and met the standard of a premier sporting competition according to a strictly defined criteria (a possible two points).

Attendances: whether the size of the average crowd was 10,000 or more and if that crowd filled more than 40 per cent of the capacity of the ground (a possible two points).

Rulebook criteria: a point would be awarded if the existing rules and regulations had been adhered to by a club.

Geographical criteria: clubs more than 20 miles from any other Super League club were awarded a final point.

Clubs that achieved a pass mark in eight or more of the 10 criteria received a Grade 'A' licence. Those scoring between five and seven would be awarded a Grade 'B' licence while clubs with four or less points would get a Grade 'C' licence.

In order to apply for a Super League licence for 2009, clubs had to be playing in either Super League, National League One or the French Elite League during the 2008 season. Nineteen clubs submitted an application for a licence by the time the deadline closed at the end of March 2008. As expected, all 12 existing Super League clubs submitted an application, as did Celtic Crusaders, Featherstone Rovers, Halifax, Leigh Centurions, Salford City Reds, Toulouse Olympique and Widnes Vikings.

It was rumoured on a message board in 2009 that a former National League coach claimed that all the Crusaders had to do was get into National League One to be awarded a Super League licence.

However, nothing could be further from the truth. The club staff all worked overtime in the office in the weeks leading up to the application deadline date in order to work on the licence application with chief executive David Thompson especially tireless in putting in the hours.

The application document that the club submitted to the RFL was bigger than a telephone directory. "The Crusade for Super League" was in the end a 158 page 26,630 word document plus the appendices which covered roughly the same amount of pages. The document was supported by a DVD that was specially produced by S4C (in English) highlighting all the major plus points of the Crusaders' licence bid and a letter from Welsh First Minister Rhodri Morgan.

Over a period of 19 weeks, Angela Powers from Sky Sports' magazine programme *Boots 'n' All* put the spotlight on all of the licence candidates and she gave the club four points thus theoretically awarding the Crusaders a higher 'C' grade licence. For the record, solvency, junior development, no salary cap breaches and obviously location were the points that Ms Powers gave the club.

David Thompson was interviewed on the programme: "What is happening here is very exciting," he said. "Everything we have achieved up to date has been achieved in National League Two. We were amongst the nominations for Welsh sports team of the year, which for a rugby league club based in Wales is impressive.

"The RFL mission statement is to promote the game of rugby league. There is no better way of promoting a sport than by putting a team in a new country. We would not be representing a village, a town, a city or even a region. Celtic Crusaders in the Super League would represent a whole nation."

So on 30 March 2008, the club's application was couriered up to the RFL headquarters in Leeds and all the club staff and players could do was sit back and wait. The staff kept a couple of copies of the application of course, but agreed not to look at it until after the decision had been made, just in case they spotted any glaring errors that they would regret making.

A new season would once again mean change. Eight new signings were originally announced – Hull Kingston Rovers trio Mark Lennon, Luke Dyer and David Tangata-Toa, three more from Widnes Vikings – Jordan James, Aaron Summers and Ian Webster, former London

Bronco Steve Thomas was acquired from Neath rugby union while Ben Flower was signed from Bedwas rugby union.

Lennon was especially keen to come down to Wales. He has a great passion for the country and was always keen to play for a Welsh club: "I'd spoken about it with John Dixon back in 2005 in Dublin over a pint of Guinness following the Ireland versus Wales match," Lennon remembers. "But I was still under contract then and the time wasn't right. 2008 was the right time for me and when I my contract was up with Hull KR, it was very easy for me to make the decision to sign for the Crusaders. A lot of my family still live in Gwent and they've now been able to watch me play on a regular basis."

In fact, all of the players, bar Tangata-Toa, were Welsh qualified with only Flower, who had previously played rugby league for Cardiff Demons' junior sides, not having played for the Welsh senior side.

There was a minor set-back when Steve Thomas wasn't able to sign in the end following a contract dispute with Neath, but the club signed a unique replacement – a French American Footballer by the name of Philippe Gardent who had never played rugby league before. Gardent was keen to learn and progress as a rugby league player.

He was 28 when he signed for the Crusaders, took up American Football when he was just 17 years old and rose to prominence in NFL Europe with Berlin Thunder and then Cologne Centurions where he was voted the competition's defensive Most Valuable Player in 2006. He spent a year with the Washington Redskins before moving to the Carolina Panthers which is where he made his NFL appearances.

"Philippe is obviously going to attract a lot of interest because he has such a different background," John Dixon said at the time. "But he's a talented athlete who'll compare well with anyone in the sport. He's intelligent and a very strong player so we hope he'll pick the game up quickly and make a valuable contribution."

Gardent commented: "It was a great experience playing in the best league in the world in American Football. I'm glad of what I did, but I'm trying to move on. I now have to learn rugby league like I did with American Football at 17 years old. It's another challenge, another opportunity for me to grow up as a man and an athlete. I will play wherever the coach wants me."

Eleven players left the club. Josh Cale, Luke Young and Rob Toshack all returned to Australia to sign for Lavington Panthers, MacKay Cutters and Woolgoolga Seahorses respectively.

144

Two players returned to their respective countries. Andy Boothroyd went back to England and Batley Bulldogs while Aurélien Cologni returned to France to play for Lezignan and starred for them in their 2009 Challenge Cup run.

A few Welsh-based players chose not to sign the compulsory full-time contract as they didn't want to give up their careers outside of rugby. Four of them went to local rugby union clubs – Dean Fitzgerald and Hywel Davies both signed for Tonmawr, Lee Jones went to Pyle and also excelled in local darts tournaments while Grant Epton carried on playing at the Brewery Field, but for Bridgend Ravens. Although released from the club, Phil Cushion stayed, but played only for the Crusaders' new second string side, the Crusaders Colts in 2008. Finally, Richard Johnston moved to Reading to join the police force.

Everyone at the club knew that the Crusaders had to perform on-and-off the field in National League One throughout 2008 to support our application. The club had no idea when the RFL would be making their decision so Super League level performances on and off the field were needed at all times.

Promoting the club was the order of the day at all times. The club was grateful for the Co-operative for sponsoring 500 free family tickets per game for the Sky live games. That certainly helped in our promotions around the schools and local businesses. The schools and other community work that had started has been one of the primary focuses for the club with Gerald McCarthy and Kevin Ellis getting the ball rolling in 2006 before Dave McNally was appointed as the first full-time community development officer in 2007. Matthew Pritchard has more than continued his excellent work from 2008 onwards.

The highlight of 2008 was a magnificent schools tag festival held before our Sky live game against Featherstone Rovers where 22 schools sides from Rhondda Cynon Taff, Bridgend, Merthyr and Caerphilly played. Their attendance helped to boost the crowd to a record 6,152 which must have impressed the visiting RFL officials who were in the area for the second Millennium Magic tournament.

"The tag festivals are just part of our work in the community," commented Pritchard. "We had a couple of them in 2008 and staged four in 2009 plus a finals day. It's all part of our Primary School programme which was one big programme in 2009 which has developed rapidly. Two schools from each festival were chosen for the finals day based on how well they contributed and did on the day.

"There are many other successes. We started up street rugby league which is for areas that don't have the accessibility to play rugby league. This is supported by South Wales Police and Safer Bridgend. Almost 100 secondary school teams from Newport to Tenby play in the Champions Schools competition which we help to run in association with the Welsh Rugby League and the RFL. Our players make visits to schools, hospitals and other organisations, we run promotions with local businesses and we even run non-sporting competitions like our Community Talent Battle which was very successful throughout 2009.

"Community Crusaders is more than just getting the Crusaders' name known. It's even more than about getting them involved in more sport. The government's aim is to get more kids and adults into playing sport and we're trying to do that as well. In addition to that, on the back of everything we do, yes our name is going to get known and that can only help the club and rugby league.

"In all community work, there's a business side but there's a fine line between community work and business side and I think we've got that just right. We are pushing our name but we're out there in the community, we're helping kids get fit and we're bringing companies together to work together. Onwards and upwards."

On the field in 2008 the club was making the step up to National League One and were tested with a pre-season friendly at home to Harlequins. The match was uniquely played in 15 minute quarters to allow the coaches to try out their new formations and it looked like the Crusaders coped better than their London opponents as they ran out 28–6 winners against a Quins side who fielded quality international players like Julien Rinaldi and Henry Paul.

"It's important to play against quality opposition pre-season, which is what we did today," John Dixon said in the post-match interview.

"We've played against a Super League side and not only won and scored some wonderful tries and only conceded one.

"What's also important is the depth of our squad was demonstrated. I'm very pleased with the youngsters who turned out today, players like Tom Burnell, Chris Vitalini and Ben Flower. Ben played his first ever game of senior rugby league today and was terrific. He was very strong and carried the ball well. If they can go out there and play against Super League opposition and be as technically good and as physically committed as they were today, then the season bodes well for us."

146

Crusaders' stalwart scrum-half Jace Van Dijk in action against Locomotiv Moscow in the Challenge Cup in March 2008 (Photo: Ian Lovell)

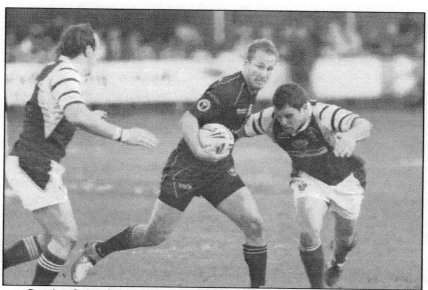

Damien Quinn fights off two Featherstone defenders in the Crusaders' 28–18 home win in May 2008 (Photo: Ian Lovell)

Philippe Gardent was given a debut earlier in the game than expected after replacing the injured Gareth Dean in the first quarter of the game, and Dixon was equally as happy with his performance.

"Phil had never even seen a game of rugby league before let alone played it," Dixon added. "To see him hold his positions in the line and do the job as well as he did was terrific. He's a long way from being the finished product for us but some of his carries off the line were strong and his understanding of what he had to do showed that he's been listening and working really hard. Down the track, I'm certain there's a place for Phil in our team."

The wins kept on coming as the Northern Rail Cup started. Once again the Crusaders were drawn in a group with London Skolars while Doncaster RLFC and Sheffield Eagles were their other opponents.

Sheffield Eagles at the Don Valley Stadium was the first game. Crusaders had played there twice in 2006 and lost on both occasions so it hadn't been a happy stamping ground for them in the past. However, a 22–12 win against what looked to be their hardest group game gave them the start they wanted in the competition.

Next was away to London Skolars and they showed how well they'd improved by making the Crusaders work hard for a 26–10 win. A 34–14 win at home to Sheffield was followed by a very hard-fought 30–22 win at Doncaster. The home side were 22–20 up with three minutes left but tries from Josh Hannay and Ian Webster gave the Crusaders the points in the end.

Doncaster's new coach at the time was one of the legends of rugby league, Ellery Hanley and, never afraid to be outspoken, he commented on his team's performance at the end of the game: "When you're a part time side playing against a full-time side, you have to play at your best for 80 minutes and not 20 minutes," he said. "Fitness proved to be the factor today and that was where Celtic excelled and they were composed right up to the end. I was pleased of my team today as we pushed them all the way."

The Crusaders finally came a cropper in the sixth game of the season after London Skolars ruined the St David's Day celebrations by beating the Crusaders for the first time in 10 attempts thanks to a late Jermaine Coleman try.

It was the Londoners' second win in as many weeks away from home against National League One opposition following their 50–32 victory at Sheffield Eagles the previous week. Their coach Tony

Benson claimed that this amazing double was just reward for their efforts: "We're probably the only people that expected to win today," said Benson. "We played well against Sheffield last week although it's funny, people said Sheffield were rubbish. However I think we proved this week that we'd be very lucky to have played two rubbish teams in a row. We've worked hard in recent weeks and improved a lot and that came off today. When it started raining we decided to tighten up, play the percentage game and it came off in the end. It was a bit of a lucky try that won us the game, I'll admit that, but we'll accept it."

Just an Ian Webster conversion separated the sides with two minutes to go and the Crusaders thought they'd done enough for a narrow win. However, they did not account for Skolars' determination. In my opinion it was a great shame that they were beaten by Sheffield Eagles a week later as it would have been good to have seen them progress to the knockout stages.

The final group game was against Doncaster at home. This game was difficult to promote as the Welsh rugby union side were at home to France in the Six Nations that same day and were looking for a win to seal a Grand Slam. However, that game was at 5.30pm so the Crusaders match was scheduled for 8pm so all fans who wanted to watch that and the other two union games could do so in the club bars and then go out into the stands to see the Crusaders take on Ellery Hanley's team.

However, mother nature had other ideas as the rain poured down both that day and the day before and the pitch was looking more and more unplayable. Ellery Hanley, bucket in hand, tried to scoop water off the field to get the match on. But despite his and efforts by others from both sides, the game was called off. At least the club made a lot of money in the bars from fans celebrating Wales' union win.

In an unprecedented move, the game wasn't replayed as both teams had progressed to the knock-out stages which was an open draw, so it didn't matter who had won the group.

A pretty good run in the knock out stages followed. In the first round, while Cardiff City were beating Barnsley 1–0 in the FA Cup semi-final, Crusaders edged past Halifax 30–24 in a snowstorm at The Shay. The quarter-finals gave the Crusaders a home draw against holders Widnes Vikings who were slammed 50–18 before the team were knocked out at home to Salford City Reds in the semi-final. The

36–20 scoreline was not a fair reflection of how close the game had been. Salford went on to hammer Doncaster 60–0 in the final.

In the Carnegie Challenge Cup, the Crusaders were drawn against Locomotiv Moscow for the second time in three seasons and just like in the first encounter, the Russians were given a rugby lesson losing 58–10. Ian Webster led the way with a hat-trick of tries.

The fourth round of the Cup is when the Super League sides enter the fray and the draw hadn't been good to the Crusaders in the past. However, this changed after the club was drawn away to Super League and World Club Champions Leeds Rhinos. Gerald McCarthy was present at the draw in Leeds and remembers the scene: "The draw was made by the England coach Tony Smith and when we came out of the hat after Leeds, all the reporters then descended on me like a flash. People were coming up and congratulating me like we'd already won the game and saying what a pity that it wasn't at our place while Doncaster's chief executive came up to me asking if we could swap as they'd been drawn at home to Widnes. Everyone wanted to face Leeds and there we were making the trip.

"The game was on a Friday night which was tough for the fans, but we still took a couple of coach loads up and they shouted themselves hoarse. We may have lost 38–16 but we were only 14–10 down at half-time. Anthony Blackwood got a couple of great tries before the break and we had confidence that we could pull off a shock here."

Andy Wilson from *The Guardian* spoke highly of the Crusaders in the following day's paper: "They gave an admittedly below-strength Leeds team a far stiffer contest than the final scoreline suggests, and it took a couple of pieces of brilliance to secure the Rhinos' passage into the last 16.

"The Crusaders have made rapid strides since they were founded in Bridgend three years ago, winning the National League Two title last season and recently assembling a Colts team of young Welsh talent who have already claimed a couple of impressive scalps.

"The Rugby Football League will announce in July whether they have done enough to claim one of the three-year licences that will determine Super League membership from next season... this display should do wonders for their credibility in Wales and beyond."

The National League One season had got off to an average start. The team sneaked a 14–12 home win against Dewsbury which considering they finished bottom was the least that could have been achieved. This was followed by beating Halifax at home 26–18 which was a very good result, but there had also been two poor away performances, a 25–6 defeat at Sheffield and a 44–16 loss at Whitehaven before facing Leeds.

The Challenge Cup performance at Leeds kick-started the season. A tight, but deserved, 16–14 win at Widnes was followed by a 28–18 defeat of Featherstone in front of the Sky cameras. A 24–22 defeat at Salford followed, again live on Sky Sports, but the next four league games resulted in wins, scoring 171 points in the process. That included another Sky game which was another defeat of Widnes at the Brewery Field. This time the score was 38–6 with Aled James re-entering the limelight.

The Welsh international was currently working for the Welsh Rugby League as a development officer, but injuries had meant John Dixon was down to bare bones so he earned a recall. He did not disappoint as he scored one try, created another and had a potential second of his own cruelly disallowed by referee Thierry Alibert. Ben Flower's try in the final minute wrapped up the win and Dixon was naturally happy with his young Welshmen.

"We've had some injuries this week," Dixon said in the post match interview on Sky Sports. "When you miss players like Josh Hannay and Darren Mapp on any given day you depend upon your young players to come in, put their hands up and have a go so I thought Ben Flower and Aled James played their parts for the Crusaders. They did the job that was expected of them and credit to them. I'm really pleased for them and pleased for us as a club that we can have players like that who come in and play that well."

The first game of that quartet of wins was a 56–28 win at home to Batley. It was try fest that would have delighted those who saw it at the ground or on S4C, but the game was marred by a tackle by Danny Maun on Jace Van Dijk that broke the Crusaders' skippers' jaw in three places. Jace would be out for 11 weeks while Maun only received a six-match ban for his tackle

Announcement day was approaching. Wednesday 22 July was the when everyone would fine out who was to be given the three-year Super League licences. The nerves were showing all round the club both on and off the field. July hadn't started well as the Crusaders lost their first two matches and were fourth in National League One as the club staff assembled in their offices at Dekor PLC to await the decision.

The national and local media were all there. Sky Sports, BBC, ITV and S4C had all turned up to film the occasion. Sky's cameras were hovering over David Thompson and his computer, waiting for the email to come through while the rest of the staff were pacing around the office like expectant fathers. At 10am the computer beeped and David uttered the immortal words "We're in!"

The celebrations started as the cameras continued rolling. The players sang their celebration song normally reserved for post-match following a win, before giving interviews galore to the patient members of the media.

All 12 Super League sides had, as expected, retained their places for another three years while favourites Salford joined the Crusaders in the elite. Widnes were unlucky to lose out but at least their officials took the decision gracefully, the gentlemen that they are. Another of the clubs who lost out, Leigh Centurions, didn't take it so well and made a public statement saying that it was a disgrace that the Crusaders had been selected.

It was nice to receive an email from Whitehaven's chairman Gordon Grace later that day congratulating the club. He was just one of many though as a countless number of famous Welsh men and women had already emailed in their congratulations.

Rhodri Morgan's official statement said: "Rugby league is a great game with a big following in Wales based on our long standing 'export' of our rugby union stars to go north to play rugby league. Just think of the contribution that Jim 'Buller' Sullivan, Gus Risman, Billy Boston, Clive Sullivan, David Watkins, Jim Mills, John Devereux, Jonathan Davies and countless others have made playing for clubs or the Great Britain Rugby League team over the years.

"More recently top quality rugby league has come to Wales, while Wembley was unavailable from 2000 to 2007, with the Challenge Cup being played in the Millennium Stadium. Weekends of Super League club Millennium Magic have followed on after Wembley's rebuilding was finished.

"With rugby league mainly a summer sport and rugby union being a winter sport, the Welsh public will now be able to watch top flight rugby all the year round."

Jonathan Davies added: "We missed the boat in both 1995 and 1998 when a Super League side could have been placed down here but this decision more than makes up for it. Now, more of an infrastructure is in place with teams at all levels in Wales from schoolboys upwards, which wasn't the case 10 years ago.

"When teams like Wigan, St Helens and the like have visited Wales in the past for one-off Super League games, they've always been well attended. The Welsh public love top level sport and I'm sure that Celtic Crusaders will be a great success in Super League. I'd like to thank the RFL for giving us the opportunity and roll on 2009."

Former dual-code Wales and Great Britain captain David Watkins said: "The game is spreading far and wide now and for the first time ever, the prejudices against rugby league in Wales are being removed. More people down here have seen rugby league over the last 10 to 15 years thanks to Sky, their eyes have been opened to the game and they appreciate it for the great game that it is.

"...Everyone has done a lot of hard work behind the scenes to get this and I'm sure that the Crusaders will be well supported in Super League and will go onto bigger and better things."

Former Wigan and Great Britain star Shaun Edwards, the current defence coach of the Wales national rugby union team was very pleased at the decision.

"This is really good news," he said. "I know a lot of the people involved at the Crusaders and I have a strong friendship with their coach John Dixon. I'm sure that everyone at the Crusaders will give it 100% to make sure it's success to replicate the excellent work that has already gone on in France."

Edwards' bosses at the Welsh Rugby Union joined him in congratulating the club with an official statement from the WRU reading: "The Welsh Rugby Union is supportive of all sporting activity and we congratulate Celtic Crusaders on their achievement."

Make no mistake, this decision is and will continue to be a massive boost for the international game as a whole. A Super League club in Wales opens the door for Welsh players to play Super League and then represent Wales. This will eventually enable a stronger Welsh national side to be built leading to more competitive European and World international tournaments.

Anthony Seibold, who returned to the club at the start of the season as football manager / assistant coach said that this decision will benefit the game in Wales as a whole from grass roots level right up to the full international side: "This is a great boost to the game in Wales as a whole," he said. "Every player in Wales from juniors right up to seniors now know that they've got something positive to aim for when they're playing rugby league. There are hundreds of rugby league players in Wales right now and they will all want to play Super League in Wales and then play for the Welsh national team.

"We have already had 57 Welsh-born players turn out for the club for either the first team or the Colts in the last two years. We have seven home grown squads throughout Wales feeding into the Crusaders and with this decision today, this number will surely grow and the future of rugby league in Wales is now secure."

The RFL graded all clubs into 'A', 'B' and 'C' licence statuses and the Crusaders were awarded with a 'C' with the official comments being: "Whilst well maintained, the ground is limited and old fashioned but there is a commitment to immediately enhance the current facilities. In the medium term the club recognises the need to develop a new facility and appears to be working with the local public agencies to deliver this. As with any new venture, financial projections are more subjective but the club has demonstrated financial stability during its progress through the National Leagues. The club has built good relationships with commercial partners and television channel S4C offers exciting opportunities. There is supportive independent market research for Super League in South Wales, although inevitably this can only be fully tested by the club's actual participation in the competition. The playing infrastructure is very good in places but the club is understandably at the early stages with its scholarship and academy teams."

The hangover lasted until Sunday as the team lost a game they were expected to win on the sloping pitch at Batley. This was a poor defeat and John Dixon was very disappointed in the team, stating in the post-match interviews that Batley won because they were better than the Crusaders and there were no stand-out performers for the club that day. To become top of the league was a goal now out of reach but the players were determined to come second. That was the good spirit inside the club. Celtic Crusaders may have got a place in Super League but were not going to sit back on their laurels. Everyone at the club wanted to reach the Grand Final and win it.

The Crusaders needed four straight wins to secure second place and three of the games were at home. Sheffield Eagles were first up and live on S4C they were demolished 42–6. The next two games were a lot tougher – Leigh at home and Halifax away – both sides had lost out to the Crusaders in the race of Super League licences and had to points to prove. Both games were struggles and both ended up 38-28 wins. The Fax win was exceptionally good as they were in second place before the day started. The Crusaders' win meant that they leapfrogged over Halifax into second place.

However, to stay in second place, the Crusaders had to beat confirmed league leaders Salford. Second place meant a bye in the first round of the play-offs and a trip to Salford in the second round.

The game was one worthy of two Super League clubs. A Luke Dyer try gave the Crusaders the lead on eight minutes and while the game was a tight contest all the way, the Welsh side were never behind and ended up winning 20–10.

After the game, John Dixon said: "When we arrived today, we thought that we could play well enough to win and that's what happened. We felt we could be a force against Salford and I'm very pleased our all-round performance across the park today, and of course, with the result. By finishing first and second both sides get a real chance to freshen up. We'll have a break, come back and train hard and we'll prepare to play at Salford which I'm sure we'll be an excellent game."

His opposite number Shaun McRae was unhappy at the result but positive about the near future: "You're never happy about losing a game but I don't think we deserved to win," he said. "We were pretty good defensively, offensively we turned over far too much ball. We went from 67 per cent completion rate in the first half to 54 per cent in the second and that's probably not enough to win a game. The Crusaders were roughly 85 per cent and 70 per cent, they were clearly a lot better with the ball than us in very tough conditions. I don't think we played anywhere near as well as we could have. However we have a few weeks off now – we haven't had many weeks off this season – so hopefully we will be fresh and ready for when the Crusaders visit in three weeks."

The play-off match at Salford three weeks later was destined to be just as tough. However no-one would have predicted just how much the Crusaders dominated the game.

They played entertaining rugby from start to finish and took the lead in under two minutes after back to back penalties in the first 40 seconds gave them strong territorial advantage. Darren Mapp was stopped after surging forward and from the next tackle, Jace Van

Dijk set up Luke Dyer to go over in the corner. Mark Lennon's conversion looked to have gone through the sticks but both touch judges ruled the goal out and the score remained at 4–0. It was very lucky that the game wasn't settled by two points as most fans believed this clearly was the wrong decision.

The lead was extended two minutes later after Salford kicked the ball out on the full from the kick-off. From the penalty, Tony Duggan ran 30 metres through to score. Lennon's kick made the score 10–0.

From a penalty, the Crusaders scored a third, Damien Quinn pouncing on a loose ball from his own grubber kick after Matt Gardner fumbled. Lennon made the score 16–0.

The final score was 44–18 as the Welsh side completely dominated. Quinn, Webster and Blackwood all added scores, with nine minutes remaining Tony Duggan sealed our Grand Final place with a 45-metre individual try, his 98th for the club while Jordan James rubbed salt into Reds' wounds with a try in the final few minutes.

It was good to get to the Grand Final early as it meant the club had time to market it properly. Salford went on to beat Whitehaven in the next round meaning that the Crusaders had a third consecutive meeting with the men from Greater Manchester. However, with the Final being played at Warrington, it meant that it was virtually a home game for them while the Crusaders had to travel north.

Hundreds of fans made it to the Halliwell Jones Stadium and they witnessed another rugby league classic. The games between the two clubs in 2008 were tied at two wins apiece before kick-off so this encounter was the ultimate decider. And it took extra-time for the teams to be separated this time as 80 minutes refused decide things between the two teams.

The Crusaders went 10–0 down after tries and Paul White and Stefan Ratchford but were back in the game just before the interval thanks to an Anthony Blackwood try. Then eight minutes after the interval came a moment of magic from Luke Dyer. Jace Van Dijk was stopped short of the line and from the next play, Dyer scored in the corner diving accurately and placing the ball down just before he was pushed into touch. The build up and the precision of the touchdown made it one of the tries of the season.

Jordan James and Karl Fitzpatrick swapped tries before another memorable Crusaders moment when David Tangata-Toa intercepted a Stefan Ratchford pass and ran faster than he's ever run before, 55 metres to the line. John Dixon couldn't believe it! Crucially Lennon missed the kick and the Crusaders were just two points up.

The drama continued until 20 seconds from the end when Salford were awarded a penalty after Darren Mapp was penalised for holding down Richard Myler. Crusaders fans believed it was a strange decision for the referee to make as he hadn't made a decision like that all game. Wilshire's long-range kick was good and extra time was played. Salford then took control, scoring three converted tries to give them a 36-18 win.

However, the Crusaders had finished in the top two and reached the Grand Final proving that they were the right team to be elected to Super League both on the field as well as off.

Damien Quinn summed up what the players were thinking following the defeat: "We were all very disappointed," he said. "Our goal as a club was to reach Super League but as a player, you play to win Grand Finals and the opportunity doesn't arise too often. It was a fantastic game and a great spectacle but unfortunately we lost that game when we were in a real position to win it."

Super League was just around the corner. John Dixon celebrated by penning an article in *League Express*. The final paragraph read: "It has certainly been an exciting journey over the last three seasons, and I think to achieve what the club has done has been a credit to all involved both on and of the field. When we started as a club there was a will to succeed, so to see what is in place now shows the benefit of vision and hard work combined. I believe the progress made at the Crusaders can only be for the good of our game as a whole."

So despite defeat in the final game, 2008 was a fantastic year for Welsh Rugby League, with success for the Wales 'A' team, under-18 side and students internationally.

And, of course, a few hours before the Grand Final defeat, Crusaders Colts, made up of the best of the young Welsh talent beat Bramley Buffaloes 26–4 to take the Conference National title.

From 2006 there was a lot of focus on the Crusaders, but the development of the game at grass roots level hadn't stopped. In fact, it had increased. The Crusaders were set for Super League but there was a massive network of talent ready to feed into the club.

Luke Dyer scores against Salford in the Co-operative Championship Grand Final at Warrington on 28 September 2008 (Photo: Ian Lovell)

11. A Welsh rugby league structure

While Celtic Crusaders were enjoying their meteoric rise to Super League, development work continued throughout Wales. The Welsh Conference grew in 2006 from seven to 10 clubs, albeit only for a brief time. "We're looking to expand the Welsh Conference Premier to 10 clubs, splitting the league into two five-team regional leagues," Mark Rowley commented. "Blackwood RFC, a semi-professional [union] club in the Gwent valleys will be opening a rugby league arm, former Hull FC player Paul Prenderville has set up West Wales Sharks and we are in talks with two central Swansea rugby union clubs to form a 10th side. This will give us even more Welsh rugby league players as we aim to build the professional and amateur national sides."

The 10th club didn't emerge in Swansea. Instead there was an announcement that Pembrokeshire Panthers, based in Tenby, would compete in 2006. However, a week into the new season, the Panthers felt that they were unable to compete due to a shortage of administration staff and volunteers, and withdrew from the competition.

This setback created havoc in the league structure, which was based on Western and Eastern Conferences, and the four remaining teams in the Western one played each other three times to form a makeshift competition. However, it was still enjoyed by all, even if the media coverage decreased somewhat – a situation that Cardiff Demons' administrator, Simon Davies called 'The Brisbane Broncos effect': "Before Brisbane Broncos were formed, the Queensland Cup was massive in that state," he explained. "Not just from a player perspective but from a media perspective too. It would have dominated the column inches in all the state's papers and received a lot of television news coverage. When the Broncos came in, the competition wasn't forgotten about, but the media focus was rightly shunted upwards a lot and as a result attendances have fallen."

The problems that the Queensland Cup faced were brought to a head in 2007 when Toowoomba Clydesdales, the club that gave Crusaders players like Tony Duggan, Damien Quinn and coaches Anthony Seibold and John Dixon a chance in rugby league, announced that they didn't have the funds to field a side.

However, Anthony Seibold said that "They are still getting coverage of the Queensland Cup in Australia. They benefited in recent years by having matches shown live on ABC in Queensland on Sunday afternoons and there is still press interest. The decrease in coverage in the Welsh Conference can also be related a lot to the Welsh Premiership in rugby union. Before the 'regions' started, clubs like Bridgend, Maesteg and Neath would get thousands watching and would dominate the papers. This doesn't happen anymore because we have the [regional] Blues, Ospreys, Dragons and Scarlets. What we have to do here at the Crusaders is support our clubs like the Bridgend Blue Bulls and Cardiff Demons as this is where the next star of Welsh rugby league could come from."

The 2006 season certainly started well with Wales Rugby League becoming self-governing for the first time after the Rugby Football League granted it autonomous status in January and the Sports Council of Wales recognised it as a national governing body in May. After years of having their destiny determined by the RFL in Leeds, Wales now had a determined professional and hard-working organisation with the sole aim of developing the sport in the country.

Mark Rowley outlined at the time: "This is a new era for our game. Super League has proved that this is a family sport and we want to develop these sort of values in our game, but also making it exciting for everyone involved, from players, coaches and backroom staff to the fans themselves."

The Welsh Rugby League launched their season on Wednesday 26 April in Que Pasa bar in Cardiff city centre. Rowley, who had recently been appointed the first executive chairman of Wales Rugby League, had been busy. He had attracted new sponsors for the Welsh Conference – Picton Jones and Costley & Partners – while a new kit, website and new logo were launched on that sunny spring afternoon.

The logo was something of a bone of contention. For years, the WRL had always used the traditional Prince of Wales feathers as used by the Welsh Rugby Union and Surrey Cricket Club. The WRU had updated their logo a few years before with a slicker, cleaner, three feathers look, but the WRL, to ensure that their look was different to rugby union, changed their logo entirely to a very well designed arty logo of a dragon holding a ball with XIII written on it.

The Welsh Conference had itself risen in status. With so many clubs wanting to join the Conference system across the length and breadth of the United Kingdom, the RFL thought that it was time to split the teams into two divisions with the best performing clubs from each area

160

going into the Conference Premier. However, there was a question over the Welsh clubs. It was put to Niel Wood that it would be unfair to split the Welsh clubs up as the game was growing here and that the regional competition should be kept as a Welsh one. It was also argued that out of the eight existing Welsh sides, at least five or six would hold their own in the Premier Division without any problems. Thankfully Niel agreed without hesitation and thus in Wales there was "The Picton Jones and Costley & Partners Welsh Conference Premier".

Before the Conference season started, the WRL organised the Scott McRorie Nines as a pre-season competition for the first time. This had been held as a post-season tournament the year before, but 2006 saw it officially sanctioned by the WRL for the first time. Played in memory of Scott McRorie, a young rugby league player with Aberavon Fighting Irish, who died in a bike accident aged 17 in 2004, the tournament caused some controversy because it was staged in Blackwood and not at what was believed to be its true home, Aberavon Greenstars RFC. Because of this, the Fighting Irish withdrew from the competition but this did not undermine an excellent eight-team contest that Cardiff Demons rightfully won as they went unbeaten throughout the day. Scott's father attended to present the trophy.

On the opening day of the Conference season, Bridgend Blue Bulls lost 32-50 to old rivals Aberavon Fighting Irish. It was a deserved result especially as Bridgend were without most of their first choice side, many of whom were on rugby union duty that weekend. One of Bridgend's debutants was one Lee Beech, who according to the report from Simon Green that appeared on the Cymru RL website and the *Wales on Sunday* newspaper, had a fine game. On the following Monday, Lee Beach (note the difference in spelling of the surname) was allegedly called into the offices of his employers, the Ospreys, and was given the sack for playing rugby league without permission. His pleas of innocence initially went on deaf ears until calls from Green and reporter Gary Baker informed the management that this wasn't a 23-year old with the surname of Beach but a 41-year old called Beech who had been drafted in for the day. Beach still plays for the Ospreys and helped to lead Wales Sevens RU side to a World Cup victory in 2009. The whereabouts of Beech is unknown.

The race for the semi-finals of the Welsh Conference Premier went right up to the final day of the season. Only favourites Bridgend Blue Bulls were guaranteed a place in the last four when it began. Cardiff

Demons and Blackwood Bulldogs faced each other at St Peters RFC knowing that the winners would take the East Wales Conference title and the losers may not qualify for the semi-finals. The Bulldogs, in their first season of rugby league, had been the surprise package of 2006 and now had a serious chance of the title.

"We had nothing to lose that season," Blackwood coach Roger Moore said. "Our aim in 2006 was to have a team playing every game. The fact that we were in contention for the East Wales title was a positive surprise to us. We went into each game to enjoy the occasion and play rugby league. There were no expectations."

The match was low scoring and eventually ended in a 10–10 draw, the only result guaranteed to put both sides into the play-offs. However, this was no pre-determined outcome. The intensity of the match showed that both teams wanted to win and finish as league leaders to avoid Bridgend Blue Bulls in the semi-finals.

Demons took the East Wales title on points difference and were due to face Aberavon Fighting Irish at home the next week while Blackwood were to travel to Bridgend. Despite a spirited comeback from an under-strength Torfaen Tigers in the other game in the East, Newport Titans stormed to a 36–20 victory. However, Cardiff and Blackwood's draw meant that they narrowly missed out on the play-offs for the third year in succession. Apparently Newport's coach Dan Clements threw down his clipboard in disgust after hearing the result from the capital.

In the Western Conference, Bridgend – who had already clinched the title – edged out Aberavon with a try in injury time. Both sides qualified for the play-offs after West Wales Sharks' 20–6 defeat of Swansea Valley Miners.

Bridgend versus Blackwood was yet another Welsh rugby league classic. The visitors looked to have secured victory when Jeremy Lloyd kicked his third penalty of the game, then a drop-goal with 10 minutes left on the clock to give them a 31–22 lead. However, Simon Mustoe, who had arrived back in Wales after a week's holiday in Greece just six hours before kick-off, scored his second try under the posts after a strong run from Tavita Manaseitava. Matthew Hutchings converted and then, from the very last play of the game, further proved his talent with the boot to kick ahead for Aaron Warner to pick up and score in the corner. The conversion was missed, but it mattered little as the full time whistle blew to give Bridgend a 32–31 win.

162

Champagne flies everywhere as Bridgend Blue Bulls celebrate winning the Welsh RL Conference 2006 Grand Final (Photo: Ian Lovell)

Unfortunately, the other semi-final didn't take place after Aberavon Fighting Irish pulled out of the competition just hours before kick-off because of a lack of players. It was a sad end to what had been developing into a great club and the Irish closed their doors soon afterwards. This was reportedly due to a lack of administrators to run the club. However, a new club, Neath Port Talbot Steelers, was formed in its place for 2007 so rugby league wasn't lost to the area.

Their new club secretary, James Davies, said: "Aberavon Fighting Irish was seen as an Aberavon Green Stars RFC club. NPT Steelers was formed to embrace rugby league as part of the region and not as a single rugby union club. Our main aim has always been encouragement and development of young rugby players throughout the locality who perhaps wouldn't have played rugby league before."
The Grand Final belonged to Bridgend Blue Bulls for the fourth year in a row. Solid in both attack and defence, they never looked like losing, while Cardiff continually failed to take advantage of their chances. The Demons actually had more possession during the 80 minutes, but Bridgend were more successful in turning their chances into tries for their 22–10 win and just had that little bit extra, which is how champions are made.

The Blue Bulls successfully defended their title in 2007 after again finishing top of the table but, in that year's Grand Final, they were pushed harder than they'd ever been before with Newport Titans almost winning the game. Newport took the lead early on through a

Tyrone Mahoney try under the sticks that Lloyd White converted but, by the 54th minute, Bridgend were 24–6 up. However, the Titans fought back with quick-fire tries from White and Mahoney.

The last 10 minutes were full of completed sets, excellent defensive work and many big hits that enthralled the large Brewery Field crowd. Vinnie Lott was close to levelling things for Newport, but he fumbled and Karl Hocking caught the loose ball. Bridgend scraped home 24–18 and their crown looked more in danger than it had ever looked before.

In 2008, something had to give and there were wry smiles from most rugby league fans in South Wales when the Blue Bulls finally lost their five-year grip on the Welsh title when they lost 50–18 to Newport Titans in the first round of the play-offs.

Minor premiers Blackwood Bulldogs reached the final as predicted with a 28–20 win at home to Cardiff Demons in a game that will be remembered most for the period of stoppage time that took the overall game time to well over 90 minutes.

However, their Gwent rivals Newport failed to join them in the Final. They were 30–18 up against Valley Cougars with 10 minutes remaining but once again failed to take a grip when it came to the big stage as they lost 32–30.

An inspired try from Tom Rees on 73 minutes spurred the Cougars on. In the next set, Stephen Parry completed his hat-trick with Ceri Cummins's conversion putting them within two points with five minutes left. The game was sealed with two minutes to go as Tom Rees flew over the line to give the home side the lead. The kick was missed, but the Cougars successfully hung on to qualify for the final.

For the nomadic Cougars, who had played at Abercynon, Pontyclun, Ferndale and Pontypridd before finally settling at Nelson RFC, this was a true rags-to-riches story. Perennial cellar dwellers in the first few seasons of the Welsh Conference, their persistence and never-say-die attitude – sometimes lacking at other non-professional clubs – had finally been rewarded.

Favourites Blackwood took the lead after a matter of seconds in the Brewery Field final when Byron Williams went in under the sticks, but there was to be no rout. Instead, the Cougars took control of the game and Steven Parry was their hero with a hat-trick of tries to give the men in light blue and pink a 26–12 win.

"This is an example to all clubs that if you stick at it, success will arrive eventually," said Cougars and Wales chief Mark Rowley after the match. "We've worked hard over the years to build a strong squad and we proved this today. Naturally I'm really pleased with the win and we look forward to representing Wales in the national play-offs."

However, like Bridgend in the previous two years, the Cougars fell in the national semi-finals, losing 32–30 in a tough, hard-hitting game against West London Sharks. But the RFL's expansion of the Carnegie Challenge Cup saw them make the headlines again in early 2009. For the first time in 100 years, there were three Welsh sides in the world's premier rugby knockout tournament and – by a cruel twist of fate – two of them drew each other in the preliminary round.

UWIC and Valley Cougars faced off in a tight match in Cardiff in mid-January. With Celtic Crusaders reserves players on both sides, the game had a State of Origin 'mate versus mate' feel about it. Arguably the two best non-professional sides in Wales served up an entertaining game which the Cougars should have sewn up earlier than they did. They won the match by five tries to three, but the scoreline was just two points in their favour after they failed to land a single conversion, compared to UWIC's Lloyd White who, as expected, had a 100 per cent kicking record. The final score was 20–18. The Cougars' reward was a trip to Portsmouth to face the Royal Navy in the next round.

The Navy were 34–6 up at half-time and looked to be coasting. However, a second-half surge from the Welsh side turned a rout into a contest and the final score was 38–28 to the Navy. The Cougars had performed well in their Cup run and chairman Mark Rowley wasn't displeased with the matches: "All of our boys played rugby union matches yesterday and four of them had to drive all the way down here this morning," he said. "We were up against things from the start so to see us end the game as the fitter side was pleasing. Our second half performance was first class and I'm really proud of everyone wearing a Cougars shirt. We congratulate the Navy who had an excellent first half performance that saw them through and we wish them all the best in the next round."

The Welsh Conference fielded nine clubs in 2009 with even more teams playing at junior level. West Wales Wild Boars were new entrants at senior level, but junior sides from Swansea, Merthyr Tydfil and Pembrokeshire played games at various age groups in 2008.

For Merthyr, it was a return for rugby league to the town where it was first played in Wales in 1907. The Tydfil Wildcats ran three junior sides in 2008 and hope to have a senior side by 2010.

The number of schools sides also increased after Celtic Crusaders' introduction. From just a handful in 2004, the number grew to almost 100 in 2008. At the time of writing, while no Welsh school side has reached a National Champions Schools Final since Brynteg's two finals in 2004 and 2005, they lost to Castleford in 2005, some schools have run a lot of their northern counterparts close and taken a few scalps along the way. From all these sides at different age groups more than 1,500 players took to the rugby league field in Wales in 2008.

The Welsh amateur side was another success story between 2002 and 2005. In the 12 home nations matches Wales played in this period, 10 were won, with losses only to Ireland and England. This gave Wales the championship every year since 2002. "It was another part of Wales's strength in depth that this happened," said Wales rugby league development officer, Wayne Williams, "No-one has been an ever present in the side. In fact we used 83 players over those four years, some of whom have gone on to play at full international level."

The 'A' team was now just one of many representative sides in Wales as the game continued growing at grassroots and junior levels. Wales now had representative teams at under-16, under-18 or 19 and student level in addition to the 'A' and senior sides.

The under-16s have only played one representative game a year, a home clash with England. For the first three years, England won the games easily but, in 2008 and 2009 the matches were very close with England winning 10–6 in 2008 and 18–16 in 2009.

At under-18 level, the Welsh success has become more apparent as the Welsh youngsters have grown both in physical stature and also in skill levels. Under-18 tournaments have been organised in two-year cycles since 2006, with the European Nations Cup one year followed by the British Championship the next. The pinnacle for the young Welsh side came in 2008, after two years' development, they lifted the European Championship trophy in Prague after wins over the Czech Republic 64–0, England 40–22 and then France in the final 38–24.

"To play three games in five days is tough to start with," said Wales under-18 coach Stuart Williams. "But to beat countries of the calibre of England on Wednesday and France today just shows how far we've come as a nation. I'm immensely proud of all of our players who have done so well out here."

Wales also took on an Australian touring side at under-18 level in 2006, losing 68–14 in the first ever international hosted by Blackwood.

166

Three of the Welsh players, Lee Williams, Chris Vitalini and Tom Burnell have gone on to represent Celtic Crusaders in the lower leagues and reserves, but 13 of the 17 Australians have played professionally in the NRL with Israel Folau, who has since played for Queensland and Australia, Mitchell Pearce who has played State of Origin for New South Wales and Joseph Paulo, who played for Samoa in the 2008 World Cup, standing out.

Rugby league is also expanding throughout the universities in Wales with sides from Cardiff, Glamorgan, Swansea and Aberystwyth now taking to the field in the XIII-a-side code. And with many Welsh-born students playing for sides like Liverpool's John Moore's and Leeds Metropolitan universities, it's not surprising that a stronger Welsh national universities side has been developed.

The 2005 Student World Cup was a little disappointing for Wales so in the next tournament, in 2008 in Australia, the players were determined to qualify for the semi-finals at the very least. The Welsh students had achieved a third-place finish in the four-team Home Nations in 2006 followed by last place in the six-team Euro Nations in 2007 so the odds were against them. However, with a strong backroom staff led by the legendary Clive Griffiths and also containing Kevin Ellis, James Davies and Kevan Tee, Wales finished second in their group, just behind New Zealand, to qualify for the last four, only to then lose 26–10 against hosts and eventual winners Australia.

The 'A' side carried on picking up championships. However, they had a blip in 2006 after losing to Ireland and England after an opening win against Scotland. All three games were close, but Wales were not as inspiring as usual, possibly because of some players signing for Celtic Crusaders, making them ineligible to play for the 'A' side.

The team started 2006 with a 22–16 win over Scotland in Glasgow with Andrew Jenkins, David James, Sean Gilbertson and John Breakingbury scoring tries. However, the home match against Ireland at the Brewery Field saw a poor 24–10 defeat for Wales with only Breakingbury and Jason Hill going over.

The result meant that Wales needed to beat England by 31 points in Featherstone to regain the title. Although that never looked likely, a fourth win over England looked possible right up until the last 15 minutes. Wales lost captain Jason Hill in the first minute after he pulled a hamstring, but shrugged that off when Adrian Owen touched down. Jon Breakingbury added to that lead after eight minutes with Jones converting both tries to give Wales an early 12–0 lead.

However, Wales gave away a penalty straight from kick-off and England didn't waste the opportunity. Marco Rossi scored under the posts and Barry-John Swindells converted. England continued to press and Paul Drake scored and converted his own try.

Wales took the lead again after 25 minutes when Gareth Jones produced his usual half-back jinks to weave his way through and also converted his own try. Wes Palmer broke through to set up Chris Roets in the corner to extend Wales's lead, but England hit back just before half-time with a Chris Spiers try in the corner.

Karl Wesley pulled another English try back on 50 minutes, but Breakingbury restored Wales's their six-point advantage with a try five minutes later. England scored again after 62 minutes with Rossi's second and Drake converted to level the scores. They took the lead for the first time in the game three minutes later with a Paul Drake goal, the same player adding another penalty soon after to give England a narrow 30–26 win.

England may have had a triple crown and their first ever title at this level, but normal service was restored in 2007 and 2008 with the Cheltenham Regency Trophy retaining its rightful place in the Brewery Field trophy room on both occasions.

An exciting 44–30 win over Scotland at Cardiff Demons' ground opened 2007. Blackwood Bulldogs' David James led the way with a hat-trick of tries while Cardiff's Gareth Jones and Bridgend's Chris Roets each added a brace.

Lee Williams, Karl Hocking and David James all scored tries in a pulsating 16–16 draw in Ireland which meant that the now traditional final match against England would again decide the title.

Wales didn't waste home advantage in Blackwood and, despite the teams being evenly matched for a lot of the game, fitness showed through in the end as Wales broke away in the latter stages of the game.

The score was 12–12 at half-time thanks to tries from Daniel Blethyn and John Bowd for Wales and Nick Mercer and Dan Reeds for England. Gareth Jones and Tom Sibley shared early second-half tries to make the score 18–18, but late tries from Mark Wheeler and David James with two settled things and Wales ran out 39–18 winners.

It was Wayne Williams's last day in charge of the Welsh squad and he was pleased to go out on a high. "It's been a very emotional day," he said. "I thought we edged it today, the penalty count was ridiculously against us but we dug in there and played really well. This title is testament to our hard work all season, not just from the boys who played day but those who have turned out all season. We didn't just turn up and play, a lot of hard work has gone into winning back this title and I thought that showed a lot near to the end today."

As a postscript to 2007, Wales 'A' also hosted France 'A' for the first time and, in torrential conditions in Aberavon, won 22–18 with Gareth David, Chris Roets, Byron Williams and Matt Entwhistle all scoring. It was an historic win for Wales as no one expected them to beat the French. It certainly made the rugby league world sit up and take notice that Welsh Rugby League was getting better and better as the years were going by.

Wales 'A' opened 2008 with another win over Scotland 'A' following an outstanding second-half performance in Glasgow. The final result was a 62–20 win after being only 18–10 up at half-time. Tyrone Mahoney led the way with tries in the 13th, 32nd and 42nd minutes but, after he'd finished, the Welsh took turns to score with Lee Williams, Matt Harvey, Scott Bessant, Trevor James, Owen Jones, Paul Emmanuelli, Martin Corley and Jason Hill also adding tries.

A 32–24 win over Ireland in Porthcawl followed. As usual against Ireland, this game could have swung either way and the visitors were actually 18–14 up on a cold afternoon by the sea. However, a strong second-half Welsh performance and tries from Wheeler, James, Bessant, Harvey, Mahoney and Carl Thomas, sealed the win.

Just days before Celtic Crusaders were awarded a Super League licence, Wales clinched their fifth home nations title in six years after beating England 24–8 at East Riding in Hull. The title was won in style as Wales racked up a 22-point lead in an hour to make the game safe. England had taken the lead after five minutes with a penalty from former Cardiff Demons full-back Matt Jackson. But Elliot Kear, playing his second game in as many days after starring for Crusaders Colts on Saturday, struck for the Welsh on the quarter hour scoring in the corner. Paul Emmanuelli, another of the seven men who turned out for the Colts the day before, added the conversion.

It was 12–2 to Wales at half-time after a 100-metre try from Mark Harvey under the posts that Emmanuelli converted. Harvey picked up the ball from underneath his own sticks and beat off all the Englishmen to score. Emmanuelli crashed over from close to the line after 50 minutes for a further Welsh try, converting it himself, before a Steve Parry individual try from dummy half near the half-way line 10 minutes later. Emmanuelli's kick made the score 24–2 and the title was safe despite a consolation try from the home side.

These Welsh players formed the backbone of the previously mentioned Crusaders Colts side. A joint venture between Celtic Crusaders and the Welsh Rugby League, the Colts were the first ever regular "second string" side for the Crusaders and played their first season of rugby league in 2008 in the Conference National, the pinnacle of amateur rugby league in the summer months.

The Crusaders had experimented with an Academy side in their first two seasons with mixed success. Following an initial trial match against Harlequins under-21s in early 2006 that ended in a 22–22 draw, a Crusaders Academy side faced Widnes under-21s, the Royal Navy and Great Britain under-21s later that year, losing every game. A further match against the Navy was played in 2007 and this produced the Crusaders Academy's first success, a 54–30 win. The foundations were in place for an Academy side, but it was decreed that this would only be full-time when the Crusaders were promoted to National League One. When the Crusaders' first team secured that promotion in 2007, recruitment began immediately for both players and coaching staff. The Welsh Conference clubs was the best place to start and the Wales 'A' side was used as a backbone for the 2008 side.

Dan Clements was appointed as coach. A Midlands-born West Bromwich Albion football fan, Clements moved to Wales in the late 1990s to go to UWIC in Cardiff and started playing for their already-successful rugby league side.

"From there I went to play for Cardiff Demons," he said. "They were only running an under-18 team then and there were only a couple of us from UWIC who were eligible. But soon after that they started a senior side so I went on to play for them too. I then got involved with the coaching and helped to start up a team in Rumney in the east of Cardiff in 2003. They then moved just down the road to form Newport Titans a year later.

"I started off coaching the Cardiff Demons under-15 side. I then got involved as assistant coach for Wales under-18s before getting the head coach position. I did that for three or four years while also

170

coaching the Newport junior set-up. From there I was offered a post at Celtic Crusaders.

"No-one expected us to do well in 2008. In fact, John Dixon said to me that as long as we have a full team every week turning out on the field and playing games then that would be a success for year one.

"The whole aim of this team was to give young Welshmen a chance to play rugby league on a consistent basis. It started off quite well and we surprised a few people including ourselves, and we went from strength to strength all year."

In the regular season, only one side seriously matched Crusaders Colts and that was Bramley Buffaloes. A side formed out of the ashes of the famous professional Bramley club that ran from 1879 to 1999, the Buffaloes had proved themselves to be one of the strongest at this level and were also serious rivals to the Crusaders in 2005 in trying to obtain a National League Two place.

The original Bramley club had a long history. They were the first club to entertain an international touring side when they faced New Zealand on 9 October 1907. Their only major honour in their original guise was the BBC2 Floodlit Trophy in 1973.

Bramley Buffaloes were formed in 2003 and were immediately placed in National League Three. After finishing runners-up in 2005, they took the title in 2006, beating Hemel Stags 30–8 in the Grand Final. They were runners-up again in 2007 when the league was renamed as the Conference National, losing out to Featherstone Lions.

Crusaders Colts did the double over Featherstone Lions with hard-fought 24–18 and 30–12 wins. Their only losses came to Bramley, 34–24 at home followed by a 19–0 defeat at the Arthur Millar Stadium.

These results meant that the Colts finished in second place to Bramley in the table, meaning a trip to the Arthur Millar Stadium again in the first round of the play-offs. A 43–24 win for the home side sent Bramley through to the Grand Final, but the Colts had a second chance to qualify with a home game against Featherstone Lions – one that they didn't waste. A 44–12 win sent the holders crashing out of the competition and the young Welshmen were in the final at Warrington.

The game was the first in a triple header of rugby league finals at the Halliwell Jones Stadium and was the curtain raiser to the televised National League Two and League One climaxes.

With three wins over the Crusaders Colts already in 2008, Bramley were hot favourites, but the Welsh youngsters dominated from almost

171

start to finish winning 24–8. Captained by Geraint Davies, a man who had been at the Crusaders since day one, the Colts romped to victory thanks to two tries and five goals from Lloyd White, one try from Gary Williams and one from Lee Williams, another player who has been at the Crusaders since inception.

It was just reward for a team that had given 42 players the chance to play rugby league in 2008. Out of those 42, 37 of them were Welsh with 30 of them making their club debut for the Colts. The most successful of these players were retained to play for the Crusaders reserve side in the Super League reserve championship in 2009.

With Crusaders Colts' success in 2008, a decision was also made to form an under-18 side to play in the winter-based Gillette National Youth League for the 2008–09 season.

"Junior development in Wales had been going on for a number of years now," said Dan Clements. "At least eight or nine years I think. It's gone from one development officer running everything to a nice little team of part-time and full-time development staff. We had junior teams over nine clubs in Wales in 2008 with a few more due to open in 2009.

"The first junior sides in Wales were from Cardiff Demons and then Valley Cougars who ran a scholarship scheme and then, as the game boomed, there was a big spread – the rest of the junior clubs came out of the Conference clubs when they were formed in 2003."

The Crusaders realised that the future of Welsh rugby league lies with the juniors. In 2008, the club announced that it would be setting up four regional home-grown squads with the opportunity to increase this to six as the numbers of players developed.

Celtic Crusaders' head of performance, Anthony Seibold, is very enthusiastic about the set-up and continuing development of these squads that enable a real pathway for young Welsh rugby league players: "Our brainstorming sessions in 2008 led us to believe that this is the way forward," he said. "Establishing home-grown development squads in and around Wales which are managed by upcoming coaches in various regions feeding through to an elite home grown squad [or scholarship program as the RFL terminology suggests] is one of our greatest achievements thus far in the short history of Celtic Crusaders.

"These development squads are based around Wales under the direction of our head of youth performance Andy Lindley and are monitored and managed by developing Welsh coaches. The first four squads are based in Bridgend, Neath and Port Talbot, Cardiff and Swansea, and Rhondda and Merthyr Tydfil. These four squads will grow into six squads over time as we establish wider networks in and around the country. Each squad has around 20 to 25 players who have been identified by our performance and development staff or the coaches themselves. The squads are rolling squads which mean players can be added as they are identified. They meet every three weeks and the three key areas that are developed within each are long term athletic development, skill acquisition and game. These squads are about growing and increasing the player tree within the sport of rugby league here in Wales while promoting the Crusaders brand.

"The players then have an opportunity to be identified and selected for our elite home-grown program based in Bridgend. This squad will look at more elite-level performance indicators such as education, nutrition and preparation, while still developing the three keys areas identified above. All at the Crusaders are excited about the structure we have put in place and believe that because we have a whole country to identify young players from we can develop home-grown players where the elite will filter through to first-team level and then hopefully the Welsh national squad. This may take some time but all the pathways are now in place in Wales for the first time ever."

Moving into 2009, Welsh rugby league had never been stronger. With the game being played successfully in schools, colleges, universities and local clubs, more players than ever were taking to rugby league in Wales. But 2009 was to become the biggest challenge yet. With all this development underneath it, Super League was at last coming to Wales on a regular basis. It would be a year to remember.

The banner at Blackwood RFC proudly announcing the arrival of the Blackwood Bulldogs. (Photo: Peter Lush)

The Crusaders mascot at the match against Leeds in August 2009. (Photo: Peter Lush)

12. International disappointment

The Welsh national side's failure to qualify for the 2008 World Cup Finals was seen by many as a disaster for the sport in Wales. Certainly it would have been nice to have brushed shoulders with the world's best out in Australia, but Celtic Crusaders' qualification for Super League more than made up for it. Of course, this should not really be the case. The international game should be the be-all and end-all in all sports but, luckily for Wales, the Welsh media barely acknowledged the 2008 World Cup. It is doubtful that many of the Welsh public knew it was going on so were unaware that Wales were missing out.

Not that it would have caused too much of a ripple. Wales football fans know what it's like not to qualify for a major event. The football team has not qualified for the World Cup Finals since 1958 and the European Championship since 1976. The rugby union side always gets to its World Cup Finals, but always flusters on the big stage. The last tournament in 2007 saw the Welsh beaten in the group stages by Fiji and Australia and fail to qualify for the quarter-finals as a result. However they do gain automatic qualification for the 2011 event for finishing third in their group of five.

The 2011 Rugby Union World Cup will again have 20 teams, 12 of them automatic qualifiers, based on their performance in the 2007 event – the right thing to do in my view. When it comes to organisation at international level, the XV-a-side game is head and shoulders above rugby league.

When it came to qualification for league's 10-team Finals in 2008, five teams were chosen as automatic qualifiers, based on their performance in the 2007 event – the right thing to do in my view. When it comes to organisation at international level, the XV-a-side game has traditionally been head and shoulders above rugby league.

However, it's pleasing to see that by mid-2009, the initial plans had already been out in place for the 2013 Rugby League World Cup that will be held in Great Britain. The international cycle that was proposed in 2007 also looks like its being kept to, which is very positive news for the game.

The Rugby League International Federation had officially announced the 2008 tournament on 6 May 2006 with further details on scheduling and dates following on 19 April 2007.

It was then the RLIF made their strange decision over who was to qualify automatically. The last two World Cups have seen the same semi-finalists – England, Wales, Australia and New Zealand – who, one can argue, have been the giants of rugby league since 1991. The RLIF rightly chose England, Australia and New Zealand, but left out Wales and instead chose France and Papua New Guinea as automatic qualifiers. It had been decided that the only the first five members of the Rugby League International Federation would be automatic qualifiers. Even though Wales played in the first ever international in 1908, they were not one of those five. France didn't come into the fray until the 1930s and Papua New Guinea the 1970s, yet they were considered to be earlier members.

So Wales had to try to qualify for the 2008 event. Qualification in Europe actually started before the official announcement of the tournament itself – such is life in rugby league – as Netherlands against Russia in the Hook of Holland officially kicked off the preliminary rounds.

European qualification was split into two stages. The first stage saw Russia, Georgia, Netherlands and Serbia play each other once with the top two teams qualifying for the second stage. The group winners were to go in a pool with Ireland and Lebanon, while the runners-up would join Wales and Scotland. The winners of each of those pools would go straight through to the World Cup and the runners-up into a play-off series.

Russia and Georgia finished first and second out of this initial group. However the final game in the group, between Russia and Georgia, was not played, as the countries were almost at war at the time. Georgia was subsequently ejected from the competition and banned for two years. It was a great shame, as the sport had been building nicely in that country since its introduction in 2004 and their win-loss ratio in internationals had been excellent: winning five and losing just two.

The Netherlands finished third in the group and by rights they should have replaced Georgia alongside Wales and Scotland. However, they also had a disagreement with the RLIF, and the game in that country also ground to a temporary halt. Another shame because the Dutch are passionate about their sport, whatever it is, and would support a decent rugby league side.

So Wales and Scotland were left in a group of their own, perhaps a major error, especially in the way the schedule was organised. The idea was that two games would be played at the end of 2006 then another two, with the play-offs at the end of 2007 which probably would have worked well if Wales were in a three-team group like Lebanon, Ireland and Russia. But Wales were in a two-team group; this meant that Wales versus Scotland was the only international game that Wales played at senior level in 2006.

Welsh preparation for the game wasn't fantastic. Initially it was reported that Keiron Cunningham and Iestyn Harris may return for the qualifiers. It would have been the first time in more than five years that they had played for Wales if that had been the case.

Iestyn had had a much publicised move to Cardiff Blues, then an even more publicised and controversial return to rugby league when he signed for Bradford Bulls, an apparent breach of contract with his former club Leeds Rhinos.

Keiron's success with Great Britain had kept him out of the Wales line up. Since 2002, Great Britain and Wales internationals had been arranged for the same weekends, not a good move in the opinion of most Welsh fans and, because of that, Keiron had been unavailable for the Dragons. He had announced his retirement from Great Britain in August 2006 and there was hope that he would make himself available for Wales. He didn't in the end, but Harris did, publicly announcing his involvement live on BBC Radio Wales in September 2006 after agreeing to change his holiday plans to turn out for his country.

"It's important to me to play for Wales and it's the start of a really long journey to the 2008 World Cup," he said to Robert Phillips on the Tuesday night *Sportstime* programme. "We need to qualify and it's worthwhile switching my holiday around.

"I don't regret my decision not to play for Great Britain. To play for Wales is really important. It's not as intense as Great Britain – it's not a seven-week tournament like the Tri-Nations. There's only one game this year, one game at the end of next year and then the World Cup in 2008. It's something really close to my heart and I really wanted to be involved in it."

There were also fears that skipper Lee Briers wouldn't make it. Briers had been selected for the initial Great Britain Tri-Nations squad to tour Australia and New Zealand, a tournament that had controversially been organised for the same time as the World Cup qualifiers. Despite scoring six goals and reportedly playing a good game in their 40–6 warm-up win over Newcastle, he missed out on a place in the full squad and was sent home. Britain's loss was Wales's gain.

"I knew the score before I went to Australia," Briers said at the time, "I was only able to stay with the squad if there were injuries to the regular half-backs. There were none so I got sent back. Training with the Great Britain squad for a week and a half was a great experience. I'm glad that I went but I'm equally as glad to be back and playing for Wales."

Briers was there to lead the team out in Bridgend, but Harris didn't follow him. He had undergone keyhole surgery on his knee before going on holiday two weeks before the tie and, with the rest he was getting, he had expected to be fit for the game. However, the injury flared up while on holiday, he was declared unfit to play while in Miami, and didn't fly back as a result.

The first that anyone outside of the Welsh squad knew about this was when they turned up at the ground on the Sunday for the game. An announcement was made to the unhappy media and fans and Wales got on with the game.

Unfortunately for Wales, the pre-match crises carried on through the game as they went down 21–14. Looking back, it can be theorised that this was the game that really cost Wales qualification for the World Cup because it was a game that Wales really should have won.

A Wade Liddell try converted by Gareth Morton gave Scotland an early lead. But Wales pulled a try back after 16 minutes. From Lee Briers's grubber kick, Richard Johnson, playing his first game in more than three months after recovering from a broken arm, pounced to ground in the corner. Briers missed the difficult conversion attempt.

Danny Brough was sin-binned for dissent after 26 minutes and Wales duly took advantage by scoring two tries in the 10-minute spell he was out of the action. Adam Hughes scored in the corner after 32 minutes following fine work from Briers and Robert Roberts. Briers did well to convert successfully from the touchline.

It was 14–6 almost immediately after the kick-off. Johnson created a chance and Briers brilliantly dodged through to score, but missed a far easier chance to extend Wales's lead when he failed to add the extras.

Scotland came out firing on all cylinders after the interval and scored two quick unconverted tries through Danny Brough and Jamie Benn to level the score. They continued to dominate and a Mick Nanyn try, that he converted himself, sealed the win, with Brough adding a further point to complete the scoring.

Lack of match practice was one reason given for Wales's poor performance in Bridgend. But the same can be said about the Scots. The fact remains that in 2006, Wales played just one full international match. Compare that to 1975 when Wales played 16 times, including warm-up games against club sides, and it was clear that there was a problem. There are many reasons why this 1975 momentum wasn't kept up – but even so playing only a quarter of the games would have been acceptable for internationals are the pinnacle of the game.

In 2007, neither Wales nor Scotland was going to make the same mistake as both teams organised warm-up games. Scotland travelled to France while Wales hosted Papua New Guinea who, as mentioned before, had automatic qualification for the World Cup.

The Kumuls, coached by former Wigan star Adrian Lam, had recently overturned a 20–0 deficit to draw 24–24 with the Australian Prime Minister's XIII so Wales needed to be at their very best to have a chance of repeating their 22–8 win from 2000.

Thirteen of their 2008 World Cup squad turned out for Papua New Guinea on a sunny, but cold Sunday afternoon, which, in hindsight, made Wales's 50–10 win all the more special.

There was just one debutant for Wales in the Scotland game the previous year, Wigan's Gary Hulse, who made his only appearance in a Welsh shirt. However, in 2007, Wales coach Martin Hall had completely revamped the side. Against Papua New Guinea, no fewer than eight players made their Welsh debuts – Phil Cushion, Dave Halley, Matt James, Sean Penkywicz, Craig Kopzcak and Crusaders-bound, Aaron Summers, Ian Webster and Luke Dyer. All bar Cushion, who was a Welsh resident, qualified via the grandparent ruling.

Some of them even got on the scoresheet. Halley scored two tries while Matt James and Penkywicz got one each. Wales stalwarts Phil Joseph, Damien Gibson with two tries, Rob Roberts and Mark Lennon also crossed.

But taking all the media attention was Iestyn Harris who finally made his Wales comeback, playing for the national side for the first time since 2000 and kicking five goals to celebrate.

"I was pleased with the game today," he said after the match. "But we've got a lot of work to do before next week's game – it's going to be tough to overcome a seven-point deficit. I was disappointed to be injured for last year's Scotland match, but this year I've had three or four week's rest so I'm raring to go. It was good to pull on the Welsh jersey once again; it's been a long time."

The win was a special one and people now find it difficult to believe that Wales beat what was a nearly full-strength PNG side in such convincing fashion. A comment posted on You Tube during the 2008 World Cup underneath a video of the tries from the game read: "This can't have been the full PNG squad - they nearly beat (should have beaten) England!"

Well it was, and that gave Wales a lot of confidence to go to Scotland and get the eight point victory needed to qualify for the World Cup Finals.

The match in Glasgow was a competitive one from start to finish. Scotland had the better of the first five minutes but Wales composed themselves and took the lead after seven minutes. Matt James was held up centimetres from the line and, after Wales won a scrum, Phil Joseph set up Luke Dyer to dive over. Iestyn Harris kicked the goal to leave Wales just a point down on aggregate.

Scotland thought they'd hit back five minutes later. Lee Patterson's grubber kick was latched onto by Oliver Wilkes, but the Widnes prop failed to ground the ball and the video referee correctly disallowed the try. The home side did get on the board on the 20-minute mark through a Danny Brough penalty goal after he had been obstructed by Damien Gibson.

Wales had a try disallowed in a similar style to Scotland's. Lee Briers kicked an inch-perfect grubber, but Anthony Blackwood just failed to ground the ball when sliding in.

Iestyn Harris restored Wales's six-point lead as he kicked a penalty following an infringement at the play-the-ball, but Wales were denied a further try from the kick-off when the unlucky Blackwood received Dave Halley's forward pass.

Scotland hit back again with a 40-metre penalty kick from Brough following an obstruction, but Wales went into half-time with a three-point aggregate lead (10 points on the day) after an Adam Hughes try that was successfully converted by Harris.

But just like in the first leg the year before, Wales blew their lead. Wales did not actually lose the game, but their eventual two-point win was treated like a defeat, and the Scots had never celebrated a loss so gratefully. A Ben Fisher try converted by Brough helped make the difference after Wales had conceded two quick penalties.

When Wales were denied two tries in five minutes through knock-ons, the multitude of Welsh fans who had travelled there knew it wasn't going to be their day. Scotland actually took the lead at one point through a Jamie Benn try converted by Brough. A Damien Gibson try with a few minutes to go made the final score 18-16 to Wales on the day, but it wasn't enough to put them through to the 2008 Finals.

There were no formal post-match interviews arranged and I declined the opportunity to interview Martin Hall after the game knowing that he would be in a stinking mood and that I would not be welcome. Dave Hadfield from *The Independent* had no hang-ups and bravely went down, arriving back a little less than five minutes later saying "That was like getting blood out of stone."

The only comments from Hall that Hadfield managed to extract were: "We had some opportunities today but we didn't take them and made some unforced errors. We had opportunities to win in this game and in the last one but we didn't take them and we now need to regroup for the Lebanon match on Friday."

Scotland coach Steve McCormack described World Cup qualification as the best achievement in his career: "I've won Northern Rail Cups and league leaders trophies with Widnes but I've had a lot of disappointment in big finals over the years," he said. "But to be associated with these people here in Scotland, the management, the crowd and the players, is something I've really enjoyed over the last three years and to help Scotland get to the World Cup is something amazing.

"We knew that Wales would chuck everything at us. The effort last year in Wales gave us that cushion though, and I said to the lads at half-time that even though we were 10 points down, we're only really three points down and that gave them a bit of a lift. I think Wales will do well in the repecharge, I hope they do win as we need all of the home nations at the World Cup."

Scotland qualified automatically as group winners while Wales had to play off against Lebanon who were runners-up to Ireland in the

World Cup action: Anthony Blackwood playing for Wales against Scotland
in a qualifying match in October 2006 (Photo: Ian Lovell)

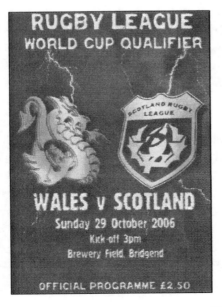

Left: The match programme. Wales's
defeat made qualification for the 2008
World Cup an uphill task.
(Courtesy Ian Golden)

182

Phil Joseph charging forward for Wales against Scotland in the World Cup qualifying match in November 2007. (Photo: Ian Lovell)

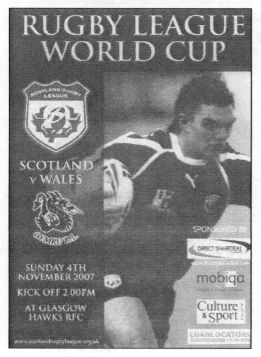

The match programme. Wales won the game, but lost the tie overall on aggregate. (Courtesy Ian Golden)

other group. The winners of this game would go on to face the winners of a match between Samoa and the USA.

Wales hoped to have Aaron Summers and Mark Lennon back for the Lebanon encounter but there was a doubt over Lee Briers's fitness after picking up a knock late in the Scotland game. Briers was fine, but neither Summers nor Lennon were able to turn out in the encounter at Widnes, something that Lennon was very disappointed about.

"Not playing against Scotland or Lebanon that year was one of the biggest disappointments of my career," he said. "To sit there in the stand watching while we were losing in both of those games and not being able to do a thing to help pained me. I'm not a very good spectator, I always want to be out there on the field so it was also tough watching the 2008 World Cup knowing that we could have and should have been there."

Warrington's Andy Bracek, who made his debut against Scotland, kept his place in the side while Wales's only debutant for the Lebanon encounter was Mark Roberts.

The evening, which started well for Wales, ended up to be my worst day ever watching sport. I've seen relegation with Cardiff City, last day mishaps against teams like Scotland, Russia and Romania that stopped Wales qualifying for the football World Cup and constant cricket defeats, but nothing could have prepared me for the defeat against Lebanon, not just the loss but the manner of the defeat as once again – the Welsh side went down like a pack of cards in the second half.

I had a premonition that Lebanon would be too strong. Unbeaten since the 2000 World Cup, a run that included a couple of wins against near-to-full-strength French sides, I knew they would be difficult, but not many people realised this. I remember the milk advert from the 1980s, "Accrington Stanley – who are they?" Well, the same thing was being said about Lebanon, especially by the Welsh media who couldn't believe that a nation who doesn't play rugby union at any level or football to any great extent, would be competitive on the rugby league field. The fact that they had run Wales close in 2000 had been forgotten. Wales were 20–10 up on 43 minutes thanks to a Damien Gibson hat-trick of tries and another from Andy Bracek, but the Lebanese then dominated with seven second-half tries and won 50–26 with just Anthony Blackwood crossing for Wales in the last 10 minutes.

The defeat saw the end of the international careers for Iestyn Harris, Lee Briers and Martin Hall. Briers announced his international retirement soon after the Lebanon defeat while Harris was always due to retire following the 2008 World Cup.

"I still consider myself Welsh through and through but unfortunately the time has come for me to quit the international scene," Briers told *Rugby League World* in June 2008.

"I've put my heart and soul into my Welsh career but I feel that I have to sacrifice something and this is it. I've loved every minute. When I was little, if someone had said to me that I'd have got to play in a World Cup semi-final against the Aussies in a side that was winning for so long, I wouldn't have believed them."

Harris, Wales's record points scorer with 12 tries, 58 goals and a drop-goal, called time on his international career just days after the full-time whistle blew at Widnes: "As far as my Wales career is concerned, that's it for me," he told the *South Wales Echo*. "Many of my best times in rugby have been playing for Wales. We achieved some great things and I have fond memories I'll treasure. What disappointed me was to be involved in poor preparation before a game of the magnitude of Scotland.

"The World Cup is the biggest stage and to say I'm disappointed that I won't be there is an understatement. It's a shame I couldn't experience another World Cup and bow out after that as it is sad to end my Wales career on such a low. But that's life."

But although Harris was retiring from playing, he was to form a new Welsh international backroom staff. With Hall's failure to lead Wales to the final stage of the competition, wholesale changes were needed and most supporters were pleased that Crusaders coach John Dixon was given the head coach job. Anthony Seibold and Hull Kingston Rovers' coach Justin Morgan were appointed assistants alongside Harris.

Typically of Dixon's modesty and his ambitions to see rugby league grow at grassroots level in Wales, this announcement wasn't made at a lavish press conference. Instead, he chose to launch his tenure as Welsh coach at an under-13 junior match between Valley Cougars and Tydfil Wildcats in June 2008 – the Wildcats first ever match at any level.

"This was the best place to launch the new set-up as we wanted to demonstrate that the long-term success and sustainability of rugby league in Wales belongs with the youth of Wales," Dixon said.

"We wanted to tell the youngsters who attended, their parents and their coaches, that this group of boys is just a sample of the much larger group of young men who have a pathway that could see them play firstly for the Crusaders and then Wales."

"To help coach Wales is a great honour," Iestyn Harris added. "The likes of Keiron Cunningham and I have had our time and now there's an opportunity for younger kids to come through.

"In the long-term, to have an opportunity to coach Wales would be up there as one of my top achievements, but at this early stage it's a great opportunity to learn from a good coach and a good person. It's my first step on the coaching ladder and we have a really good set-up.

"With us not being in the World Cup, we had to reassess what we wanted to achieve in the next four or five years and we need to start building for the future."

While Dixon and Harris were – and still are – keen to build for the future, even they didn't envisage the task that was in store for them later in 2008.

Wales were given just one game at senior level that year, a match against England at Doncaster's excellent Keapmoat Stadium. The fixture was originally going to feature Ireland, but when they pulled out midway through the year, Wales were selected in their place. Tours to the USA and South Africa had been put in the melting pot as possible fixtures before the England game was arranged and, in hindsight, these probably would have been better than a game against a strong English side who were preparing for the World Cup.

At every level of rugby league, 2008 had already been a successful year for Wales. It had started with a Home Nations win with Wales 'A' taking the four-team tournament for the sixth year in seven after beating England, Ireland and Scotland on the way.

The Welsh under-18 side continued this trend by winning the European under-18 championships with convincing victories over the Czech Republic, England and France.

The best Welsh students did well in the World Cup, reaching the semi-finals and performed admirably against the giants from down under: holders New Zealand and eventual winners Australia.

At club level, Celtic Crusaders achieved a Super League licence for the next three years before finishing in second place in National League One and were within 30 seconds of winning the Grand Final.

Their second string side, the Crusaders Colts, a team made up of the best of the young Welsh talent who would be playing in Super League reserve grade in 2009 and beyond, went one better by beating Bramley Buffaloes 26–4 to take the Conference National title.

However, because of injuries to experienced campaigners Anthony Blackwood, Luke Dyer, Aaron Summers, Gareth Dean, Gareth Price, Adam Hughes, Ian Webster, Rob Roberts, Bryn Powell and Matt James, the Welsh squad that played against England had nine players aged under 22, seven of whom were making their senior debut.

Three of them hadn't even made their professional first team club debuts. Rhys Griffiths, son of former Wales and Great Britain boss Clive, was one of them. He has been playing with Castleford Tigers while the other two, Rhys Williams of Warrington Wolves and Gil Dudson of Celtic Crusaders, had already experienced beating England that year as they were in the victorious Wales under-18 squad.

Gateshead Thunder's Matt Barron, a former Wales Students, Wales under-19 and Great Britain student international also made his debut while, in addition to Dudson, Crusaders' Geraint Davies and Ben Flower were also named for the first time as was Lee Williams, who was in the Wales 'A' squad who beat England in July 2008.

"It'll be a challenge because we've only had this week to prepare ourselves," Justin Morgan said before the match. "From the Welsh point of view we're disappointed not to be going to the World Cup and this game provides us with a good hit out.

"Traditionally, Wales have always gone well against the bigger nations like Australia and England, and I know all the players are excited by the chance of playing for Wales. We've a number of new players in the side who are keen to make an impact and where better to start than against England. It'll be a difficult game on Friday but we're going to give it a good shot."

The players went into a week-long training camp where Dixon, Seibold, Harris and Morgan were able to use their Super League and NRL experiences to ensure the perfect preparation. Aled James, back in the Welsh squad for the first time in three years was pleased with how the week went: "This was the best Welsh camp I've ever been involved with," he said. "At times in the past, Wales has been

187

considered by some to be just an end-of-season jolly but this time it was drummed into us that we were there to concentrate on playing rugby league. This was being treated just like any other professional game and rightly so."

John Dixon also instilled the players with pride in playing for their country. Those players and coaches who didn't know the national anthem were taught it and were told they had to know it by heart when they walked out against England in Doncaster.

"Well if it's a singing contest the Welsh have won it," Eddie Hemmings said on the live Sky Sports broadcast. "But it's not, it's an international rugby league match."

The singing was passionate, certainly a lot more passionate than the English who were singing *God Save the Queen*. However, passion does not win matches and England's experience proved too much for Wales's youth as England won 74–0 in a rugby league lesson watched by 11,263, the second highest attendance of an England versus Wales match since 1991.

New skipper David Mills was centimetres from crossing the English line in the first five minutes, but was stopped short. When they regained possession, England made their chance count as Rob Purdham left Dave Halley for dead, easing his way over the line to score after six minutes and convert his own try.

After that the floodgates opened as the English ran in 13 more tries. For Welsh supporters, it was a nightmare scenario. It was Wales's record defeat, but an expected one when a bunch of mainly National League, Super League reserves and Conference National players are up against some of Super League's best.

"I was over the moon to be selected as Welsh captain, it's such a massive honour," said David Mills. "There's not a lot of people who get to play for their country, let alone captain it, so this is very special for me. I take a lot of pride in knowing that I am captain of Wales and my dad, an Ely boy, is just as proud. A while before the end of the game, I got the players together and reminded them that although we got beaten by a high score, a lot of positives came out of that game. We've got four matches in 2009. This gives us a lot of opportunity to build and prepare for the next World Cup."

"It's not a good day for us in terms of the score but in terms of long-term development this is a starting point," John Dixon said in the post-match press conference.

"We've had a wonderful week. We've got a group of kids here who have come out of the National Conference and, to see them compete as well as they did, we can only grow from here. I thought the attitude and demeanour were terrific and so was the effort for 80 minutes. We were just beaten by the better team."

England went on to struggle throughout the World Cup in a complicated format that allowed the seeded teams to have an almost certain place in the semi-finals. Despite just one win, a scrape home against Papua New Guinea, England went through to the last four and were soundly beaten by eventual winners New Zealand for a second time.

The 10 teams that qualified for the Finals were separated into three groups. A group of four – Australia, England, New Zealand and Papua New Guinea, and two groups of three – Fiji, France and Scotland; and Ireland, Samoa and Tonga. The teams were split into these groups to create closer games and this was a partial success especially in the two so-called weaker groups that arguably produced some of the more entertaining and memorable games save for England versus Papua New Guinea, a game that the South Sea Islanders could have won. It also brought Jason Chan to John Dixon's attention. A try scorer against England, John snapped Chan up after the finals and he was to play Super League in Wales in 2009. The World Cup Final was also memorable as New Zealand's 34–20 win over Australia brought an end to 33 years of dominance from the Kangaroos and was celebrated by an estimated 99 per cent of the rugby league supporting world.

Over the past 100 years, the Welsh national side has built up an extensive history after facing England 65 times, France 37, Australia 13, New Zealand nine, Scotland five, Ireland three, Papua New Guinea three, USA and Lebanon twice, and Western Samoa, Russia, South Africa and the Cook Islands once each. The world of rugby league is growing fast and Wales with it. The team is due to face Serbia for the first time in October 2009 in a European Cup match with the first finals day due to be held at the Brewery Field in November. These are exciting times for international rugby league and, with a proper structure in place at last in both Wales and the world, the game can only grow and prosper.

Cardiff Blues coach and former Wales Rugby League international, Dai Young has welcomed this tournament and the development of the game in Wales as a whole: "It's good that we've now got a rugby league team playing in Wales and in Super League," he said. "Had the Crusaders not got that decision then I'd have feared for the future of the game here. But we have to use Welsh players or there's no point. When they expanded the game in London they brought in a load of Aussies. But saying that, first they have to have a team that competes – that's the short term goal. The long term goal is to produce Welsh players who are competitive. It's sad to see Wales losing the way they did against England and we don't want Wales to slip back further. We need a building stage and next year's games against Serbia and Ireland make sense. When we've built a more competitive team we can step back up again."

The Crusaders were about to embark on their first ever Super League campaign and would use a number of Welsh players, some a lot sooner than expected. The year 2009 would be one of the most dramatic in the history of Welsh Rugby League and one that no-one would ever forget.

13. Into Super League

It may have been Super League XIV for the competition, but for Celtic Crusaders it was Super League I. It was also the first time a Welsh club had competed at the top level of rugby league, as all the previous clubs had either been when there was only one division, or in the Second Division.

Pre-season

John Dixon kept to his usual routine of only announcing the new squad when he had finalised it. Now, with Super League on the horizon, the signings were more high profile as the Crusaders plunged into the deep end with the big swimmers.

The club announced its 25-man squad just days before the players went into a gruelling three-week Queensland-based training camp. There were nine new signings that included six players with more than 500 NRL appearances between them.

Mark Bryant, who was born in Cootamundra, New South Wales, the same place as cricket legend Don Bradman, arrived in Wales on a high after making his 100th NRL appearance when helping to lead Manly Sea Eagles to the NRL championship after their 40–0 thrashing of Melbourne in the 2008 Grand Final.

Bryant was a former Australian schoolboy international, as was Lincoln Withers who, along with Marshall Chalk, came from Canberra Raiders. Ryan O'Hara was a State of Origin player who had played for New South Wales in 2004. He arrived from Wests Tigers.

The final Australian was Adam Peek who had made 123 NRL appearances. Signed from Cronulla Sharks, he started his career with Adelaide Rams in the old Australian Super League before going to Canterbury Bulldogs, South Sydney Rabbitohs, Parramatta Eels and St George Illawarra Dragons.

To complete the batch of Crusaders' new recruits, Cook Islander Ben Vaeau signed from North Queensland Cowboys. However, he pulled out of the transfer due to family commitments at home and was replaced by new Papua New Guinea hero Jason Chan, who joined the club after a successful World Cup, where he scored a try against a poor England side.

Out of the three British players, two were former professional association football players – Matt Smith and Steve Tyrer, who both arrived at the club from St Helens on a season-long loan. Smith was on Everton's books as a youth and reserve player while Tyrer was a former Wigan Athletic goalkeeper. Both players had since excelled at Saints and were prominent goalkickers.

The other Super League signing was Peter Lupton from Castleford Tigers, who had more than 100 Super League games to his name for the London Broncos, Leeds Rhinos and Hull FC.

Dixon said at the time: "I'm pleased with the squad that we've assembled. We've maintained continuity on and off the field. We've retained our coaching staff and the core of players who have served this club so well over the last three years. We've addressed the key areas where we believe that we needed to improve as a club and have recruited accordingly. I'm happy with the squad and collectively we're looking forward to playing our role in Super League in 2009."

It was initially announced that seven players from 2008 would leave the club. Two players went to France, Gareth Dean to Carcassonne and Neale Wyatt to Pia. Ian Webster and Aaron Summers signed for Queensland Cup side Central Queensland Comets, Jamie I'Anson went to Oldham Roughyeds while Philippe Gardent and Paul Ballard were also released.

But again there were a couple of changes. Ballard came to an agreement with the Crusaders in the new year and re-signed for 2009 while Australian Terry Martin, who was set to come back for 2009 as a player-coach, didn't arrive after being refused a working visa.

The new rules regarding visas for overseas players were one of the major issues for the Crusaders and other clubs in early 2009, although arguably the Crusaders were the most affected. The players might have had the benefit of the Australian-based camp to get to know each other and to try out training routines. However, getting all the players back into Wales proved to be a problem.

The training camp in question took place in the first three weeks of December and achieved much. When they first set out, Anthony Seibold said that "The idea behind the camp in Brisbane is to provide the most ideal climate for pre-season training and to give the squad the best possible chance to prepare for what is going to be a massive challenge in Super League."

There was criticism from some quarters for sending the side down under but Seibold knew that it was right thing to do from the start: "We are not the first Super League club to hold a training camp in Australia," he said. "Nearly all Super League clubs have warm-weather training camps during the pre-season and the research that we conducted as a club suggested that this was the most effective physical preparation and the most cost-effective that we could have. It was also a good way to welcome our new signings into the club."

Thanks to Dixon and Seibold's links at Brisbane Broncos, the Crusaders were able to utilise some of the Broncos' off-field staff including nutritionist Holly Frail and kicking coach Graham McColm, while John himself exchanged ideas with new Brisbane Broncos first grade coach, Ivan Henjak and Gold Coast Titans coach John Cartwright.

The side also played opposed games against Queensland Cup sides, Burleigh Bears, Redcliffe Dolphins and Wynnum Seagulls and with sessions on the park daily, in the gym four times a week and run-outs on some of the many Gold Coast beaches once a week, the team seemed to have had the ultimate in fitness tests to prepare themselves for Super League.

However, just a few days before the players were about to return home, tragedy struck in Wales. On 17 December 2008, one of the club's under-18 stars, Jonathan Davies, died after his car collided with a van and another car at Stalling Down, near Cowbridge. This was just eight miles from the club and he was travelling home after a training session at the Brewery Field. The Swansea University student had also represented Wales at under-18 level.

Crusaders' Head of Youth Performance Andy Lindley said: "He was a very popular member of the squad who had a bright future. He was extremely motivated, tough physically and mentally and had a great attitude. He had a 'can do' mentality and he will be hugely missed by all. This is maybe an understatement but he was a great lad."

The tragedy shook the club. Club staff gave support to his family while his granddad, with whom he lived, was presented with his playing shirt and a photograph of him in action for the club. Every player and staff member who was in the country at the time went to his funeral. His Facebook site still remains and it's touching to see how many of his friends regularly post there. He is sadly missed.

When it came time for the players to return to Wales in late December, Tony Duggan, Josh Hannay, Mark Dalle Cort, Damien Quinn, Jace Van Dijk, Darren Mapp, Ryan O'Hara and Jason Chan didn't make it back into Britain straight away.

A tightening of procedures at the British consulate was the cause of the delay. As of 27 November 2008, sportspeople looking to play in the UK had to apply for a visa under a new points-based system for immigration. These visas would normally take a month to six weeks to come through but, with a backlog and Christmas in the way, the non-EU Crusaders' players didn't get back into Wales until the last day of January, just six days before the Super League season was due to start with an away game against the previous season's champions Leeds Rhinos.

The news that the players were finally returning actually came through on the day of the club's official media launch at Big Pit coal mining museum at Blaenafon. The launch, covered by BBC, S4C, Sky Sports and some leading local and national newspapers, was a great success and saw the players enter the mine and learn a bit of Welsh history as they prepared to represent the nation in Super League.

The team photos were taken outside with the coal mine in the background and, while it made for a classic shot, it was a freezing January day. Many of the players described it as the coldest that that they have ever been.

The British weather had a major part to play in adding to the club's frustrating pre-season preparations. A game at Harlequins was the only pre-season friendly arranged but, due to torrential rain coupled with the Quins' rugby union side having an important game on the same pitch 48 hours later, the game had to be called off.

Anthony Seibold commented: "We're really disappointed that the game had to be cancelled because it was our one and only pre-season friendly. This isn't ideal preparation for us by any means but we've overcome other issues in the past and we have always taken the positives out of any situation. We are now setting our sights fully on the Leeds Rhinos match where we are looking forward to being welcomed into Super League by the World Club Champions."

The only minor benefit arising from the pre-season problems was that the club received a lot of media attention and the negative publicity eventually became a positive. Media interest as a whole increased. The club was aware that the move from National League

One to Super League was going to be big, but naively didn't expect it to be so big. Now members of the media were on the phone for stories rather than it being the other way around. Regular weekly press conferences were planned and matches would have build ups of two to three days in local papers rather than a small column on the day of the game which had been the case for the past three years.

The Crusaders' success had a positive effect on other rugby league in Wales. For the first time in 100 years, there were to be three Welsh teams in the Rugby League Challenge Cup – the Crusaders, of course, plus Welsh Conference Premier champions Valley Cougars and top-rated university side, Cardiff-based UWIC.

By sheer coincidence, those two sides were drawn together in the Preliminary Round on 18 January with the game to be played at UWIC's Cyncoed Stadium. A scrappy game in the mud turned into a rugby league classic as the Cougars eventually won 20–18.

It was pleasing to see a very large crowd at UWIC with spectators even coming from various parts of northern and southern England to witness the clash.

With Celtic Crusaders reserve and under-18 players on each side, the game had a State of Origin 'mate against mate' feel about it as the two sides served up an entertaining game which Valley Cougars should have sewn up earlier than they did. They won the match by five tries to three, but the scoreline was just two points in their favour after they failed to land a single conversion, compared to UWIC's Lloyd White who, as expected, had a 100 per cent kicking record. Cougars were 16–0 up at half-time and 20–6 after 63 minutes, but UWIC tries after 66 and 78 minutes made for a nervous finish.

The result meant a trip to Portsmouth for the Cougars a week later to face the Royal Navy and this time it was the Cougars who were under the cosh going 34–6 down at half-time. Wales 'A' international Jim Barnes scored his second try for the Navy two minutes after the interval which was unconverted, but that was where the deluge stopped and the Cougars woke up. They scored 22 points in the second half, but it wasn't enough. The Navy were 38–28 winners.

Cougars' chairman Mark Rowley was proud of his players: "All of our boys played rugby union matches yesterday and four of them had to drive all the way down here this morning," he said. "We were up against things from the start so to see us end the game as the fitter side was pleasing. Our second-half performance was first class and I'm really proud of everyone wearing a Cougars shirt. We congratulate the Navy who had an excellent first-half performance that saw them through and we wish them all the best in the next round."

February

Celtic Crusaders' overseas players were finally back in the country but the off-field setbacks continued. Chief executive David Thompson announced his resignation a week before the season opener and marketing manager Mike Turner, who had only been at the club a couple of months, was given the responsibility of running it. He had plenty of experience, having worked in major roles for Leicestershire and Somerset cricket clubs, Bristol Shoguns rugby union club, the English Premier Rugby organisation and Sheffield Eagles rugby league club, where he was responsible for bringing in their record shirt sponsorship deal and was part of the backroom staff that guided them to Super League status and a Challenge Cup Final win over Wigan.

A trip to Leeds Rhinos would never be easy but the club's first ever Super League game, with all these kind of troubles behind them, was going to be nearly impossible to win.

The match was originally scheduled for St David's Day weekend, but because Leeds were involved in the World Club Challenge against Manly on 1 March, the game was brought forward three weeks.

Once again, the media were lapping it up. BBC and ITV sent cameras down to training sessions in the week before the big night. Sky Sports showed the game on television, while live radio coverage came from BBC Radio Wales and BBC Radio Cymru.

The players were given a baptism of fire on that cold winter's night and lost 28–6. However, they did exceptionally well in the second half because, after being 22–0 down at half-time, the score after the interval was only 6–6 and Leeds only scored their six points with 28 seconds remaining.

It couldn't have been easy for the Australians in the sub-zero climate of the British winter, seven of whom had walked off a plane from home less than six days earlier. They had been more used to the heat at Bondi or Brisbane rather than unwelcoming Yorkshire ice.

Luke Dyer scored the Crusaders' historic first Super League try after getting on the end of a trademark Jace Van Dijk grubber kick. Josh Hannay kicked the conversion.

196

After such a poor run-up to the season and a tough opening game, the club deserved some positive news. And despite another staffing setback which saw long-time operations manager Gerald McCarthy leave to work for the new Brewery Field stadium company, who were in the process of buying the ground in preparation for a new multisport complex in the future, the positive news was starting to come through.

At grassroots level, the first ever Welsh Finals Day in the national Carnegie Champions Schools competition was held at the Brewery Field in February, with both finalists going through to the knockout stages of the national competition. St Joseph's Roman Catholic High School from Port Talbot had the most success during the day, winning both the Year 7 and Year 9 competitions while Crusaders' stars Damien Quinn and Lincoln Withers and coaches John Dixon and Anthony Seibold were on hand to present the trophies. No Welsh side reached the national finals in London, but St Joseph's Year 9 side came the closest, eventually losing out to Freeston School from Wakefield in the semi-finals.

The Crusaders held a successful roadshow at the local Bridgend Designer Outlet which was hailed as one of the best public appearance events it had ever organised. Thousands of new and old fans were in attendance to meet the team less than 12 hours after arriving back in Wales following the Leeds Rhinos encounter, many of whom had watched the Crusaders for the first time on Sky Sports the previous night and had liked what they had seen.

The club also announced new media partners, with games being reported in Welsh from the ground for the very first time thanks to Siân Couch from *Y Cymro* and *Y Dinesedd* newspapers while Kiss 101 were unveiled as the club's official radio station.

Kiss's involvement was to be a success all season. While other radio stations had come forward in the past and had presented impressive packages, Kiss – whose logo was on the first team's playing shorts throughout 2009 – offered more of a hands-on approach.

In the lead up to the Super League season, they broadcast an advertising campaign on their radio station as well as sponsoring the press packs for the media launch at Big Pit. They also provided all the music and presentation at the Brewery Field on matchdays with long-time rugby league fan, Reece Carter, presenter of Kiss 101's *The Weekend Edge* becoming the new stadium announcer.

197

All this positive news was helping to promote the first home league game against Hull FC on 21 February but, before that there was a second away game, this time against Salford City Reds, familiar opposition from 2008. Crusaders had beaten them twice and lost three times, the third defeat being the National League One Grand Final after extra time.

It was a game that the Crusaders thought they had a good chance of winning and one that could have kick-started the season, but it wasn't to be. Salford stormed into a 20–0 lead after 21 minutes thanks to tries from Craig Stapleton, Richie Myler and Mark Henry, all converted by John Wilshere. "You can't give a side a 20-point start," John Dixon said after the game. "It was too big a lead to reel back."

Peter Lupton and two Tony Duggan tries helped cut the lead to four points midway through the second half but Ian Sibbit's late try and two Wilshere penalties eased Salford to a 28–16 victory. The only bright note to celebrate in this game was Tony Duggan scoring two tries to reach his century for the club.

Duggan scored the club's first-ever try in Crusaders' inaugural game at Hemel three years before and this, being just his 85th appearance, marked a tremendous feat. "I'm always just pleased to play rugby league and turning out in Super League in 2009 has been tremendous," said Duggan. "To reach 100 tries was a memorable moment for me when it happened but it wasn't something that was at the forefront of my mind. I'd have given all my records up for a few more wins in 2009."

Following two defeats and two backroom staff departures, Crusaders' chairman Leighton Samuel spoke live on BBC Radio Wales to assure fans that all was well with the club. "People are bound to take a pop at us," he said. "Here we are. A rugby league franchise in South Wales and people will obviously want us to fail. But we're not going to fail. We are going to be here and we are growing from strength to strength.

"I don't think we have any problems on the field. The [playing] infrastructure's there from the development right up to the top tier. We have to put the infrastructure off the field into place and that's going to take the time. People have done very, very good jobs and they've moved on and we wish them all the best. I don't know who's worried about that – the club is sustainable. We've needed to take a backward step, if you like, and look at it and put in disciplines and a structure that we have to adhere to.

"The initial response and initial reaction to us from most people is very, very positive and we've got to build on that and we've got to make it grow. We're going to be here a long, long time to come because the development structure underneath the Crusaders is so strong. We've got some very promising youngsters coming through so basically I think there's a massive future for us."

The week before the inaugural home Super League game against Hull FC was very busy for everyone at the club. While the players were training hard hoping to get a first win, the backroom staff was inundated with orders for tickets for both this and the second home game against St Helens a fortnight later. Merchandise was selling well and season ticket sales were having a late surge.

The demand for press tickets was also higher than in the past with many of the national media wanting to experience the Brewery Field atmosphere for the first time. And bar a few teething problems, they all seemed to enjoy themselves, Angela Powers from Sky Sports especially. Her feature on the club on Sky Sports's *Boots 'n' All* in the week following the game was very positive. As well as focussing on the game, she reported on the Crusaders' Family Village – something that was to make a regular appearance throughout 2009.

The Family Village, situated behind the posts at the open end of the Brewery Field, was a great opportunity for different companies and organisations to showcase themselves. For example, at the first game against Hull FC, the Welsh Regiment attended, bringing with them an assault course and climbing wall. Local company Really Welsh had an exhibition display and provided daffodils all around the club. Engage Super League title sponsors engage Mutual Assurance, who brought along their mascot Super Sid the Savings Pig, had a bungee run and some inflatable games. Eurovehicles ran a competition in which fans had to guess how many of first team players were able to fit in their van. Bridgend College brought along a samba band, Rural Foods provided a cooking demonstration while The Hogfather provided a tasty hog roast to warm up all fans on that first February evening.

The pre-match pyrotechnics added to the occasion and this, coupled with 5,272 fans in the ground, made for a wonderful atmosphere and inspired the team to take an early 10–0 lead. But it wasn't enough. Hull were 18–10 up at half-time and with the second half an even contest, they ran out 28–20 winners.

"It was a good start for us today and credit to Hull in that they fought back into it very well and the try just on half-time was one of the important actions of the game," John Dixon said afterwards.

"If we'd got that win today, then we would have convinced everybody we have a footy team here. Now we have a break next week because of the World Club Challenge. We can recharge our batteries and set our sights on a nice easy game against St Helens."

March

The first team may have been without a game on St David's Day but the reserves kicked off their season with a trip to Leeds Rhinos, with their game being played on the same day as the World Club Challenge game, just across the city.

Anthony Seibold knew how big this game and the whole season, was for the reserves: "The leap from winning the Conference National title to playing against the next generation of Super League stars was a massive learning curve for our young Welsh players," he said.

"Going from playing – with all due respect – teams and players from the Bramley Buffaloes and Hemel Hempstead to facing the best youngsters from Leeds, Wigan and St Helens and the many years of expertise coaching and playing experience the youngsters from those teams have, was difficult.

"Facing Leeds first up was a massive test against arguably either code of rugby's best academy set-up and system. The Rhinos have developed the blueprint for all academy set-ups with their partnership with Leeds Carnegie University.

"Led by head of youth performance and former international Barrie McDermott, Leeds have a great tradition in players coming through their academy and reserve team set-ups to international and Super League honours. Current names like Maguire, Burrow, Sinfield, Bailey, Smith, Hall and Diskin have all come through this system.

"What a result it was in defeating Leeds Reserves 48–40 in our first-up effort. It was great to see 13 Welsh-born kids on the field doing their best, led by some experienced first-team players. That is what reserve teams and academy set-ups are all about, producing players not winning championships or even games – that is a bonus.

200

The Crusaders reserves side who beat Leeds Rhinos 48-40 in the club's first ever Super League reserves match. (Photo: Ian Golden)

The enthusiasm, experience and work ethic of Mark Lennon, Geraint Davies, David Tangata-Toa, Steve Tyrer, Aled James and Paul Ballard in helping the team in the win against Leeds were very positive. I'd give special mention to Steve Tyrer on his 32-point effort with four tries and eight conversions while Lee Williams, Lloyd White and Lewis Mills were other young players who performed well during the game."

The first team returned to action against St Helens on Saturday 7 March. It was a day that could have gone absolutely perfectly for the club. The marketing had gone extremely well and the telephones were even busier than before the Hull FC game. A club record crowd of 6,351 packed into the Brewery Field as every corporate box was sold for the first time in the club's history.

The game was also one of the most remarkable on record as outstanding defence from the Crusaders' backline ensured the first ever Super League half-time score of 0–0. The deadlock lasted for nearly an hour and was eventually broken when Saints winger Tom Armstrong grounded the ball in the left corner.

With the final score at just 4–0 to St Helens, the visiting fans applauded and cheered the Crusaders players off at the end. A lot of fans congratulated John Dixon was after this game, despite the Crusaders losing. At the post-match press conference, he was certainly happier than his opposite number Mick Potter.

A week later, in the club's 100th game, they lost 48–18 away to Hull Kingston Rovers following an outstanding second half from the Robins. A number of the Crusaders' fans were a few minutes late into the ground having stayed in the bar to witness Ross McCormack's dramatic equaliser for Cardiff City FC live on Sky Sports. They were treated to a plucky display that was not enough to get the team's first-ever Super League win.

John Dixon knew what he was up against before the game started. In that morning's *Wales on Sunday* newspaper he described Craven Park thus: "The wind howls straight across the sea and across the park and the debris blows straight at you. You've got to get out the passenger side of the car if it's blowing against you.

"The ground lies east-west, not north-south, so you're playing into the sunshine, and they've got the most warm and loving fans up there, so it's a terrific place to go and play footie.

"But seriously, we got a really warm welcome from Justin Morgan and his board when we went to look at how they ran their franchise last year. They'd been promoted from National League One and made some progress, so they were very good mentors for us in those early days of applying for Super League."

The Crusaders took the lead after 13 minutes with a try that just looked too easy. Matty Smith opened up a gap for Marshall Chalk. He in turn laid the ball off to Peter Lupton who had an easy run to the line to score the club's 600th try. Josh Hannay's kick made the score 6–0.

However, Rovers went into half-time with a 16–12 lead and then went try-crazy in the second half scoring six to win 48–18.

The match a week later against Wakefield Trinity Wildcats was meant to be Crusaders' first home game to be broadcast live on Sky Sports, but other events took their toll in what turned out to be arguably one of the saddest days for rugby league in living memory.

Preparations for the match had not been good, especially the timing. On that weekend, the Welsh rugby union side were due to have a possible championship decider against Ireland at the Millennium Stadium. The club knew that this would be detrimental to its attendance and had requested, if possible, not to have a match on this weekend.

Unfortunately, the fixture compilers had produced a home match that weekend and it was not possible to swap it, so it was decided to make the best of a bad deal. The Wales union game was due to kick off at 6.30pm so the Crusaders set the time of their game for 3pm so fans could see it before watching the rugby union afterwards.

But Sky Sports wanted to show the match live. They set the kick-off time at 6.00pm, directly clashing with the rugby union. When this happened, most of the Crusaders office staff got on the phone to their respective departments in the RFL asking for Sky to choose another game or at least show it at 3pm. Sky came back with a 7pm Sunday kick-off which, although it wasn't the best of times, was better than the original planned.

The reserve match between the two sides was played just up the road at Maesteg RFC three hours earlier. The first half was an even and exciting affair with the Crusaders youngsters going into the break 15–10 up. That was when I left the ground to go and set up for the first team game at the Brewery Field.

About 40 minutes later, my partner Siân, who was reporting on the game, called me to say that she was on her way to the Brewery Field because the match had been abandoned. My immediate thoughts were that there had been a mass brawl as that's the only reason I could think that a match would be abandoned. But no, she told me that a player had made a tackle, got up, then collapsed again. An ambulance had been called and the referee abandoned the game.

By the time that Siân got to the Brewery Field, there were reports that the player, who we later learned to be 21-year old Leon Walker, had died. However at the time, this was completely unconfirmed.

I went about my business at the club as usual. By this time it was 6.00pm, an hour before kick-off, so I'd collected the team sheets and typed them up. I then received a phone call telling me to get down to the dressing rooms immediately. The confirmation had come through regarding Leon's death. The match was instantly postponed, however we were unable to tell the supporters and media the reason for the postponement because no-one had yet been able to inform Leon's parents.

Sky Sports showed a replay of the 2008 Grand Final, and it was halfway through that when we were told that his parents had at last been contacted. Wakefield's CEO made a public statement live on Sky Sports at 8.50pm that night and the media were then informed officially. A post-mortem was held that week and while the tests failed to establish the cause of death they did rule out any injury caused by playing rugby league.

A minute's silence was held at every game the following weekend. Wakefield bravely chose to play on and their match against St Helens went ahead as planned on the Friday night live on Sky Sports.

The Crusaders travelled to Warrington Wolves' Halliwell Jones Stadium, and just like the Grand Final there the previous year, it was a close encounter that the visitors really should have won.

In 2008 against Salford, the Crusaders gave away a penalty with seconds to go when they were two points up. In 2009, against Warrington, the scores were level with eight minutes to go when Ryan O'Hara was sin-binned when following through after making a tackle, leaving the Crusaders with 12 men for the rest of the game. This proved crucial as it gave Warrington that extra space in a final period where players were tiring.

It looked like that a drop-goal from man-of-the-match, former Welsh captain Lee Briers, would be the score that would break his fellow countrymen's hearts, but a final try from Chris Hicks sealed a 27–22 win. "We let ourselves down a little bit," John Dixon said after the game. "We're not in a position to have 13 players against 12. A lack of discipline hurt us."

April

The following month saw another change around in the backroom staff at the Brewery Field as Thibault Giroud, the strength and conditioning coach over the past two seasons, departed to take up a similar role at top French rugby union side, Biarritz Olympique. This led to Maesteg RFC's head coach and director of rugby, Kevan Tee, being appointed as the new football manager and Anthony Seibold taking on a new role as 'head of performance'.

Seibold said at the time: "This role is going to be a wonderful challenge for me and one I am looking forward to. It will allow for a much greater hands-on role within the first team and I think it will allow me to use more of my strengths as a person and as a professional. I am excited and looking forward to the change."

Kevan Tee's background had mainly been in rugby union. He was a WRU level 3 coach, former WRU tutor coach, former director of rugby and head coach at Tondu RFC and was also the team manager at both the Celtic Warriors and the Ospreys regional age grade teams.

His initial involvement in rugby league was as tour manager for the Welsh Students side in their 2008 World Cup campaign in Australia where they finished fourth after losing narrowly to both New Zealand and champions Australia. He also assisted Wales Rugby League's national teams and was manager of the Celtic Crusaders' homegrown squad - Bridgend Region.

"I'm pleased to be joining the Crusaders full-time," Tee said. "To have an opportunity to work at a Super League club was something that I couldn't turn down. I've had a great time at Maesteg RFC and long may this continue as the support from the Old Parish has been superb but this will be a whole new challenge for me and it's one that I'm relishing."

Tee didn't have a good first month in the role when it came to first-team results. Five games were played culminating in another five defeats and morale in the office was reaching an all time low.

Out of the five games, the players came closest to winning the fifth. The game against Castleford Tigers was there for the taking as Celtic were 10–0 up after 15 minutes and 16-12 ahead at the interval. But with five minutes remaining the Tigers were 34–16 ahead and a consolation try from Ryan O'Hara wasn't enough.

It was a tough month all round for the side. John Dixon had a number of selection problems thanks to injuries with Tony Duggan, Jace Van Dijk, Darren Mapp, Matty Smith, Anthony Blackwood, Mark Lennon and Geraint Davies all missing for during the month with one ailment or another.

Crusaders' physiotherapist Ben Stirling was one of many involved in rugby league who was calling for a change in the Easter programme that forces teams to play two games in less than 72 hours with a game on Good Friday and one on Easter Monday. "I have contemplated the benefits of this programme and struggle to find any that are truly meaningful for any of the Super League teams," he said. "The game of rugby league continues to develop with players becoming faster, stronger and fitter. This not only makes for a more captivating spectacle, but also comes with a physical price, heavier collisions and therefore more trauma to the body.

"Two days is not enough time for the body to recover and replenish itself in preparation for the next game. Consequently, players suffer from fatigue and more importantly increased risk of injury. Also, with a squad of only 25 players, teams can be forced to field players that are carrying niggles or minor injuries which could result in more damage and a more prolonged absence, something that could have been avoided with a six or seven-day turnaround.

"In an age where the science behind sport has become the foundation for all aspects of physical performance and governing bodies impose strict medical guidance to ensure player welfare and safety, it surprises me that such a short turnaround still exists.

"After reading articles by the likes of Hull Kingston Rovers coach Justin Morgan and Warrington assistant coach James Lowes, I realise that I am not alone in my viewpoint that this tradition is one that needs to be scrapped."

But there seems to be no chance of that happening in the near future. In *Rugby League World* magazine in June 2009, the RFL's chief executive Nigel Wood said: "The contracts have been negotiated and are sacrosanct for a three-year period. One of the issues about Easter is that every club gets a home game. Reducing that to one wouldn't be insurmountable but it's actually the third game where most people think the standard drops off."

Welsh Rugby League had to accentuate the positives in April, so it was good that there were many. At development level there was a lot to shout about. Playing three games in a week leading up to Easter, Wales Students beat Scotland, Ireland and England to win the Student Home Nations title.

Wales were 12–0 down in the first game as Scotland looked the most likely winners following tries from Mike Scott and Charlie Paxton each converted by Robbie Smith. But Wales turned the tables in stunning fashion forging a 14-point lead early in the second half with two tries from substitute Owain Brown, touchdowns for centre Daniel Phillips, winger Lloyd Stapleton and substitute Iwan Brown, three of which Rob Montgomery converted. Scotland scored two tries with Jordan Rice and Paxton crossing in the 50th and 60th minutes, but Wales won 26–22.

Wales followed that up with a 36–16 win over Ireland. The Irish, although never in front, were only 12–10 adrift early in the second period, but fell away to a Lloyd Stapleton brace, supplemented by late tries for Lloyd White, who also added five goals, and Rhys Griffiths. Iwan Brown scored a try and a goal in the opening period and Jason Mossop nipped over.

Favourites England were seen off in the final game 31–16 after having battled back from seven points down to within a point. Wales were never behind, stand-off Lloyd White the man-of-the-match kicking four goals to embellish a fine all-round display. Curtis

Cunningham crossed twice and there were touchdowns for Rhys Griffiths, Craig Foy and Christiaan Roets, with Foy adding a conversion and a drop-goal.

The Welsh supporters almost enjoyed a double Welsh victory that day. At under-16 level, Wales were facing England in the annual Good Friday international which, in 2009, was being held at Blackwood Bulldogs. Both teams scored three tries each but as Wales converted just two of them, England won 18–16. It was the closest Wales had ever got to beating England at this level.

The final weekend of April was a big one for the Crusaders as no less than four sides – or five if you add the supporters' tag team, the Celtic Barbarians – represented the club over the two days.

Saturday saw a double header in Treforest where the reserves beat Castleford Tigers 34–24 and the club's foundation academy (under-16) played for the first time, and took on Widnes Vikings.

The under-16 match resulted in a 60–10 defeat, but it mattered little. The fact that they were playing in the first place was a step forward for the development of the game in Wales.

The Crusaders youngsters were 42–4 down at half-time and impressed in the second half with a more solid performance once they'd found their feet. They scored one try in each half, Sam McComb in the opening period and Josh Ramsey, younger brother of the Arsenal midfielder Aaron, with a breakaway try near to the end of the game which was converted by Liam Harris.

Crusaders under-16s assistant coach Wayne Williams said: "This was a total and utter learning experience for all of our lads. We didn't have a great deal of preparation and for a lot of these players it was their first full rugby league match. For all the players, going up against a side like Widnes was very challenging. However, there were a lot of good individual performances, they showed promise, and we're going to get better. This is a brand new team and, despite the scoreline, this was a good first outing for us."

The biggest success of 2009 for the club came the next day when the under-18s took on Leigh Miners Rangers in the Gillette National Youth League Grand Final at Widnes and won 32–0.

It was the culmination of a year's hard work for the Crusaders' head of youth performance Andy Lindley and his side who had chosen to compete in this winter competition against the top amateur clubs in Great Britain, in a similar fashion to Crusaders Colts in the summer of

2008. The aim was to gain experience in rugby league and be ready to compete at Super League under-18 level in 2010.

It had been a season of success for the under-18s. Starting off with just 14 players in the squad for the first game of the season, they lost 24–18 to an experienced Featherstone Lions side. After that it was all systems go and 14 wins on the bounce followed as they finished in second place in the final table.

Their success had seen some of the players win Great Britain under-18 call ups against France and Australia with Mark Wool captaining the Lions. Antony Symons, Dalton Grant, Jamie Tibbs, Rhys Fenton, Gil Dudson, Ross Wardle and Loren Quick also won caps.

The Grand Final result was unexpected. While all 17 Welsh-born youngsters were fantastic, Alex Webber stood out with three tries and six goals with Dan Godwin and Kyle Blackmore also going over.

Andy Lindley said: "This was a fantastic result for us, especially as we beat a Leigh side that hadn't lost in over a year. We dominated the game from start to finish and were the better side at every level today. We're delighted to have won the title as it was the result of a long season where we've worked extremely hard.

"We've replicated the Colts' honour from last year. They were in their first season and finished in second place, just like we did this year, and were awesome when they beat Bramley in that final. I didn't think that we'd match that today but credit to our boys and with no disrespect to last year's Colts, I think we excelled them.

"We're building nicely as a club now. Our foundation academy played their first game yesterday and that's the level that the under-18s were at this time last year. The future looks bright for us and today's result proves it."

The Wales Students side after beating England to win
the 2009 Home Nations competition (Photo: Clive Griffiths)

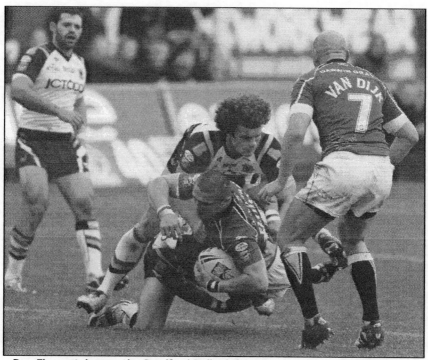
Ben Flower takes on the Bradford Bulls defence in the Crusaders' first Super
League win on 17 May 2009 (Photo: Ian Lovell)

Crusaders' Mark Lennon prepares to convert Damien Quinn's try against Harlequins at The Stoop on 6 June. (Photo: Peter Lush)

Crusaders on the attack against Harlequins in the same match.
(Photo: Peter Lush)

14. Super League wins and more

By the end of April 2009, despite no wins for Celtic Crusaders in Super League, there had already been much to cheer about in the world of Welsh Rugby League. The Wales Students side had won the Home Nations tournament, the Crusaders under-18 side had won the Gillette National Youth League title, the Crusaders reserves had beaten Leeds Rhinos and the club's under-16 side had played for the first time.

The under-16s continued their challenges into May and while they failed to win a game in their short five-match season of friendlies, they improved week-by-week and the experience gave them a lot to build on, both as individuals and as a team.

Improvement was shown in their second game, as they went down 24–13 to Harlequins at Penallta RFC. Owain Rees and Efan Ellis scored the Crusaders tries with Rhodri Lloyd kicking two conversions and a drop-goal. The side kept up their record of scoring one try in each half in their third game, but they were taught a rugby league lesson by the experienced St Helens side at Knowsley Road.

Saints' under-16s had too much firepower for the young Welsh lads running in nine tries, five of them before the interval. Brad Thyrer and Tom Davies scored for the Crusaders with Rhodri Lloyd converting both to leave the final score 58–12.

Against Salford City Reds, they took the lead for the first time. It was from a good passing move just after the quarter hour mark which Scott Gibson scored. "They showed signs of further improvement in that game," said Anthony Seibold. "The youngsters went down 16–4, but again we had a number of players we have identified only playing their fourth game of rugby league, while playing against kids who have played the game since they were six or seven. These kids are the Crusaders' future. I cannot praise enough the work of Andy Lindley, Dan Clements and others including Stu Williams who are leading from the front when it comes to grooming our lower-grade players."

The conclusion came with the ultimate in tough games, a trip to Leeds Rhinos and, to their credit, the youngsters scored more points that in any of the other four games, but still lost 56–24.

Crusaders took the lead again in this match and the half-time score was level at 14–14, but the Leeds side's fitness showed in the end.

Owain Rees and Jack Pring each scored two tries with Rhys Watkins also crossing and Rhodri Lloyd kicking a conversion in each half.

"Although the scorelines were disappointing to the eye, the boys showed a gradual progression throughout their games," Andy Lindley said. "Now they're now putting on Wales shirts and training for the under-16 European Nations Championships in Serbia in August. After that, it's Super League Junior Academy 2010, at under-18 level, for a lot of them. We'll be offering pro contracts to a number of these players. This has been a good start for them and they're all going forward."

Also at junior level, the Welsh Conference was expanding with new clubs in Swansea, Penallta and Pontyclun, the last, nicknamed the Panthers, staging an six-team under-13 tournament in May, winning it after beating the Bridgend Blue Bulls 10–4 in the final.

"It was great to see so many new players enjoying rugby league today," said Welsh development officer Dan Clements. "The standard was really impressive, especially as many of the players were playing their first game. Pontyclun in particular have been fabulous hosts and it was nice to see them performing so well in the tournament."

There was also a new side at senior level with the St Clears Wild Boars in West Wales bringing the total number of rugby league clubs in Wales to 14. The game had never been so healthy.

The Wild Boars joined the eight other senior level Conference clubs in the annual Scott McRorie Nines tournament in Cardiff where the hosts were unable to secure a third successive title – last year's league champions Valley Cougars beat Bridgend Blue Bulls 22–20 in the final.

Back in Super League and a large following from Wales travelled up to Edinburgh for the third annual Magic Weekend. For the last two years, Magic Weekend had been held in Cardiff under the moniker of 'Millennium Magic'. But due to a number of reasons, which included poor co-operation from the WRU and the opportunity to develop the game north of the border, the showpiece weekend was moved to the Scottish capital.

And it was a big success. A supporters' tag tournament was a great way to open the weekend. The mascot highland games proved much hilarity with the newly named Colyn the Crusader finishing a creditable 11th out of 15.

Celtic Crusaders' 19-man squad flew to Scotland on Friday morning to prepare to take on Huddersfield Giants at Murrayfield on the

Sunday. However, they did not recover from a poor start, losing 40–16 with tries in the last quarter from Chris Beasley, Anthony Blackwood and David Tangata-Toa saving their blushes.

The team was more fired up than ever for a trip to three-times World Club Champions Bradford Bulls a fortnight later. There was no game for the team in the weekend in between the fixtures, but the players weren't given a rest and carried on training, including a well-publicised boxing session at Fight Academy Wales in Pontyclun.

The session was very well attended by the media with BBC Wales, ITV Wales, Media Wales (publishers of the *Western Mail* and *Echo*) and national newspaper representatives in attendance.

Darren Wilson, who opened the boxing gym 18 months previously, is a big Crusaders fan, regularly attends matches at the Brewery Field and was a matchball sponsor on one occasion in 2008. "It was the Crusaders' second visit to us," Wilson said. "They came to us last year when they were in National League One, again in the middle of the season. This session was really good. The boys put 100 per cent into everything they do. It looks like they got a lot out of it. Boxing, like rugby league is a tough and physical sport and they were worked hard this morning.

"I do like watching rugby league and I enjoy going down to the Crusaders. It's an explosive sport, always on the go and that's why it's a favourite of mine."

Despite the disappointing news that Tony Duggan would probably miss the remainder of the season due to an ankle injury that needed an operation, the team travelled to Bradford in a confident mood and proved it by taking a 10th-minute lead with a Chris Beasley try.

Josh Hannay, who had missed the conversion, made up for it when he kicked a 30-metre penalty following interference at the play-the-ball. In a highly defensive first half, the Crusaders excelled. A classic example came on the half-hour when Bradford's Jamie Langley passed to Matt Cook who was brilliantly tackled by Lincoln Withers and Josh Hannay. Luke Dyer picked up a high bomb from the next play to completely defuse the attack.

Soon after, it was 8–0. Van Dijk kicked another grubber aiming for Withers who was brought down by Ben Jeffries. Hannay kicked the resulting penalty. Bradford's try just before the interval could have proved to be a sucker punch for the Crusaders, but thankfully it didn't affect the players. Andy Lynch's touchdown had brought Bradford to within two points and a lot of sides may have folded then. But the Crusaders kept going and earned their first victory in Super League and 2009.

It took the visitors just three minutes to get on the board in the second half. After the tackle count had been reset when the Crusaders were five metres from the line, Damien Quinn played the ball to Neil Budworth at dummy half and David Tangata-Toa forced his way over. Hannay converted.

Another try for the Welsh side came after 50 minutes. Matty Smith made a fine kick under the sticks allowing Withers to slide over. Hannay kicked the conversion. After the Crusaders defended superbly following two complete sets of six within their 20-metre line, Michael Worrincy finally scored a try on 56 minutes. Bradford's Paul Deacon kicked his second goal to put the Bulls just eight points behind.

However, the Crusaders scored straight away with a very well-taken tries. Van Dijk kicked a high bomb, Dyer caught the ball in mid-air while outjumping the Bulls defensive line. Somehow he managed to scrambled over his opponents high in the air and touch down before being pushed over the dead-ball line. Hannay missed the kick so the Crusaders just had a two-try cushion.

Bradford capitalised on Damien Quinn having to take the ball into touch on his own five-metre line. The home side played a fine set following the scrum culminating in Steve Menzies twisting and turning his way through to score. Deacon kicked the extras again.

A third Hannay penalty, kicked from the halfway line following a high tackle on Ryan O'Hara put eight points between the sides with seven minutes to go.

But the Bulls fought back again with Sykes on the end of a string of passes converted by Deacon. That try came with just two minutes remaining and Bradford knew they had to fight hard for a winner. However, from the kick-off, Ben Jeffries took the ball into touch giving up possession that the Crusaders did not waste and Jason Chan set up Luke Dyer in the corner to seal the win.

John Dixon was understandably ecstatic with the Crusaders' first ever Super League win: "This makes a change coming into a press conference with a smile on my face," he said. "I need something new to say to now. Today was the first time we were able to match execution to effort. I thought our execution was the best it has been.

"I always felt we could compete but this will give us a bank of knowledge to say yes we can, and that we can survive an onslaught and come through it. There's now a smile and belief in the dressing rooms and a spring in their steps. They all train hard and work hard. Today we got the rewards."

The day could have been even more perfect as the reserves almost collected a victory against their Bradford counterparts before the main game. In a close match, the young Welshmen gave a good account of themselves after a shaky start. The home side went into the interval 10–4 up thanks to tries from Jodie Sheriffe and Johnny Horton with Paul Ballard replying for the Crusaders. Bradford were first on the board in the second half with an early try from Elliott Whitehead but for the final half hour the Crusaders were in complete control.

Mark Wool was close to crossing but was pulled into touch after receiving a pass from Geraint Davies, who was playing his first match for two months following a broken hand. The Crusaders regained the ball straight away and a loose pass allowed Ashley Bateman to run over. Lloyd White converted to put the Crusaders within four points. Despite further Crusaders' pressure, Bradford hung on to win 14–10.

The Kenfig Hill Male Voice choir had been at Odsal and their singing before, during and after the Super League match was outstanding. They were invited back to a home game two weeks later, against Wakefield, but were unable to inspire again as the Crusaders went down to a very disappointing 50–6 defeat in the rescheduled match on the last Saturday in May after its postponement in March. This defeat, coupled with a 30–18 loss at home to Catalans Dragons the week before, brought the Crusaders back down to earth with a bump.

June

If there was ever such a thing as a perfect day for Welsh Rugby League, Saturday 13 June was very close to it. Four matches were being played in the Bridgend area that day – at Maesteg RFC, the Wales under–18 side was facing their English counterpart at 10.45am while Crusaders reserves took on Wigan at 2.30pm. At the Brewery Field, also at 2.30pm, the Wales 'A' side – newly named as the Dragonhearts – took on the England Lionhearts with Celtic Crusaders versus Wigan Warriors providing the conclusion at 6pm.

The day was promoted heavily in the local and national media with ITV Wales also getting in on the act with a good match preview on their Friday night news programme. All this, coupled with some hefty marketing from the Crusaders – the corporate boxes and match hospitality had been sold out for weeks - led to one of the biggest crowds of the season at the Brewery Field.

The Wales under-18 side was a strong favourite to beat England following their European Championship success the year before and Celtic Crusaders' Gillette National Youth League triumph. Many players from both of those sides lined up against England and while the visitors gave them a contest in the first half, Wales did enough in the second half to win the game 34–20.

Wales were 20–4 up at one stage thanks to early tries from Chris Davies and Loren Quick, the first of a hat-trick of tries from the loose-forward, who also converted three times. Dafydd Carter and Adam John also scored for Wales in the first half. England fought back hard and their determination was rewarded by first-half tries from John Frodsham and Danny Gaskel, the two lynchpins in the England side, as well as one each for Mike Sharett and Josh Jackson. Ben Mullen kicked two conversions. Quick completed his hat-trick in the second half and Dan Godwin finished the scoring with a try as the pace slowed because of the intense heat.

Crusaders reserves fought hard in the next game at Maesteg but were unable to win against the unbeaten Wigan reserve team. The Welsh lads may have gone down 40–22, but coach Dan Clements said: "There was a great deal of improvement from the team this week. Considering that Wigan are top of the reserves league as well as being unbeaten, we didn't do too badly and put in a massive effort. We were always in contention and didn't let Wigan run away with the game."

Better was to come the week after when the Crusaders beat Hull KR reserves 40–22, fielding their youngest ever side against a team that contained two World Cup players, a number of first team semi-regulars and the captain of Wales, David Mills.

Back to 13 June and onto the Brewery Field. Wales Dragonhearts were looking to open their campaign in style against the English and, despite an early equalising try from England after Jamie Murphy had given Wales a fifth-minute lead, the home side did just that. Murphy added a second try on the half-hour, while his Bridgend Blue Bulls team-mate Matthew Hutchings also scored two tries as Karl Hocking,

Craig Fox and Adrian Owen all crossed. Jamie Murphy kicked seven out of seven conversions and Wales romped home 42–4.

"I'm really pleased at how well the lads played today," said Wales coach Mike Healy. "We got one or two early tries which settled us down a bit and our game plan was perfect after that. It was an outstanding performance."

This game, along with the Crusaders versus Wigan climax, was billed as "Brewery Field's biggest ever double header" and a number of first-time fans were in Bridgend to see exactly what rugby league was all about as a result of the promotion work.

The Crusaders had come into the game on the back of a 26–6 defeat at Harlequins where they finished the game with just 13 fit men. Luke Dyer had been carried off after picking up a head injury on the hour, taking no further part in the game. He joined Aled James who left the field after 10 minutes, Ryan O'Hara after 16 minutes and David Tangata-Toa after 50 minutes.

The training programme during the following week was focused on recovery with only 12 players actively taking part after the Harlequins game. A number of key personnel were missing throughout the week with Friday's team run being the first time the Crusaders had anything that represented a competitive squad for the Wigan match. The odds were heavily stacked against the Crusaders because they were eight points adrift of Salford in the league table at kick-off.

However, they finally got it right, although they could have found themselves well behind had Wigan not squandered chances and had wing Luke Dyer not pulled off a tremendous try-saving tackle to deny Shaun Ainscough.

Instead, both sides turned on a fantastic half of rugby in which there was not one penalty conceded. Crusaders went in front when Welsh international Mark Lennon made a decisive break down the left, passed to the excellent Peter Lupton who put scrum-half Jace Van Dijk on a 20-yard run to the posts for Lennon to convert. Wigan hit back when second-row Harrison Hansen drove over as Wigan put the pressure on the home team inside their '20' with Pat Richards converting, but a huge crossfield kick by Van Dijk sent Lupton over near the posts and, with Lennon's conversion, the dream was on and Crusaders were 12–6 ahead at the interval.

The Crusaders drew first blood in the second half. It was a truly outstanding try that got the crowd on its feet. Jason Chan had a massive hand in the score. After it looked like he'd been tackled, he was soon back up on his feet to create a possible chance on the left wing. Blackwood was tackled and from the next set, it was Chan's pass that set up Dalle Cort. Dalle dived onto his own cheeky grubber to score in the corner and Lennon was unlucky with the conversion.

Wigan got back into the game after winning a crucial refereeing decision that gave them a scrum on the home side's 10-metre line allowing Cameron Phelps to run over with Richards converting. An Amos Roberts try brought the scores level before Lupton's late second try made the final score Celtic Crusaders 22 Wigan Warriors 16.

"I'm elated for the players and the club," said John Dixon. "We talked during the week about Wigan coming down and to play as well as they did was terrific. This is what you play footy for. It is a special place to be with the team at the moment. It was about effort and execution. That is what it was about today. We hung in.

"Our ball control in the first-half was nothing short of outstanding. We tried to simplify things this week and maybe that has raised their execution and we got the result at the end. This win is huge, not just for this club but for rugby league. I talked to the players afterwards and said they have to understand what they have done. To win against such a high-profile club will do wonders for the game in Wales, there is no doubt about that."

The local media loved it. "No, your eyes are not deceiving you, and the score at the top of the page isn't a misprint," wrote Simon Kendal-Williams in the *South Wales Echo* as the centre pages of Monday's paper were devoted to the win.

BBC Wales's Celtic Crusaders correspondent Gareth Rhys Owen was also delighted to witness the win and wrote a celebratory article for the BBC website. He pointed out the significance of the win not just to the Crusaders but to the Bridgend area and also talked about how the club was bringing the youngsters through.

The enthusiasm of people like Simon and Gareth has been vital to the club. With all media outlets running at lower budgets than ever due to the credit crunch, placing a new sport in the area can't have been welcomed by any cash-strapped organisation. They, along with a number of other media partners, tried their best to promote the club against the odds they faced. While they were successful during the summer months, once the rugby union and football seasons started again late August, it was the same old story. Coverage dramatically decreased and was a partial cause of the low attendance for Crusaders' final home game of the 2009 season – the fact that a lot of the general public who watched the news or read the papers wouldn't have known that there was a game on. This is something that has to be addressed in the future.

Others from the media who were regular attendees throughout 2009 included Y Cymro's Siân Couch, GTFM's Ioan Dyer, Radio Cardiff's Francis Taylor, Real Radio's Mark Poyser as well as independent reporters Phil Cadden and Gary Baker.

Baker, who runs Wales and West media company deserves special credit. He is the only one who has not only supported the Crusaders from the start, but the Welsh Rugby League Conference before that. He, just like the players and administrators who have battled their way up to work in Super League, is now getting the rewards for his hard work over the years.

A loss to Hull Kingston Rovers followed a week later but the ramifications from that match concerned more than just a 32–18 scoreline. The injury list was already big and a few more knocks in that match meant that it was going to get bigger. There were long-term injuries to Steve Tyrer, Matt Smith, Tony Duggan, Marshall Chalk and Darren Mapp while Josh Hannay and David Tangata-Toa had definitely been ruled out of the forthcoming trip to St Helens. There were also serious doubts over a few other players. Realistically, the Crusaders were facing the fact that they only had 13 fit first-team players for an away trip to the Super League leaders. Indeed, new shirts had to be ordered for young Welshmen Lloyd White and Gil Dudson.

Dudson didn't play at St Helens but White did. He and Geraint Davies made their Super League debuts on the ultimate stage. Both played well but Saints were too good, winning 30–0.

While a home game against Warrington Wolves was next on the agenda, promotion had started for the three home games following that match. This was of a massive campaign involving adverts on buses, billboards, throughout newspapers and on the radio. The community department, headed by Matthew Pritchard, went into schools to promote each event. The *South Wales Evening Post* gave the Crusaders a two-page special, which complemented the two other paid-for specials that appeared in other papers earlier in February. The *Echo* had included an eight-page pull-out and the regional papers that were owned by Media Wales had four-page specials. The Leeds Rhinos game in August was moved to Newport so it could be marketed to a new audience. By the end of June, pre-ticket sales for this match were already more than 1,000, which looked promising.

Despite all the strategies that were planned by the club's chief executive Mike Turner and marketing guru John Oates, more were needed. The club needed the support of the fans more than ever. So 'Super League Challenge 1000' was launched. This challenged supporters to see if they could put up 1,000 posters in Newport, Cardiff, Bridgend, Pontypridd and Swansea advertising all three games. The games were also advertised online on the official website and also through Facebook – the fans' help was also needed to spread the word and invite their friends to the game through this medium.

Supporters were invited to a meeting so this could be discussed further and a small, but enthusiastic, bunch gathered, willing to help out. This was the second supporters meeting held in 2009. The first, a couple of months earlier, was to allow supporters to discuss concerns with John Dixon, Leighton Samuel and Mike Turner, and most people went home happy, pleased by the honesty of the three men in charge.

July

The club were going to need all the support that the fans could give, especially in the month of July and August 2009 – two of the most turbulent in the history of the club. At the start of the month, a national newspaper ran a story – which they had allegedly held onto for a week – saying that the club was in financial trouble.

Leighton Samuel immediately responded to the claims saying: "When I was approached in 2004 to start up a club that was capable of getting into Super League by 2009, I was 100 per cent committed to that cause. That commitment has never waned and now we're in Super League, there's no way that I and Dekor PLC are going to walk away from it.

"Granted it has been a tough first season but we didn't expect anything less. We knew it would be a learning curve for us both on and off the field and we were ready for all the challenges that we have faced.

"We're now planning in earnest for 2010 and are currently restructuring the club both on and off the field. We have the best and most hands-on chief executive that the club has ever had in Mike

220

Turner and I'm very confident that with him at the helm we have a good future.

"As far as Dekor PLC is concerned, despite a difficult trading period to year end 31 May 2009, the company's UK turnover remained static, but it posted a pre-tax profit of £374,000 compared to a small loss the previous year. That's what I call a result!"

It had been a tough season – that was certain. The attendances hadn't been as big as had been expected and there were a lot of contributing factors to that. Despite an increase in media attention and coverage, it still wasn't enough when compared to other sports and week-on-week it was a struggle to get the club on television, on the radio or even in some newspapers. The local papers always featured the club, but increased coverage was often dependent on whether the writer or sub-editor at the time was rugby league friendly and stories could sometimes end up being on the same page as the racing – if that happens, the sport has been classed as very low importance with the Crusaders being a Super League club, that certainly wasn't right.

In South Wales, there is always going to be competition with other sports and that includes televised sports such as the British and Irish Lions rugby union tour of South Africa with two of the three tests played on the same day as Crusaders home matches. Even though these games kicked off at 2.00pm and the Crusaders at 6.00pm, in Wales the rugby union culture often revolves around two hours of rugby enveloped by approximately six hours or more of socialising. When the Crusaders faced Hull Kingston Rovers in June, the attendance suffered because of this, despite the team beating Wigan the week before. The Lions lost their second test on the day after the Crusaders lost at St Helens, otherwise the attendance for the Warrington home match could have been a complete disaster. As it was, the crowd was around 200 more than Hull KR despite the opposition bringing far fewer fans. Thank you Springboks for that one.

Also, historically the Bridgend public had failed to attend matches in great numbers at the Brewery Field, despite successful sides being played there. In the early part of this decade Leighton Samuel wrote in the Bridgend RFC match programmes commenting on there being such low attendances despite being top of the league. Also, the Celtic Warriors' attendances at the Brewery Field, European Cup aside, were lower or similar to the Crusaders' crowds in 2009. However, the Crusaders draw their crowds from a much larger catchment area.

Obviously the worldwide recession had a lot to do with the state of everyone's finances in 2009. This had affected sponsorship and corporate income in many clubs and associations, not just the Crusaders. The Rugby Football League acknowledged this and they said that they would help the club meet its challenges.

"It was always going to be tough for the Celtic Crusaders in their first year as an engage Super League club and the RFL is lending its expertise to provide the support they need," said RFL director of development Gary Tasker. "When their Super League licence was first approved, the world was a very different place to what it is now and no-one at Celtic Crusaders could have anticipated many of the difficulties they have faced. However, they are in it for the long haul and we are determined to do what we can to help them find additional investors. We are trying to establish a Super League club outside the traditional rugby league heartland, which would have been a tough ask at any time, never mind in the depths of a worldwide recession. We are taking a holistic approach to helping the Crusaders and they are proving very receptive to the work we are doing. This is an ongoing process which is not exclusive to Celtic Crusaders."

Other reports to appear in the media throughout the month involved claims of irregularity in some of the Australian players' visas, departures of top players, and one from the RFL that pointed out that the Brewery Field wouldn't be suitable to get the Crusaders a licence again in 2012.

There was no option, the Crusaders had to find a new ground with Newport, Cardiff and Llanelli being mooted as favourites for a temporary home at least until a new stadium could be built in Bridgend. There was no way that the RFL would give the Crusaders a licence again based on hear-say. Before the month ended, Crusaders' chief executive Mike Turner spoke on Sky Sports' *Boots 'n' All* programme: "We're negotiating with them [Newport Gwent Dragons] at the moment and hopefully within the next 10 days we'll have a contract signed and we'll be moving to Newport," he said. "We're hoping that we will have our own stadium built by 2012 and there are two possible sites in Bridgend for that."

On a purely co-incidental basis, on 11 July, the Newport Gwent Dragons president David Watkins was unveiled as the new president of the Crusaders. This fuelled rumours that the club was definitely going to Newport, but no deal had been agreed by that point. Outgoing president Jonathan Davies had actually announced his intention to quit in December 2008 with Scott Gibbs initially accepting the new role. This was going to be announced in February 2009, but his increased work commitments, that were starting to take him out of the country, meant that he decided not to accept as he felt that the role deserved someone who could be there on a regular basis. Watkins certainly fitted that role. He was approached mid-season and it was decided to delay the announcement until the day that the Crusaders were facing his old club, Salford City Reds at the Brewery Field.

Watkins, the only player in history to have captained both the British and Irish Lions rugby union side and the Great Britain rugby league teams, said: "I'm delighted to be the new president of Celtic Crusaders. I've enjoyed watching them since their inception and I'm now pleased to be officially involved. I really want this to be a huge success. Celtic Crusaders are now a fully professional outfit, they have the right backing, the right press and hopefully soon we will get the right sort of results too."

After all the excitement off the field, the crowds in Wales continued to be entertained on it. The Crusaders beat Salford 25–12 on a day that could have been a PR disaster. 2008 Britain's Got Talent winner George Sampson was due to entertain the crowd before the game with his *Singing in the Rain* dance moves, but ironically had to cancel due to inclement weather. However, he organised a signing and photo session instead to satisfy the fans that had turned up and another thing that could have gone wrong had been saved.

Earlier that day at the Brewery Field, the finals of the Crusaders' first ever season-long Primary Schools rugby league programme were held. A staggering 54 primary schools were involved in 2009, taking part in four sessions which included team building work, rugby league skills and game scenarios with the last session being a competitive festival before a Crusaders Super League match. Ten schools from the programme were chosen for Finals Day with Nant-y-Moel Primary School, situated in the valleys, 10 miles from Bridgend and 15 miles from Pontypridd, eventually taking the "Roddy Cup" trophy that was sponsored by Martin Roddy MBC. The day was a huge success with Anthony Seibold doing a speech to all parents and children at the conclusion, Crusaders' starts Mark Bryant and Jason Chan presenting certificates and awards and John Dixon presenting the trophy.

There was further joy earlier that day in Blackwood when Wales under-18s and Wales Dragonhearts beat their respective Scottish counterparts at Blackwood RFC. As Ireland hadn't entered an under-18 side in that tournament, Wales' 30-6 win gave them that title while the 32-12 win for the Dragonhearts over the Bravehearts all but gave them that championship. Two tries for Matthew Hutchings and one each from Liam Williams, Byron Williams, Grant Epton and Paul Boden meant that all Wales Dragonhearts needed to do was to avoid a 34-point defeat in Ireland on 8 August to be crowned champions for the seventh time in eight years. It was also good to see Tydfil Wildcats make their open-age debut in July while it was announced that five Welsh players, Kris Wilkes, Anthony Symons, Alex Webber, Rhys Fenton and Mark Wool were all to tour Australia with the Great Britain under-18 side, the latter being appointed captain. All bar Wool played in a warm up game against the first ever representative side from Pakistan, winning 46–0 at Odsal in Bradford with Symons grabbing two tries.

August

The Crusaders may have been glad to see the back of July. Two more defeats followed in Super League and another set of injuries meant that, like the St Helens away match in June, just 18 first team players, including Lloyd White, were able to travel to France to face Catalans Dragons on 1 August. The weakened team were unable to compete with the French and a 34–0 defeat was a fair reflection of the game. The injuries continued to mount with Peter Lupton being ruled out for the season with other top players like Marshall Chalk, Lincoln Withers and Luke Dyer all joining him on the injury list during the month.

However, July's problems were to follow the Crusaders into August. A big shock hit the club on Tuesday 18 August when the club received information that six of the star Australian players were to be deported due to irregularities in their visas in previous years, couldn't play again for the Crusaders again and were unable to return to the United Kingdom for 10 years. Their visas for 2009 were fine, it was their applications in previous years that were the problem. The Crusaders were not the only club in this situation. Reports in *League Weekly* and *League Express* said that up to 13 other clubs could have players on incorrect visas from 2006 to 2008 but by 2009, all of those players had left the country.

The Crusaders players involved were Tony Duggan, Jace Van Dijk, Damien Quinn, Darren Mapp, Mark Dalle Cort and Josh Hannay. The Crusaders were cruelly given no time at all to inform these lads of their fate. As soon as an email was sent to the club, the UK Borders Agency also sent a press statement to the BBC and despite the club's best efforts in trying to prevent that organisation from placing the report on their website before the players were fully informed, they did so anyway. John Dixon and Anthony Seibold had started phoning round the six and had hopefully managed to get through to all or most of them at a similar time to BBC Online printing their 'exclusive'.

To say that it hit the players and everyone involved in the club hard is an understatement. Two days later, Anthony Seibold volunteered to make a statement: "The news from the UK Border Agency this week has hit the club like a brick," he said. "Those six players have been terrific servants for the Celtic Crusaders for the past three to four years. Tony Duggan, Jace Van Dijk and Damien Quinn were here from the first training session and were teaching Welsh rugby union players how to play-the-ball, so it's been an emotional few days for us all."

A few of the players spoke out about the situation. "Obviously, we breached some guidelines and it appears we are here illegally, but we did NOT do it knowingly. We are not cheats," Damien Quinn told the *News of the World*. Mark Dalle Cort said to the BBC that "Having to pack up your life in the space of two weeks is hard. It's a big deal and the other boys are devastated as well. It's pretty sad because we've formed some bonds with team-mates but we've had no real opportunity to say goodbye. When I first heard about the investigation I didn't think anything of it as I didn't think we had done anything wrong. Then I got a call on Tuesday and saw the papers. They said: 'As of this date you are no longer able to be employed in this country'."

At any time, news like that is devastating to any club, but in the week before being due to play Leeds Rhinos at their new home for 2010, it brought the Crusaders' situation into a whole new dimension. Out of the 25 squad members originally declared by the club at the start of the season, just 13 were able to turn out against the Rhinos. It gave the club the opportunity to field up-and-coming reserve team players like Lewis Mills, who had made his debut at Wakefield the week before, Gil Dudson, who had already played full international rugby league, and Elliot Kear, who had a sensational debut against the Rhinos with many reporters making him the Crusaders' man-of-the-match for an outstanding performance at full-back.

Anthony Seibold had also spoken about the Leeds game in his press statement. "We need your support more than ever this Saturday," he said. "We know that there will be a number of new fans coming to Rodney Parade, but the team that you will see will not be representative of the side that we have fielded this season, that beat Wigan and Bradford, and nor will it be a representative of what we will field in Super League in 2010. There are some players who are now having the chance from our reserves and academy and we have to make sure that they learn over the next three weeks and try and make it a positive environment for them."

The fans didn't let the players down. In an amazing show of passion, over five and half thousand turned up and cheering on not only the Crusaders players out on the pitch but also the players who were to be sent home with "Justice for the Saders Six" ringing around the ground on many occasions throughout the game as well as after the match when they walked out onto the field. It didn't really matter that the score was 68–0 to Leeds, it was simply an emotional experience for everyone who was there.

John Dixon summed up the day in an interview with BBC Wales: "I must give the crowd a sincere thank you," he said. "They understand the situation. They cheered the players on and didn't boo and jeer. They realised that they were watching an investment in the future. That to me is something very heartwarming for the players and really appreciated by the club.

"We've grown fantastically as a club, maybe too fast. We had wonderful success at National League Two and National League One level. Maybe there was a belief here that we could just come in and be successful again at Super League level in our first year and that's a bit tough. We've found week-in, week-out that the challenges are greater than anticipated but this is year one, a stepping stone, we must learn and grow from this.

"There'll be some changes next year for sure, some forced rather than considered. I think what those young men have done [Duggan, Quinn, Mapp, Van Dijk, Hannay and Dalle Cort] is set down the foundations for the club and there's no doubt that the club will move on. The club will look back and thank them, the sadness of it all as that they won't be around any more. They've done a wonderful job over the last four years and the club is going to thrive because of them."

September

The Crusaders had two games left to complete the season in September. In both of these, the side were up against the odds due to the complete lack of strength in depth. The final home game, against Huddersfield Giants, also doubled up as a farewell to the Brewery Field, so it was a disappointment that the lowest crowd of the season turned out to watch them. Despite a 42–16 defeat, John Dixon praised his team for the way that they stuck in there and never gave up. "For two thirds of the match, there was only one team in it (Huddersfield) but, for the last third, there was only one other team in it (Celtic Crusaders)," he said, which was a fair reflection of the performance.

The final week saw the Crusaders travel up to Castleford for their final match in a long Super League season, but the day before the game, news broke that John Dixon was being released from the club as coach and would return to his native Australia.

Dixon gave a number of farewell interviews that weekend, to the national media, to the BBC, but arguably the best was given to Simon Kendal-Williams in the *South Wales Echo*. "I'm very disappointed, but I hold no grudges and I have nothing against Leighton Samuel," he said in the edition of Monday 14 September. "As a coach, you have to tell young men the bad news that they're not playing this weekend, or that they're being released. I've been doing that for the last 10 years at various clubs. This time, the boot is on the other foot. The chairman has given me the bad news – it's his turn to say, 'thank you very much for your efforts, but we're making a change.' It goes with the territory. This is elite sport; there's no room for personal emotion.

"We've had a really good four years and have a lot to be proud of. We've made massive strides, not just for the Crusaders but for rugby league in Wales as a whole. When I arrived here, I was underwhelmed by how little rugby league there was. But we had a dream, a dream which many people shook their heads at – but look at what we achieved. Our mandate was to be competitive on the pitch, which we were. We were also charged with putting down foundations so the club could grow and that's what we've done.

"I'd like to thank the supporters and everyone at the club. I only had their best wishes from the start, and I leave wishing them best wishes in return."

Against Castleford, the Crusaders players looked like that they were giving their all, for John Dixon, one last time. It was a game that was slightly reminiscent of Wales's performance against Australia in 2000 where for an hour the challengers ran on pure adrenalin but in the end the technically better team secured the victory.

This game completed the Crusaders' grand tour of all the professional rugby league grounds in England. The only teams that they hadn't played against in a league match in their four years were Rochdale and Doncaster, but Challenge Cup and Northern Rail Cup games respectively at their stadiums ensured the set was complete.

The Crusaders took a deserved lead on 11 minutes. Matty Smith laid the ball off to Mark Lennon who played it inside to Lloyd White who ran over for his first ever first team try. Castleford took a 10–4 lead with two tries, but the Crusaders were 16–14 up at half-time thanks to two Lincoln Withers tries, both converted by Steve Tyrer, the first being the club's 500th goal. Crusaders were first on the board in the second half as Crusaders' player-of-the-season Ryan O'Hara scored under the posts with Tyrer easily converted. However that was to be the last time that the Crusaders would score in 2009. Castleford scored three more tries and a drop-goal in the second half to win 35–22, a score that slightly flattered them.

The future

In mid-September 2009, it seemed to be a case of "where do we go from here?" for Welsh Rugby League. But, as discussed throughout this book, the game of rugby league continues to strive at grassroots level. In early August, Wales 'A' secured their seventh Home Nations title in eight years despite losing 28–26 to Ireland. The Dragonhearts were never in front, but tries from Jamie Murphy, Dafydd Hellard, Dave Norman and Liam Williams kept them in the game right until the end. The title was won on points difference from the Irish, and such was the closeness of the 2009 tournament that had England beaten

Scotland by 78 points then they would have been champions. As it happens, they lost 40–24 and picked up the wooden spoon.

Blackwood Bulldogs won the 2009 Welsh Conference Premier Grand Final with a thrilling deserved 38–22 win over Bridgend Blue Bulls. The youngsters continue to develop with successful under-13, -15 and -17 Grand Finals taking place on a magnificent day in Blackwood with new sides Pontyclun Panthers and Penallta Storm taking the under-13 and under-17 titles respectively. Neath Port Talbot Steelers won at under-15 level. Internationally, the Wales under-16 side travelled to the European Championships in Serbia in August but lost to both England and France, while five Welsh players toured Australia with Great Britain under-18s with Mark Wool from Pontyclun captaining the side.

The Crusaders finished their season with three Super League wins and the reserves echoed this exactly, performed admirably and developed some players for the first team. Crusaders under-18s, the 2008–09 Gillette National Youth League champions, started the defence of their title in September 2009 with a 56–4 win over Hemel Stags and will enter the Super League Academy in 2010.

The whole on-field scenario certainly looks good for the far future, but how long will it take for the future to become the present? In an appendix in this book, Anthony Seibold writes and explains that it could take up to six years to develop a strong Welsh international side and a Welsh-dominated Crusaders side. However, players are already starting to break through, with one specific example being Lloyd White. Lloyd's name appears throughout the latter chapters of this book, being mentioned in Conference, Challenge Cup and international reports. He made his Super League debut at St Helens and scored his first Super League try at Castleford. Injuries to other players may have given him his debut, but there's no doubt that he, along with many other Welsh-born players such as Elliot Kear, Gil Dudson, Ashley Bateman and Lewis Mills, who also made Super League debuts in the latter weeks of the 2009 season, will continue to star in both Crusaders and Wales sides in the years to come.

The day before the Celtic Crusaders versus Leeds Rhinos match in August 2009, the Crusaders finally sealed the deal that was to take them to Rodney Parade in Newport for the 2010 and 2011 with the club also promising to retain a strong presence in the Bridgend County Borough through training, youth development and community work.

"Unfortunately the Brewery Field clearly does not meet the requirements set by the RFL for all Super League teams," said chief executive Mike Turner. "Brewery Field was constructed in a different era and for a different sport, amateur rugby union. Super League is a professional sport watched by millions around the world on digital television. Both the RFL and host broadcaster Sky Sports want to ensure that the facilities that host Super League games reflect the right image for one of the world's fastest growing professional sports. Rodney Parade filled the criteria and ticked every box. The people at Rodney Parade have also been very welcoming and helpful to us on all accounts, especially the promotions and community side of things. Next season, we'll play at least 10 games at Rodney Parade with three on the road. We're certain to go to Wrexham and we'll also play a game in Bridgend and central or West Wales.

"Rodney Parade is an excellent facility. We can work with the training ground in front of the stadium to do lots of festivals and get the kids more involved. Car parking is fantastic at Newport, there are multi-story car parks all round the area and they've been used to getting crowds of 5,500 and more, so they can deal with those figures. Given Newport's location, hopefully we'll be able to persuade people to come from over the Severn Bridge as well as in Wales as we're the closest Super League team to a lot of people in the South West. Hopefully we can retain the fans who have supported the club from day one too. We are talking to Veolia Transport to arrange low price transport direct from Bridgend to Newport and back on matchdays.

"We've signed a contract for two seasons at Newport. There will be an option to renew but it all depends on where we are on new stadia in 2012. Our long term aim is to return to Bridgend and play in a purpose built stadium which will be a credit to rugby league in Wales. Given its central location, good transport links and rugby heritage, we believe that Bridgend can develop into a major centre for rugby league in Wales. In recent months, we have held a number of discussions with Green Bank Partnership who were responsible for the construction of the innovative Leigh Sports Village that includes a magnificent new stadium for Leigh Centurions. They have proposed to build a stadium for Super League in an exciting regeneration project on a site already selected by the local council for a new stadium in a letter of support for our Super League application last year.

"We at the Crusaders, along with our professional advisors, believe that the Green Bank scheme offers the only realistic chance of a purpose built stadium for Super League and other sports in the Bridgend area. We also believe that, as at Leigh, the stadium could act as a catalyst for the transformation of a site that has been derelict for years. We are hoping that the new stadium will be constructed in time for the 2013 World Cup as we know that the RFL want to have a group in Wales."

2009 was a difficult year for rugby league in Wales, but the problems are always there and have always been sent to test the code. However, the one consistent factor is that rugby league in Wales refuses to die. Whatever knocks that the game takes, it comes back and grows stronger. The full Welsh international side were due to face England, Serbia, Ireland and one other side at the end of 2009 and those games should produce exciting rugby and perhaps another European Championship win for Wales. *Rugby League World* magazine unveiled their Top Ten Rugby Union Converts in their October issue, and it's no surprise that six of the 10 are from Wales (four from Cardiff). Due to rugby union allowing professionalism in 1995, the days of players of the rugby union calibre of Jonathan Davies (number 10 in the chart) and Billy Boston (number 3) converting to rugby league are now probably long gone.

The Welsh game has had to look to youth to develop a new generation of players to the 13–man code. 2010 will see a new-look Crusaders team at a new ground. It also could see up to 10 sides compete at open age level in the Conference and another few more at junior levels. Rugby league will continue to be played in schools and youth clubs throughout South Wales and even more schools will take it up in 2010 and beyond. The Crusaders and Wales will both continue to operate teams at reserves or 'A', under-18, -16 and -14 levels. Rugby league will continue to grow in universities, both on campus and at international level. Community work will continue to grow throughout South Wales too. Further afield, there are now rugby league teams across the length and breadth of the United Kingdom playing competitive matches at various levels and there is a structure to be proud of. Internationally, at last the sport has a major plan to go forward and a structure of tournaments and fixtures planned until 2013 and beyond. The organisation of this by the RFL, RLEF and

International Federation has never been more solid and it bodes well for the far future of the sport.

"The plan has always been for a Welsh Super League populated by Welshmen," said Anthony Seibold. "This was the charter set in December 2005 at the birth of the club. Against Wakefield in August, we had four born and bred Welsh players playing Super League in a Crusaders jersey - Lloyd White, Ben Flower, Geraint Davies and Lewis Mills, while Aled James had played six games this season before his shoulder reconstruction.

"I feel this is a big step forward. Having a reserve team (under-20/21), an academy team (under-18), foundation cup under-16 team and the home grown squads will only enhance the Welsh presence in our squad going forward. This will not happen overnight and some players will not be ready for the step up as seen in the last few games, but this is all part of the process of long term development. We have not looked at quick fixes by bringing in loan players. That is not our charter. Developing Welsh players to play Super League has been and is the charter."

"It's going to be a rollercoaster ride over the next five or ten years," said Iestyn Harris, whose appointment as coach to the Welsh international team will be an inspiration to young players. "There'll be times that we'll have to dig in and work hard to achieve what we want to get out of it. Long term, we want to be amongst the elite of the international game and competing against the likes of Australia, New Zealand, England and France week in week out throughout every international season. There's a lot to do and Celtic Crusaders are a big addition to us as they're doing really well in bringing the youngsters through and that's essential for the game to prosper."

Wales Rugby League announced that Harris was to take over as head coach of the national side for 2009's international matches following John Dixon's departure from Wales to take over as head coach of Queensland Cup side Redcliffe Dolphins. As a new chapter begins for rugby league in Wales, the administrators looked to the past for his assistant – Clive Griffiths, the man who had led Wales to all those successes from 1991 to 2000.

"I'm very please to be involved in the Wales set-up once again and I'm delighted and honoured to be helping Iestyn in his first coaching role," Griffiths said. "I feel like everything has gone full circle. I was part of the coaching staff who gave Iestyn his debut for Warrington then of course I gave him his debut for Wales and was part of the coaching team when he made his Great Britain debut in 1996 and his Welsh Rugby Union debut in 2001. It's amazing now that after all this time we're still working together but now it's Iestyn who calls the shots. I'm very excited about the future."

A lot of hard work has gone into taking Welsh Rugby League to the position it is in now, but it doesn't stop here. The game will continue to grow, Welsh players will come through and the sport will continue to make in-roads into Welsh society. It's an exciting time and I've been pleased to be involved in one form or another for the last 20 years. Long may it continue.

Appendix 1: Cardiff Demons

This article was written by Simon Davies in the autumn of 2004 for the booklet, *A History of Rugby League in Cardiff* that was published in December of that year. It is reprinted here in full with his permission.

Simon comes from West Kirby in the Wirral and lives in North Somerset on the English side of the Severn Bridge, and can therefore say he has spent much of his life living near the Welsh Border without ever having lived in Wales! A rugby league enthusiast for over 20 years after running an American Football Club as a teenager, Simon has been involved in the administration of Cardiff Demons since the 2002 season. He has previously written for *Open Rugby*, *Rugby League World* and *Rugby League Express* about development of the game in Wales, Liverpool and the South of France.

Cardiff Demons, South West Division Champions 2003, Welsh Shield Winners 2004 and British Shield Winners 2004. A club which in its short history has reached the third round of the Challenge Cup, has appeared on Sky TV, has produced a Super League player and can boast as many season ticket holders as Rochdale Hornets. But despite this apparent success, the Demons' last two seasons have been a roller-coaster ride, illustrating the ups and downs of rugby league development and the special circumstances which apply to the spread of the game in South Wales.

Unlike most of the newer Welsh clubs, the first years of the Demons' development saw slow, but consistent, progress based on five factors which taken together are much more typical of development in England than elsewhere in South Wales. The factors are

1) General rugby league enthusiasts including those who come from traditional areas and those who do not but have a longstanding love of the game.

2) Union players who have no league experience but wish to give league a try.

3) A local development officer funded by the RFL.

4) Current and former students who have played the game at the local university (in this case UWIC).

5) An established junior development programme from which players have graduated to the open age squad.

In many ways, Cardiff had by 2003 become a classic example of rugby league development in the 'English model' as they had all five of these key factors in place, genuine 'enthusiasts' providing an impetus for the club on both the administrational and playing side, a crop of promising players from UWIC who had gone on to succeed at open age level with some such as John Breakingbury and Aled James even succeeding in the professional ranks, a reasonable supply of local union players keen to represent the club and of course, a series of development officers, most recently Stuart Singleton and Wayne Williams, who were willing to be involved in the coaching of the club (despite the fact that this has never been an official paid role of the development officer), and finally, through the excellent efforts of Pete Gooding and his co-workers, a thriving junior set up producing young players who were attracting interest in the rugby league heartlands.

Thus by 2003, Cardiff, firing on all cylinders on the development front, were able to sweep English rivals like the longer established Oxford, Worcester and Gloucester aside for the second successive season, and inflict three heavy defeats on new arrivals Bristol Sonics, such that a new challenge was clearly required.

The new challenge of course, was to come from Welsh Conference which had begun in 2003 with six clubs. The first season was dominated by Bridgend who went unbeaten in Wales and pressed on to achieve a perfect season by winning their five play-off games, lifting the British Conference title in their debut season, Aberavon who finished second and Torfaen, who came from nowhere to finish third and reach the British Shield final, underlined the impression that the top clubs in the Welsh Conference, despite being in their first season, were a match for anyone.

Cardiff went into the 2003 play-offs with the confidence of achieving the South West Division Championship, a perfect regular season being spoilt only by a last day defeat at Somerset when the title was already safe. But successive defeats to Bridgend, 36-16, and Aberavon, 45-21, provided a rude awakening for the Demons. The confidence was gone, as the reality dawned that the top Welsh Conference sides were clearly operating at a higher standard than the Demons and the 'comfort zone' of the South West Division, in which only Somerset and Gloucestershire had provided any real test, had been a poor preparation for the playoffs.

Worse was to come in the opening weeks of 2004, following the much anticipated move to Taffs Well. After a memorable comeback resulting in a last second win over National League 3 outfit Coventry in a friendly, hopes were high especially among the enthusiastic new support based consisting of villagers and club members who were only too happy to share their excellent new ground with a successful rugby league club.

But the season proper opened with defeats to Torfaen, Bridgend and Aberavon. At least each game was close and well contested, victory in Aberavon game being denied only by a late penalty condemning the Demons to a 27–28 heartbreaker. But all optimism was finally removed by a crushing 52–10 defeat at the hands of newcomers Newport in week four. The game had started well with the Demons having three clear chances to score but taking only one for a 6–0 lead after 20 minutes. But an unfortunate clash of heads deprived Cardiff of their talismanic stand-off Gareth Jones, and as morale slipped on the rock hard Pill Harriers pitch, Newport came from behind to run in an avalanche of points.

Key members of the Demons club met in Cardiff Bay later that week to take stock of the situation. While matters were healthy off the pitch, with crowds at Taffs Well encouraging, especially for the Aberavon game, which had been played the night before the Wigan versus St Helens Challenge Cup Final, and attracted a crowd of around 300, there was a feeling that on the pitch the club was in decline. Why were the Demons failing to compete in the Welsh Conference when they had graduated to be a real force in the South West Division? The statistics spoke for themselves, in the past two seasons the Demons had played 10 RLC games against English clubs, and won nine, but against Welsh opposition they were yet to register a victory in six attempts.

On the one hand there were factors in the Demons' on-field problems which could be explained from within the club. The proliferation of new teams in South Wales had meant that several players who had originally been committed to the Demons as the only open age rugby league club in the region were now faced with the option of representing a more local club. The likeable Scott Hirene for example, who had played for Cardiff in 2002 was one of the founders of the Newport club who made a big impression in the 2004 Welsh Conference in their debut season. Rob Dodgson, an ever present in the Demons' line up in 2003 became disgruntled early in 2004 and opted to join Newport, his local club. Another significant, albeit temporary, loss was the loan for a season of Pete Gooding to Swansea Valley with a view to setting up their junior programme.

But the more intriguing question was as to how relatively new clubs like Aberavon, Bridgend, Torfaen and the debutants Newport had been able to overtake Cardiff on the field, despite the Demons having applied the 'English model' more successfully than any English club within 100 miles of the Severn Bridge. Clearly, there must be factors at play in South Wales, which have enabled a whole clutch of new clubs to reach a high standard quickly.

The answer it seems lies with the willingness of many people in the smaller towns of the region, most obviously Port Talbot (Aberavon), Bridgend, and Pontypool (Torfaen), to see rugby union and rugby league as two complementary activities which can be pursued by any community with the purposes of promoting sporting excellence, making bar money and furthering social activities in the localities they represent. For this reason the development of rugby league in Port Talbot, Bridgend, Torfaen and to some extent Newport has been achieved at a faster pace than almost anywhere else in Britain, as communities built around sports clubs have opened their eyes to the many advantages that summer rugby league can bring.

Thus through people like Chris O'Callaghan at Aberavon, Kevin Wheeler at Torfaen and the former professionals in Bridgend; Ellis, Devereux and Bateman, rugby league clubs have benefited from the support of whole sections of the community and the new clubs have been able to draw on a wide selection of potential players from a wide range of sporting backgrounds. Some such as the excellent Mark Burke at Aberavon have tried league and come to the conclusion it may be the best game for their talents, and at the time of writing this promising young forward from Port Talbot has a number of trials lined up at Super League clubs, including Union Treiziste Catalan.

The Demons, by contrast, have developed very much as a rugby league club and have drawn praise from many for their mastery of league skills. But competing against teams who can draw on players who regularly turn out for high ranking union clubs in the winter will never be easy when the Cardiff club has drawn most of its players from UWIC and lower division union outfits like Old Penarthians.

Thus one outcome of the Demons' crisis meeting in week 4 of the 2004 regular season was to aim to close the gap on the Welsh Conference sides by fostering closer links with higher ranking local union clubs. But herein lies a problem, unlike the smaller towns, where union club officials may be supportive of league for the good of club and community, Cardiff RFC, perhaps the most old fashioned and pro-establishment of all Welsh union clubs, would have no interest in promoting league.

As a capital city Cardiff is a much more diverse society both in social and sporting terms, and there is none of the cohesion and togetherness that can be found in places like Port Talbot or Pontypool which might prompt important figures in the community to get behind a league club. Perhaps for these reason, until the inception of the Demons, rugby league clubs based in the Welsh capital have never been blessed with much success in 90 years of trying, leading many to suggest that the real 'heartland' of Welsh rugby league lies along the coast in the Bridgend/Port Talbot corridor. By contrast Taffs Well supplies exactly this kind of support and community cohesion, but Taffs Well is only a small village with a union club at Division 3 level. Thus the most obvious immediate answer would be to look to form a collaboration with the nearest Welsh premier club, Caerphilly, a mere three miles up the hill from Taffs Well. But even this possibility has its pitfalls, in that trips to distribute flyers at Virginia Park have often met with the response from some that the citizens of Caerphilly are extremely unlikely to support a team called 'Cardiff' however close to Caerphilly they may play.

As a long-term strategy, collaboration with a club like Caerphilly and perhaps eventually Cardiff RFC would do much to boost the Demons' chances in the Welsh Conference. As the season progressed the club were pleased to be joined on the administrative side by Caerphilly's John Haigh, an excellent web designer and Ian Lovell, a professional photographer and for the juniors to be bolstered by young players from the Caerphilly area.

Another outcome of the crisis meeting was to underline the need for club spirit both on and off the field. With disaffected players having left the club and familiar faces returning, week five proved a time of renaissance with a healthy home win over Swansea, inspired by another Caerphilly man Lee Mullane, followed by a fine win at Pontypridd over near neighbours the Valley Cougars, leaving the Demons with the more respectable record of two wins from six from the first half of the regular season.

However, the return fixtures were again to prove that much work needed to be done, with narrow losses at Torfaen and Aberavon interspersed by heavy home defeats to Bridgend and again to Newport. The trip to Swansea Valley's ground, some 12 miles outside the city itself in the village of Ystalyfera, provided a second low point of the season as inspired by on-loan Demon Pete Gooding, the Miners came from behind to register an unlikely victory and leave the Demons looking down the barrel of a last place finish if they were unable to defeat the Valley Cougars in the regular season finale.

But after a solid, workmanlike performance at Taffs Well one week later in which the Cougars were dismissed and fifth place secured, the Demons never looked back. In the Shield play-offs, the home tie they had earned against Swansea presented no problems and they went on to a season-defining Welsh Shield Final against the Newport Titans. Having now lost all 10 of their encounters with the top four clubs in South Wales, the Demons could have been forgiven for approaching this game with trepidation, but two straight wins and a settled squad had restored self belief. The final itself was a classic with Cardiff finally defeating the Titans by 38-35 thanks to Gareth Jones's last minute try. The Demons had at last proved themselves on the field in Wales with a victory over a top four club when the chips were really down, and in winning the Welsh Shield had secured their first piece of silverware in a Welsh competition.

As though to underline the high standard of the Welsh Conference, the Demons met little resistance in the British Shield until they reached the final. Telford Raiders and St Albans Centurions were dismissed in the quarter- and semi-finals respectively, leaving an intriguing clash with South Yorkshire's Thorne Moor Marauders - a new English club built more on the South Wales model of development that the typical English one in which a whole community whether footballers, rugby league or rugby union players had been brought together to get behind a team for the benefit of all. Whereas earlier in the season the Demons might have folded up when the Marauders mounted an extraordinary comeback from 26–0 down to 27–20, by now morale was sky-high and marshalled by Pete Moore, Mark Bow and Graham Hughes Cardiff hung on for their first national trophy.

And so, by sheer hard work, team spirit and excellent rugby league coaching, the Demons' first season in the Welsh Conference was an on-field success after all. And the awards continued as Pete Moore made the conference dream team in the same week as he signed for Sheffield Eagles and the club carried off the prestigious Conference Media & PR award in recognition of the work done promoting both the Demons and the wider game in South Wales and beyond over the previous year.

Perhaps most importantly, the club has come through the potential traumas of adjusting to life in the harsher environment of the Welsh Conference with heads held high. Morale is such that players are committed to future seasons and the likelihood of the 'player drain' that was a feature of the opening weeks has much receded. Clubmen of the year, Andrew Jones and Neil Thomas come from Swansea to represent the club and their infectious enthusiasm carried many through the more difficult moments. Kyle Blake and Pat Howell graduated from the junior Demons set up to play a full role in the five game unbeaten run culminating in the British Shield final, and in them and those who have come through UWIC like Gareth Jones and Idris Evans the club can be confident of a supply of true Rugby League players for the future.

So we are left with the intriguing question as to whether the Demons, with their true rugby league skill-base underpinned by coaching from development officer Wayne Williams and others who have taken up the coaching mantle such as Anthony Loxton, their recognised excellence in administration, their flourishing junior set-up, which will be bolstered in 2005 through the return of Gooding, and their productive links with UWIC, will be able to compete with the 'town/community' rugby clubs in Bridgend, Aberavon and Torfaen.

Perhaps in the short-term, the key will be in retaining all of these factors and developing them, for instance by widening the pool of recognised coaches, attracting a broader group of administrators, continuing the great work that has been done in junior rugby league and fostering the links with UWIC. Additionally sponsors such as Walkabout, who put a four-figure sum into the club in 2004 must be retained. But the one missing component, the ability to attract or gain access to top grade athletes who currently play union in the winter, whether achieved through collaboration with Caerphilly, Bedwas or even Cardiff RFC, must remain an important goal if the club are to prosper on the field and challenge the top three in the Welsh Conference.

And what are the wider lessons for rugby league development? Clearly the 'South Wales model' of 'town/community' rugby clubs like Aberavon could

238

accelerate the standard of rugby league development across Britain if it could be replicated elsewhere. The experiences in Aberavon, Bridgend and Torfaen should be documented carefully, published and disseminated to allow sports clubs elsewhere in the UK to consider whether running a summer rugby league club could benefit both the host club and the wider community. The extra revenue generated through spectators and bar takings, extra skills accrued by players who may then apply them in their original sport or choose to further their career in rugby league, and community cohesion all provide persuasive arguments for introducing summer rugby league.

The 'South Wales model' could be applied to smaller communities in the south west of England. In this region, the existing clubs are city based and despite much hard work their application of the 'English model' of development clearly lags behind the Demons and the majority of Welsh Conference clubs. Yet the counties of Somerset, Gloucestershire, Devon and Cornwall contain many smaller towns renowned for their prowess in football or rugby union.

The knock-on effects of seeking out individuals who, like O'Callaghan and Wheeler, would see a value in promoting sport in these communities through summer rugby league could be very productive, providing both a better level of competition for the existing South West teams and a more balanced natural rivalry with the South Wales clubs over the bridge. Since both South Wales and South West England are equally remote from the rugby league heartlands of Lancashire and Yorkshire, a long term aim of the RLC must be to have a 'Wales and West Premier' league to create a thriving cross border competition between the best clubs in each region whist keeping travelling time still reasonably low, which cannot be said for an all-Wales Conference which would eventually have to incorporate teams from the north like Wrexham and Colwyn Bay.

However, much work is required to bring the south west teams up to Welsh standards and only the Gloucestershire Warriors would be worthy of inclusion at this time. But to those who say that 'Wales is Wales' and the Welsh conference clubs should be left to compete only with each other, this final point should be considered; if the delegates from Lancashire and Yorkshire who met at the George Hotel in 1895 had had the same view, that their two regions were separate and trans-Pennine leagues not practical, rugby league development may have been stopped in its tracks and 109 years later we would have been looking back at a short-lived rebellion rather than the birth of a top quality sport played to a high standard on both sides of the world.

In summary, the Demons have come through a difficult time in their development with credit, and emerged from a season which threatened to yield nothing with two trophies, a prestigious award and a real head of steam in terms of self belief and support. With so many new developments both within the club and in Welsh rugby league, the coming seasons promise to be filled with much interest for anyone who has the development of the game at heart.

Appendix 2: Development in Wales

This article was written as a blog entry on the Celtic Crusaders website on 17 January 2009 by Celtic Crusaders' head of performance manager Anthony Seibold. It is an interesting insight on the development of rugby league in Wales and was reprinted in many guises throughout the national and international press. It is reprinted here with small edits with his permission.

Many supporters and onlookers from in and around the Crusaders and South Wales and also in the wider rugby league community in the north of England offer many and varied opinions on the Welsh presence within our squad and what the club should and should not be doing with regards to having more Welsh players playing at Super League level and within our squad. Some are ill-informed and many not so practical in producing a competitive rugby league team or player capable of playing at the highest level. I am going to be a little controversial and offer some thoughts and opinions and try to spell out our charter for producing more Welsh players who are up to the standard and capable of competing in Super League.

That last statement is the key statement, players of **Super League standard**. What does it take to produce a Super League player who is capable of competing and succeeding against the best Super League has to offer at clubs like Leeds, St Helens, Bradford, Wigan, Warrington, Hull FC etc? A player may be able to lift himself for a one-off game as seen in some Challenge Cup performances or one-off friendlies as we have seen over time, but what does it take to then for that player to be able to compete and play well against Leeds the next week, then Wigan the week after that then Hull KR the week after that then Huddersfield the week after that and so on and so on for 27 games?

Let me take you back a little and give you a historical lesson on Celtic Crusaders from a recruitment perspective. In three years, the Crusaders have used 57 Welsh born players in the first team in National Leagues One and Two. That is 57 players who would not have had the opportunity to taste professional rugby league unless they migrated to the north of England. Of those players, how many have shown that they could compete at the level required for what is effectively the second and third tiers of the professional game in the UK and be regulars in the starting 17?

We have also had a Colts squad who played in the National Conference last season and, with the exception of Philippe Gardent, was full of young Welsh lads playing the game at a level that was sound, but well below National League Two and the professional arm of the game. So how many of these players could come on and play Super League? There were some signs for the future with some individual performances from players such as Lloyd White, Gil Dudson, Geraint Davies and Mark Wool that suggested that in the right environment they may be able to compete at the higher levels. But what a jump for a young man from what is effectively the fifth tier of the game in the UK (although BARLA would argue that their elite level amateur competition is far stronger then the Conference National and from my observations when living in Hull is that would be the correct assumption). That is in no way to disregard what the young guys did last year as they were playing men in what is a very competitive League and they did a tremendous job under coach Dan

Clements. So when people suggest it is simply a matter of adding a player from the Colts team to the Super League squad it is not that simple as the player's welfare and development must be taken into account.

The idea behind putting our colts in the Conference National last year was to give them some experience of playing rugby league week-in week-out in a environment we knew that was not beyond them (we look like we got that decision correct as we had great tussles all year with Bramley Buffaloes and our first victory against them game in the Grand Final) over a season and to get some playing history behind them. For many it was year one in their rugby league education. How do we create young players to play Super League?

In 2006 in taking on the role of head coach at the Celtic Crusaders, John decided that he needed to recruit some players and staff that he had worked with previously in Australia in order to assist him in developing the Welsh players and in making the side more competitive at National League 2 level initially and to see what he had at his disposal here in Wales.

History shows that Jace Van Dijk, Damien Quinn and Tony Duggan have been here from the start and no one could argue against their contribution to the Crusaders and rugby league in Wales in general. Jace Van Dijk won the National League Two Player of the Year in 2006, Tony Duggan won the same award in 2007 and Damien Quinn won the National League One award in 2008. Along the way the Crusaders have achieved promotion from National League Two, made the Grand Final of National League One and received a Super League licence. Is this luck or did John get his recruitment correct in developing a competitive outfit initially before concentrating on development?

In 2009 their faith, perseverance, determination and hard work pays off with them getting an opportunity to play at the highest level of the game here in the UK. Before coming to the UK they had a combined total of one NRL game between them (Tony debuted for the Brisbane Broncos in 2004 versus Canterbury) and there was some criticism within the rugby league fraternity in the north of bringing in players who had not played at the highest level in the NRL and putting them in front of British players. The success of Jace, Damien and Tony has been something you could write a book about.

What this shows is that they have come through the right development structures in Australia, gained experience along the way at each level they played (NRL, first team squads, Queensland Cup, NSW Premier League, NL2 and NL1) and they are more rounded players and I would argue better players now then when they arrived in 2006 as they have come through and developed at the right pace and are ready for Super League and to compete week in week out against the best. Rugby league is a late specialisation sport, and for all those who think that you can't make it if you have not played at NRL level or Super League level before you are 20 are thinking with their fiscal head on rather then their development head. I will take great pride and satisfaction in watching these three guys make their debuts in Super League in 2009. They deserve every success that comes their way.

Back to producing Welsh players capable of competing at Super League level. When John and I arrived, we looked to the Welsh rugby union Premiership and the Welsh rugby league Conference for players who may be able to compete at National League Two (the third tier of professional rugby league). This did not really eventuate in producing the right standard of

241

player. The Premiership union competition prior to the introduction of the regions had a proud history and showed it was capable of producing international rugby union players and also some players who were able to cross codes successfully at clubs such as Salford, Widnes and Warrington. The standard of competition from speaking to those with more knowledge then me of the Welsh game have said the standard of rugby at that level has dropped alarmingly in recent times.

In 2006 we recruited players spread far and wide throughout the Welsh Premiership including players from Neath, Aberavon, Bridgend, Maesteg, Pontypool etc. Famous clubs in Wales with proud histories. How many of these showed they were capable of playing at National League Two?

Hywel Davis, Richard Johnson and Grant Epton were regulars in our 17 over the first two years of National League Two and gave a great contribution to the Crusaders and guys like Lee Jones and Dean Fitzgerald were good squad players who also made a contribution towards our success in the first two seasons. The large majority of players we recruited from the Premiership could not handle the intensity, speed and skill level of the National League Two and this showed that the introduction of regional rugby had left behind the game at Premiership level in Wales. Some players could simply not handle the professionalism required at the third tier of the game. How could they handle Super League? How do we produce Welsh players for Super league? The Welsh Premiership and the Welsh Conference was not the answer.

So do we go to the regions? Perhaps? There will always be players who are more suited to rugby league then rugby union and also the other way round due to body shapes etc. Therefore we will always have one eye on players who we think fit the mould and could successfully make the transition from union to league. Ben Flower, for instance, who we recruited from the Dragons, is far more suited to league (because of his height and lineout throwing ability) due to his running game and aggression and he will be a Super League player in 2009. He played at international level at every age group for the WRU but his future is in league. The other problem we have when looking to the regions for possible recruits is a logistical one. They finish their season in May, we start ours in February. How do we contract a player who will miss half the season? Tough isn't it? Not as simple as some suggest in going out and buying union players.

What about international players? What incentive do they have to leave union at present when they are part of the international set up? In my opinion, there are some suitable players from the Welsh international squad who would make great rugby league players because of body shape and their abilities which could transfer. If I had a wish list, the four guys who would be at the top of it when looking at Welsh international rugby union are Lee Byrne, Andy Powell, Mike Phillips and Gavin Hanson, who from my observations would succeed at both games because they could transfer their skills, running games and defensive abilities between either code. But why would they come to the Crusaders at present? All are integral members of the Welsh rugby union squad and they don't need to take the risk to test themselves in rugby league.

And it is a risk as they would not be guaranteed to be successful at Super League level against teams such as Leeds and St Helens. What a challenge it would be though for them to play another sport at the highest level. Maybe that would be a challenge they would like to take before they retire (Byrney you know my number)? Who knows? That is not the answer to producing Welsh players capable at competing at Super league level. What is?

The Welsh presence at Super League level will be a gradual one and one that increases over time, not overnight as we set about producing more players capable at playing the elite level of the game. I said that right - Welsh presence. We are a Welsh club who want to produce more Welsh players. Our charter is not to produce more English players for the RFL or players for the Great Britain team that no longer exists, but Welsh players. In all our recruitment from day one we could have gone to the north of England more and more rather then for Australians we have brought in like Jace, Tony and Damien. But what is the point of going to the north of England?

If as a coaching staff we don't know what their development structures and rugby league education is like? That would have been more of a risk in putting together a competitive team at the lower professional levels. That does not produce more players who are Welsh.

We will always look for quality out of the north like Budworth, Blackwood, Lupton, Smith, Tyrer, James etc, but we wanted to recruit players who we know had been developed the right way and through systems we thought could add something to the development of our young players here in Wales. That meant recruiting Australian players that both John and I had worked with, played or coached with or against or know have come through the right development systems in the NRL. Their charter is to make us more competitive in the short to medium term. The longer term it is about producing Welsh players who are capable of competing at Super League. Therefore recruiting players like Lincoln Withers, Mark Bryant, Adam Peek, Marshall Chalk and Ryan O'Hara and keeping guys like Jace Van Dijk, Tony Duggan and Damien Quinn is so instrumental in making the Crusaders competitive at Super League level initially and for their experience and professionalism to rub off on the young Welsh players. But where are these Welsh players?

The Welsh players are here! They are four to seven years away from being Super League players not four to seven months as some would like to think, players who can compete each week against the best Super League has to offer. It is not easy. One good game against the Bramley Buffaloes does not mean that we have a player who can play week in week out against the best of Super League. The Crusaders' future are the kids between 12 and 16 who are in our four regional home grown development squads based in and around Newport and Cardiff, Bridgend, Swansea and Aberavon and RTC and Merthyr. We are a Welsh club. They are the kids who are not in those squads yet, but are out there waiting for our head of youth performance Andy Lindley, with assistance from Dan Clements in his role of development officer and the other home grown squad coaches, to identify. They are the 24 elite kids who will be part of our elite home grown squad (Scholarship programme) based at the Brewery Field this coming summer. They were the 90 kids from all around Wales who trialled for the Crusaders foundation under-16 team on Saturday at St Joseph's School at Newport. They are the kids playing in 114 schools teams as part of the WRL/RFL led Schools Challenge Cup here in Wales.

For the long term sustainability of the Celtic Crusaders in Wales we have to put time and resources into these kids to enable them to gain the training history, playing experiences in the correct professional (don't think money think best practice) environment in order to develop into players who can compete at Super League level. They all wont make it and it is just a pipe dream if we think this is just going to happen and we will have 17 Welsh born and bred players running out the tunnel of our brand new stadium in 2012 with 15,000 screaming fans watching the team as it sits on top of the Super League competition! It would be great, but not realistic at present.

Look at teams like Wigan, Hull KR and Bradford. They have had over 100 years to develop home grown players and I would not know the last time Wigan ran out with 17 players all born and bred in Wigan. That is not a criticism of the famous club, just a fact and Wigan understand they need players from other areas of the UK and also overseas to compete each week in Super League and be successful long term. That is a silly argument from many who are misinformed that each side will have only those born and raised in their city or town (country in the Crusaders and Catalans case) playing for their club at professional level. As I said a nice dream, but not realistic at a professional sports level. When Wakefield played Castleford in the game to decide who was relegated in 2006 14 of the 17 Wildcats were antipodeans (Kiwis and Australians). Hull KR are one of the most proud and historical clubs in the UK game yet they still had 10 antipodeans in their squad last year and this from the most rugby league cultured city that I have seen in the UK.

If we can have one or two graduates a year from our scholarship program that go on to play Super League level then it will have been a remarkable success, almost unparalleled. Between one and three percent of all kids recruited as part of development squads or scholarship schemes in professional rugby league, go on to play one NRL or Super League game let alone enjoy a career at Super League level. (What constitutes a career? One season, 50 games, 100 games? Careers will become shorter and shorter as the intensity of the game increases but that is for another blog).

It is a small window isn't it? That is not much of a conversion rate for the amount of time and money invested, but it is a necessary investment. There will always be exceptions to the rule, but that is what current research suggests. Leeds Rhinos are a shining example for all to see with the success they have at bringing through players from within their systems. We have a challenge at the Crusaders and it is a medium to long term challenge in producing the right players from within Wales to co-exist with the right players we identify from elsewhere to make a competitive team. But what an exciting challenge! It is one that the Crusaders are up for and a challenge that we have to up for, in order for the club to be sustainable.

We will always need players from the NRL and other Super League clubs to supplement our Welsh players in order to gain success and improve results at first team level and for us to compete as a club year upon year – fact! That is going to happen whether people like it or not, those who think otherwise have never worked in a professional sporting environment.

So to answer my question where are we going to find Welsh players capable of competing at Super League level? Well we have found them and they are there here in Wales. We know they are here and we know how old they are, we just have to uncover them. Over to you boys.

244

Appendix 3: Statistics and Records

Wales international team

Results 1991 to 2008

Date	Opponent	Type	Venue	Result	Score
27/10/1991	Papua New Guinea	T	Swansea	W	68–0
22/03/1992	France	F	Swansea	W	35–6
27/11/1992	England	F	Swansea	L	11–36
13/12/1992	France	F	Perpignan	W	19–18
03/11/1993	New Zealand	T	Swansea	L	19–24
04/03/1994	France	F	Cardiff	W	13–12
30/10/1994	Australia	T	Cardiff	L	4–46
01/02/1995	England	EC	Cardiff	W	18–16
05/03/1995	France	EC	Carcassonne	W	22–10
11/06/1995	USA	F	Philadelphia	W	66–10
18/06/1995	USA	F	Philadelphia	W	92–4
09/10/1995	France	WC	Cardiff	W	28–6
15/10/1995	Western Samoa	WC	Swansea	W	22–10
21/10/1995	England	WC	Manchester	L	10–25
05/06/1996	France	EC	Carcassonne	W	34–14
26/06/1996	England	EC	Cardiff	L	12–26
19/07/1998	England	F	Widnes	L	12–15
15/10/1999	Ireland	TT	Swansea	L	17–24
22/10/1999	Scotland	TT	Glasgow	L	16–36
19/10/2000	South Africa	F	Johannesburg	W	40–8
29/10/2000	Cook Islands	WC	Wrexham	W	38–6
02/11/2000	Lebanon	WC	Llanelli	W	24–22
05/11/2000	New Zealand	WC	Cardiff	L	18–54
12/11/2000	Papua New Guinea	WC	Widnes	W	22–8
19/11/2000	Australia	WC	Huddersfield	L	22–46
31/07/2001	England	F	Wrexham	L	33–42
03/11/2002	New Zealand	T	Cardiff	L	22–50
26/10/2003	Russia	EC	Aberavon	W	74–4
02/11/2003	Australia	T	Bridgend	L	4–74
09/11/2003	England	EC	Leeds	L	4–22
17/11/2004	Ireland	EC	Aberavon	L	12–25
24/11/2004	Scotland	EC	Glasgow	L	22–30
16/11/2005	Scotland	EC	Bridgend	W	22–14
29/11/2005	Ireland	EC	Dublin	W	31–10
05/11/2005	France	EC	Carcassonne	L	16–38
29/10/2006	Scotland	WCQ	Bridgend	L	14–21
28/10/2007	Papua New Guinea	T	Bridgend	W	50–10
04/11/2007	Scotland	WCQ	Glasgow	W	18–16
09/11/2007	Lebanon	WCQ	Widnes	L	26–50
10/10/2008	England	F	Doncaster	L	0–74

Key:

WC	World Cup
WCQ	World Cup qualifier
EC	European Championship
TT	Triangular Tournament
T	Tour match
F	Friendly international

Welsh players 1991 to 2008

	Apps	Tries	Goals	Drop-goals	Points
Ian Watson	22	5	1	0	22
Iestyn Harris	20	12	58	1	165
Anthony Sullivan	20	6	0	0	24
Lee Briers	18	9	20	5	81
Damien Gibson	18	8	0	0	32
Paul Atcheson	18	5	0	0	20
Rowland Phillips	17	4	0	0	16
Chris Morley	17	2	0	0	8
Paul Moriarty	16	0	0	0	0
Kevin Ellis	15	5	0	1	21
Dai Young	15	0	0	0	0
Allan Bateman	14	6	0	0	24
Adam Hughes	13	9	3	0	42
Mark Lennon	13	4	13	0	42
Keiron Cunningham	13	7	0	0	28
Jordan James	13	3	0	0	12
John Devereux	12	3	1	0	14
Adrian Hadley	11	5	8	0	36
Kris Tassell	11	6	0	0	24
Mark Jones	11	4	0	0	16
Gareth Price	11	1	0	0	4
Gareth Dean	11	0	0	0	0
Phil Ford	10	4	0	0	16
Jason Critchley	10	2	0	0	8
Martin Hall	10	0	0	0	0
Jonathan Davies	9	3	39	5	95
Mark Perrett	9	0	0	0	0
Paul Highton	9	0	0	0	0
Justin Morgan	9	0	0	0	0
Wes Davies	8	3	0	0	12
Gerald Cordle	8	2	0	0	8
Hefin O'Hare	8	2	0	0	8
Robert Roberts	8	2	0	0	8
Ian Marlow	8	1	0	0	4
Anthony Farrell	8	1	0	0	4
Aled James	8	1	0	0	4
Ritchie Eyres	8	0	0	0	0
David Mills	8	0	0	0	0
Jason Lee	7	4	0	0	16
Anthony Blackwood	7	3	0	0	12
Neil Cowie	7	1	0	0	4
Phil Joseph	7	1	0	0	4
Bryn Powell	6	3	0	0	12
Jonathan Griffiths	6	2	0	1	9
Dean Busby	6	1	0	0	4
Dave Whittle	6	0	0	0	0
Lenny Woodard	5	3	0	0	12
Mick Jenkins	5	3	0	0	12
Rob Ackerman	5	2	0	0	8
Steve Thomas	5	2	0	0	8
Paul Sterling	5	2	0	0	8
Chris Smith	5	1	0	0	4

Kelvin Skerrett	5	0	0	0	0
Barry Eaton	5	0	0	0	0
Gareth Davies	4	5	0	0	20
Scott Quinnell	4	3	0	0	12
Martin Pearson	4	2	2	0	12
Richard Webster	4	2	0	0	8
Richard Johnson	4	2	0	0	8
Dave Halley	4	2	0	0	8
Gary Pearce	4	0	3	1	7
Barry Williams	4	1	0	0	4
David Bishop	4	1	0	0	4
Sean Penkywicz	4	1	0	0	4
Craig Kopzcak	4	0	0	0	0
Gareth Stephens	4	0	0	0	0
Byron Smith	4	0	0	0	0
Daio Powell	3	2	0	0	8
Luke Dyer	3	1	0	0	4
Matt James	3	1	0	0	4
Andy Bracek	3	1	0	0	4
Ian Stevens	3	0	0	0	0
Paul Williams	3	0	0	0	0
Peter Kennett	3	0	0	0	0
Scott Gibbs	3	0	0	0	0
Karle Hammond	3	0	0	0	0
David Luckwell	3	0	0	0	0
Gareth Carvell	3	0	0	0	0
Neil Davies	3	0	0	0	0
Ian Webster	3	0	0	0	0
David Williams	2	1	0	0	4
Gavin Price-Jones	2	1	0	0	4
Mark Sheals	2	1	0	0	4

2 appearances, no points scored: Mark Moran, Mark Lee, Craig Makin, Keith Mason, Jon Aston, Damien Hudd, Dave Clarke, Barry Pugh, Nathan Strong, Paul Morgan, Phil Cushion.
1 appearance, no points scored: Matthew Silva, Diccon Edwards, Steffan Hughes, Tom Brown, Lewis Taylor, Karl Hocking, Jon Breakingbury, Gary Hulse, Aaron Summers, Mark Roberts, Lee Williams, Rhys Williams, Ben Flower, Geraint Davies, Rhys Griffiths, Matt Barron, Gil Dudson.

Top try scorers: Iestyn Harris 12, Damien Gibson 8, Keiron Cunningham 7
Top goal scorers: Iestyn Harris 58, Jonathan Davies 39, Lee Briers 20
Top points scorers: Iestyn Harris 165, Jonathan Davies 95, Lee Briers 81

N.B. In the above table, appearances includes players who started the match and came on as a substitute.

Super League Nines – played at Suva, Fiji on 22 and 24 February 1996
Day 1: Wales 10 Cook Islands 8, Papua New Guinea 14 Wales 12, Wales 8 Fiji 6.
Day 2: Wales 16 Tonga 6, Wales 12 Western Samoa 8 (Trophy Final).
Squad: Iestyn Harris, Mark Jones (both Warrington), Paul Atcheson, Neil Cowie, Scott Quinnell (all Wigan), Allan Bateman (Cronulla), Jason Critchley, Gareth Cochrane (both Keighley), Gareth Stephens (Castleford), Gavin Price-Jones (Swinton), Ian Watson (Salford), Mark Perrett (Halifax), Rowland Phillips (Workington), John Donno (Widnes).

Wales 'A' (Dragonhearts) in the Home Nations tournament

2002

Wales	3	3	0	0	120	60	6
England	3	2	0	1	108	46	4
Ireland	3	1	0	2	100	94	2
Scotland	3	0	0	3	40	168	0

15 June	Scotland 22 Wales 40	Glasgow Hawks RUFC
16 June	Ireland 10 England 32	Waterford City RUFC
20 July	Scotland 8 England 58	Glasgow Hawks RUFC
21 July	Wales 52 Ireland 20	Old Penarthians RUFC, Cardiff
18 August	Ireland 70 Scotland 10	Malone RUFC, Belfast
15 September	England 18 Wales 28	Prince of Wales Stadium, Cheltenham

2003

Wales	3	2	0	1	104	72	4
England	3	2	0	1	80	62	4
Scotland	3	1	0	2	90	96	2
Ireland	3	1	0	2	66	110	2

21 June	England 28 Scotland 20	Haworth RLFC, York
28 June	Ireland 32 Wales 28	Clontarf RUFC, Dublin
27 July	Wales 48 Scotland 22	Brewery Field, Bridgend RUFC
27 July	England 34 Ireland 14	Prince of Wales Stadium, Cheltenham
9 August	Scotland 48 Ireland 20	Queens Park, Glasgow
14 September	Wales 28 England 18	Aberavon RUFC

2004

Wales	3	3	0	0	124	70	6
Scotland	3	1	0	2	76	78	2
England	3	1	0	2	63	88	2
Ireland	3	1	0	2	56	83	2

15 May	Wales 56 Ireland 12	Cardiff Athletics Stadium
13 June	Scotland 26 England 28	Hamilton RUFC, Glasgow
3 July	Scotland 26 Wales 34	Hamilton RUFC, Glasgow
3 July	Ireland 28 England 24	Clontarf RUFC, Dublin
22 August	Ireland 16 Scotland 24	Navan RUFC
12 September	England 32 Wales 34	Coventry Bears RLFC

2005

Wales	3	2	0	1	120	54	4
Scotland	3	2	0	1	69	102	4
England	3	1	0	2	60	75	2
Ireland	3	1	0	2	52	70	2

12 June	Wales 70 Scotland 8	Celtic Crusaders RLFC
2 July	England 8 Ireland 26	Halifax RLFC
16 July	Ireland 10 Wales 18	Terenure College, Dublin
23 July	England 16 Scotland 17	London Skolars RLFC
14 August	Scotland 44 Ireland 16	Braidholm RUFC, Glasgow
11 September	Wales 32 England 36	Celtic Crusaders RLFC

2006

England	3	3	0	0	120	63	6
Ireland	3	2	0	1	85	84	4
Wales	3	1	0	2	58	70	2
Scotland	3	0	0	3	60	106	0

3 June	Ireland 38 Scotland 30	St Marys RUFC, Limerick
15 July	Ireland 23 England 44	Terenure College RUFC, Dublin
16 July	Scotland 16 Wales 22	Lochinch RUFC, Glasgow
13 August	Scotland 14 England 46	Braidholm RUFC, Glasgow
19 August	Wales 10 Ireland 24	Celtic Crusaders RLFC
10 September	England 30 Wales 26	Featherstone Rovers RLFC

2007

Wales	3	2	1	0	99	64	5
Ireland	3	2	1	0	72	56	5
England	3	1	0	2	81	107	2
Scotland	3	0	0	3	88	114	0

16 June	Wales 44 Scotland 30	Cardiff Demons RLFC
23 June	England 22 Ireland 28	Leigh Centurions RLFC
30 June	Wales 22 France 18	NPT Steelers RLFC (not tournament game)
14 July	Ireland 16 Wales 16	Carlow Crusaders RLFC
14 July	England 42 Scotland 40	Gateshead Thunder RLFC
11 August	Scotland 18 Ireland 28	Glasgow Hawks RUFC
19 August	Wales 39 England 18	Blackwood Bulldogs RLFC

2008

Wales	3	3	0	0	118	52	6
Scotland	3	2	0	1	74	112	4
Ireland	3	1	0	2	86	76	2
England	3	0	0	3	56	86	0

21 June	Scotland 20 Wales 62	Cartha Queens Park, RUFC, Glasgow
6 July	Wales 32 Ireland 24	Bridgend Blue Bulls RLFC, Porthcawl
20 July	England 8 Wales 24	East Riding RLFC, Hull
26 July	Ireland 26 Scotland 28	North Dublin Eagles RLFC
16 August	Scotland 26 England 24	Lasswade RUFC, Edinburgh
6 September	Ireland 36 England 24	Tullamore RUFC

2009

Wales	3	2	0	1	100	44	4
Ireland	3	2	0	1	70	76	4
Scotland	3	1	0	2	74	86	2
England	3	1	0	2	56	94	2

13 June	Wales 42 England 4	Celtic Crusaders RLFC
13 June	Scotland 22 Ireland 30	Preston Lodge RUFC, Edinburgh
11 July	Wales 32 Scotland 12	Blackwood Bulldogs RLFC
11 July	England 28 Ireland 12	Broughton Park RUFC, Manchester
8 August	Ireland 28 Wales 26	North Dublin Eagles RLFC
8 August	England 24 Scotland 40	Staines RUFC

Celtic Crusaders fixtures and results

2006

Date	Opposition	Match	Venue	Result	Score
12 February	Hemel Hempstead Stags	NRC	A	W	50–10
19 February	London Skolars	NRC	A	W	40–6
26 February	St Albans Centurions	NRC	A	W	72–0
5 March	London Skolars	NRC	H	W	78–14
12 March	Lokomotiv Moscow	CC3	H	W	64–4
19 March	Hemel Hempstead Stags	NRC	H	W	72–14
26 March	St Albans Centurions	NRC	H	W	62–0
1 April	Rochdale Hornets	CC4	A	L	8–32
9 April	Workington Town	NL2	A	W	50–18
14 April	London Skolars	NL2	H	W	70–0
17 April	Sheffield Eagles	NL2	A	L	20–22
23 April	Rochdale Hornets	NRC	H	L	6–34
30 April	Barrow Raiders	NL2	A	L	16–32
7 May	Hunslet Hawks	NL2	H	W	36–18
14 May	Keighley Cougars	NL2	A	D	30–30
21 May	Blackpool Panthers	NL2	H	W	52–16
28 May	Dewsbury Rams	NL2	A	L	4–42
4 June	Keighley Cougars	NL2	H	W	58–18
11 June	Swinton Lions	NL2	A	W	50–18
18 June	Sheffield Eagles	NL2	H	W	28–12
25 June	London Skolars	NL2	A	W	48–4
2 July	Swinton Lions	NL2	H	L	10–21
9 July	Hunslet Hawks	NL2	A	W	34–12
16 July	Barrow Raiders	NL2	H	W	42–12
23 July	Blackpool Panthers	NL2	A	W	52–0
30 July	Dewsbury Rams	NL2	H	L	18–38
6 August	Gateshead Thunder	NL2	H	L	22–26
13 August	Featherstone Rovers	NL2	A	L	10–11
20 August	Workington Town	NL2	H	W	38–10
3 September	Gateshead Thunder	NL2	A	W	28–16
10 September	Featherstone Rovers	NL2	H	W	14–11
22 September	Sheffield Eagles	PO2	A	L	16–26
1 October	Swinton Lions	PO3	H	L	26–27

Top appearances: 30 by Paul Morgan, Damien Quinn and Luke Young
Top try scorers: Tony Duggan 37, Carl de Chenu 22, Michael Ryan 20
Top goal scorers: Damien Quinn 85, Jace Van Dijk 52, Luke Young 14
Top point scorers: Damien Quinn 242, Tony Duggan 148, Jace Van Dijk 140

2007

Date	Opposition	Match	Venue	Result	Score
9 February	Widnes Vikings	NRC	H	L	6–56
15 February	Brisbane Broncos	BOCC	H	L	6–32
18 February	London Skolars	NRC	H	W	44–28
25 February	Leigh Centurions	NRC	A	W	26–22
4 March	London Skolars	NRC	A	W	28–4
10 March	Eastmoor Dragons	CC3	H	W	50–10
18 March	Leigh Centurions	NRC	H	W	22–14
25 March	Widnes Vikings	NRC	A	L	10–32
1 April	Rochdale Hornets	CC4	A	L	16–20

6 April	London Skolars	CNL2	A	W	42–18
9 April	Blackpool Panthers	CNL2	H	W	68–0
15 April	Keighley Cougars	CNL2	A	W	62–12
21 April	Hunslet Hawks	NRC	A	W	28–14
28 April	Swinton Lions	CNL2	H	W	82–4
4 May	Oldham Roughyeds	CNL2	H	L	26–34
13 May	York City Knights	CNL2	A	W	26–4
20 May	Workington Town	CNL2	A	L	16–28
26 May	Halifax	NRCQF	A	L	18–30
2 June	Featherstone Rovers	CNL2	H	W	36–28
9 June	Barrow Raiders	CNL2	H	W	26–14
17 June	Hunslet Hawks	CNL2	A	L	16–23
23 June	Workington Town	CNL2	H	W	26–12
30 June	York City Knights	CNL2	H	W	30–16
7 July	London Skolars	CNL2	H	W	50–6
15 July	Swinton Lions	CNL2	A	W	26–20
22 July	Blackpool Panthers	CNL2	A	W	54–8
26 July	Featherstone Rovers	CNL2	A	W	32–12
5 August	Barrow Raiders	CNL2	A	W	26–24
11 August	Hunslet Hawks	CNL2	H	W	84–10
18 August	Keighley Cougars	CNL2	H	W	34–12
26 August	Gateshead Thunder	CNL2	H	W	64–26
30 August	Oldham Roughyeds	CNL2	A	W	32–18
9 September	Gateshead Thunder	CNL2	A	W	60–16

Top appearances: Mark Dalle Cort 30, Damien Quinn 30, Jace Van Dijk 29
Top try scorers: Tony Duggan 40, Paul Ballard 26, Damien Quinn 20
Top goal scorers: Damien Quinn 86, Jace Van Dijk 62, Luke Young 7
Top point scorers: Damien Quinn 252, Tony Duggan 160, Jace Van Dijk 156

2008

Date	Opposition	Match	Venue	Result	Score
26 January	Harlequins	F	H	W	28–6
1 February	Sheffield Eagles	NRC	A	W	22–12
10 February	London Skolars	NRC	A	W	26–10
16 February	Sheffield Eagles	NRC	H	W	34–14
22 February	Doncaster RLFC	NRC	A	W	30–22
1 March	London Skolars	NRC	H	L	14–18
9 March	Lokomotiv Moscow	CC3	H	W	58–10
15 March	Doncaster RLFC	NRC	H	P	P–P*
21 March	Dewsbury Rams	CNL1	H	W	14–12
24 March	Sheffield Eagles	CNL1	A	L	6–25
29 March	Halifax RLFC	CNL1	H	W	26–18
6 April	Halifax RLFC	NRC1	A	W	30–24
11 April	Whitehaven	CNL1	A	L	16–44
18 April	Leeds Rhinos	CC4	A	L	16–38
27 April	Widnes Vikings	CNL1	H	W	16–14
2 May	Featherstone Rovers	CNL1	H	W	28–18
15 May	Salford City Reds	CNL1	A	L	22–24
24 May	Widnes Vikings	NRCQF	H	W	50–18
31 May	Batley Bulldogs	CNL1	H	W	56–28
8 June	Leigh Centurions	CNL1	A	W	45–22
14 June	Salford City Reds	NRCSF	H	L	20–36
22 June	Dewsbury Rams	CNL1	A	W	32–10
26 June	Widnes Vikings	CNL1	H	W	38–6

251

Date	Opposition	Match	Venue	Result	Score
13 July	Featherstone Rovers	CNL1	A	L	30–42
19 July	Whitehaven	CNL1	H	L	22–26
27 July	Batley Bulldogs	CNL1	A	L	22–30
2 August	Sheffield Eagles	CNL1	H	W	42–6
10 August	Leigh Centurions	CNL1	H	W	38–28
17 August	Halifax RLFC	CNL1	A	W	38–28
23 August	Salford City Reds	CNL1	H	W	20–10
11 September	Salford City Reds	PO2	A	W	44–18
28 September	Salford City Reds	POF	N**	L	18–36

*Match not rearranged. **Halliwell Jones Stadium, Warrington

Top appearances: Damien Quinn 30, 29 by Mark Dalle Cort, Jordan James, Ian Webster
Top try scorers: Tony Duggan 21, Damien Quinn 16, Luke Dyer 15
Top goal scorers: Mark Lennon 96, Jace Van Dijk 10, Damien Quinn 7
Top point scorers: Mark Lennon 225, Tony Duggan 84, Damien Quinn 78

2009

Date	Opposition	Match	Venue	Result	Score
29 January	Harlequins	F	A		P–P
6 February	Leeds Rhinos	eSL	A	L	6–28
14 February	Salford City Reds	eSL	A	L	16–28
21 February	Hull FC	eSL	H	L	20–28
7 March	St Helens	eSL	H	L	0–4
15 March	Hull Kingston Rovers	eSL	A	L	18–48
22 March	Wakefield Trinity W	eSL	H		P-P
29 March	Warrington Wolves	eSL	A	L	22–27
3 April	Hull Kingston Rovers	CCC	A	L	6–32
10 April	Huddersfield Giants	eSL	A	L	10–30
13 April	Harlequins	eSL	H	L	18–40
19 April	Wigan Warriors	eSL	A	L	10–44
26 April	Castleford Tigers	eSL	H	L	22–34
3 May	Huddersfield Giants	eSL	N*	L	16–40
17 May	Bradford Bulls	eSL	A	W	30–24
23 May	Catalans Dragons	eSL	H	L	18–30
30 May	Wakefield Trinity W	eSL	H	L	6–50
6 June	Harlequins	eSL	A	L	6–26
13 June	Wigan Warriors	eSL	H	W	22–16
20 June	Hull Kingston Rovers	eSL	H	L	18–32
26 June	St Helens	eSL	A	L	0–30
4 July	Warrington Wolves	eSL	H	L	6–22
11 July	Salford City Reds	eSL	H	W	25–12
17 July	Hull FC	eSL	A	L	6–22
25 July	Bradford Bulls	eSL	H	L	12–34
1 August	Catalans Dragons	eSL	A	L	0–34
16 August	Wakefield Trinity W	eSL	A	L	12–46
22 August	Leeds Rhinos	eSL	H	L	0–68
5 September	Huddersfield Giants	eSL	H	L	16-42
13 September	Castleford Tigers	eSL	A	L	22–35

*Murrayfield

Top appearances: Ryan O'Hara and Neil Budworth 28 each, Mark Bryant 27
Top try scorers: Luke Dyer and Lincoln Withers 6 each, David Tangata-Toa and Anthony Blackwood 5 each
Top goal scorers: Josh Hannay 25, Damien Quinn 12, Mark Lennon 8
Top point scorers: Josh Hannay 58, Damien Quinn 40, Luke Dyer 24, Lincoln Withers 24

All time Celtic Crusaders first team players (to September 2009)

Player	Apps	Tries	Goals	Drop goals	Points
Paul Ballard	51	40	0	0	160
Ryan Barton	28	4	0	0	16
Ashley Bateman	1	0	0	0	0
Chris Beasley	76	4	1	0	18
Anthony Blackwood	67	30	0	0	120
Andy Boothroyd	11	1	0	0	4
Steve Brown	1	0	0	0	0
Mark Bryant	27	0	0	0	0
Neil Budworth	83	11	0	0	44
Tom Burnell	3	0	0	0	0
Josh Cale	21	2	0	0	8
Marshall Chalk	14	4	0	0	16
Jason Chan	24	3	0	0	12
Aurélien Cologni	5	1	0	0	4
Phil Cushion	47	5	0	0	20
Mark Dalle Cort	83	30	0	0	120
Geraint Davies	47	8	0	0	32
Hywel Davies	53	5	0	0	20
Carl de Chenu	29	22	0	0	88
Gareth Dean	61	3	0	0	12
Neil Dixon	3	5	0	0	20
Gil Dudson	1	0	0	0	0
Tony Duggan	88	101	0	0	404
Luke Dyer	41	21	0	0	84
Carle Ellis	11	0	0	0	0
Kevin Ellis	3	1	0	0	4
Grant Epton	33	14	0	0	56
Dean Fitzgerald	39	9	0	0	36
Ben Flower	30	4	0	0	16
Philippe Gardent	6	0	0	0	0
Josh Hannay	44	11	30	0	104
Matt Hill	10	6	0	0	24
Karl Hocking	15	9	0	0	36
Michael Hook	8	1	6	0	16
Jamie I'Anson	44	2	0	0	8
Gareth James	1	0	0	0	0
Aled James	22	6	0	0	24
Jordan James	51	14	0	0	56
Matt Jobson	13	8	0	0	32
Richard Johnson	29	14	13	0	82
Lee Jones	9	0	0	0	0
Elliot Kear	3	0	0	0	0
Mark Lennon	40	9	104	1	245
Owen Lewis	2	0	0	0	0
Andy Llewellyn	5	0	0	0	0
Peter Lupton	21	4	0	0	16
Darren Mapp	61	18	0	0	72
Terry Martin	31	3	0	0	12
Lewis Mills	4	0	0	0	0
Paul Morgan	30	16	0	0	64
Lloyd O'Connor	5	3	0	0	12
Ryan O'Hara	28	3	0	0	12

Scott O'Kelly	6	2	0	0	8
Rod Peake	1	0	0	0	0
Adam Peek	18	3	0	0	12
Gareth Price	8	0	0	0	0
Damien Quinn	112	58	190	0	612
Craig Richards	10	14	0	0	56
Michael Ryan	24	20	0	0	80
Darren Ryan	1	0	0	0	0
Marcus Sainsbury	4	3	0	0	12
Dean Scully	17	0	0	0	0
Anthony Seibold	11	4	0	0	16
David Simm	16	2	0	0	8
Matty Smith	16	3	2	1	17
Aaron Summers	25	2	0	0	8
David Tangata-Toa	46	8	0	0	32
Rob Toshack	24	12	0	0	48
Steve Tyrer	9	2	5	0	18
Jace Van Dijk	94	22	125	0	338
Shawn Van Rensburg	12	0	0	0	0
Chris Vitalini	4	0	0	0	0
Ian Webster	29	7	1	0	30
Lloyd White	6	1	0	0	4
Lee Williams	6	2	4	0	16
Lincoln Withers	22	6	0	0	24
Lenny Woodard	10	4	0	0	16
Neale Wyatt	40	8	0	0	32
Luke Young	53	17	21	0	110
TOTALS		655	502	2	3626

N.B. In the above table, appearances includes players who started the match and came on as a substitute.

Celtic Crusaders tables

2006 Northern Rail Cup

	P	W	D	L	F	A	Pts
Celtic Crusaders	6	6	0	0	374	44	12
London Skolars	6	4	0	2	182	170	8
St Albans Centurions	6	2	0	4	56	248	4
Hemel Stags	6	0	0	6	60	210	0

2006 LHF Healthplan National League Two

	P	W	D	L	F	A	Pts
Dewsbury Rams	22	19	0	3	693	354	38
Sheffield Eagles	22	18	0	4	808	390	36
Celtic Crusaders	22	14	1	7	730	387	29
Featherstone Rovers	22	14	1	7	596	504	29
Swinton Lions	22	13	1	8	641	475	27
Barrow Raiders	22	12	0	10	599	481	24
Gateshead Town	22	11	0	11	547	540	22
Workington Town	22	10	0	12	558	645	20
London Skolars	22	5	1	16	406	776	11
Hunslet Hawks	22	4	2	16	411	617	10
Keighley Cougars	22	4	1	17	419	736	9
Blackpool Panthers	22	4	1	17	350	853	9

2007 Northern Rail Cup

	P	W	D	L	BP	F	A	Pts
Widnes Vikings	6	5	0	1	0	256	70	15
Celtic Crusaders	6	4	0	2	0	136	156	12
Leigh Centurions	6	3	0	3	2	192	120	11
London Skolars	6	0	0	6	0	72	310	0

2007 The Co-operative National League Two

Celtic Crusaders	22	19	0	3	3	918	345	60
Featherstone Rovers	22	18	0	4	2	819	366	56
Barrow Raiders	22	17	0	5	4	769	387	55
Oldham Roughyeds	22	16	0	6	5	661	420	53
Workington Town	22	12	0	10	7	655	515	43
York City Knights	22	10	0	12	6	488	470	36
Swinton Lions*	22	11	0	11	6	605	649	33
Hunslet Hawks	22	8	0	14	7	368	591	31
London Skolars	22	8	1	13	4	448	610	30
Keighley Cougars	22	6	1	15	4	407	692	24
Gateshead Town	22	6	0	16	3	381	822	21
Blackpool Panthers	22	0	0	22	6	332	984	6

* 6 points deducted

2008 Northern Rail Cup

Celtic Crusaders	5	4	0	1	1	126	76	13
Sheffield Eagles	6	3	0	3	1	144	142	10
Doncaster	5	2	0	3	2	112	114	8
London Skolars	6	2	0	4	0	124	174	6

Celtic Crusaders versus Doncaster was postponed and not replayed

2008 The Co-operative National League One

Salford City Reds	18	12	3	3	3	614	302	45
Celtic Crusaders	18	12	0	6	4	511	391	40
Halifax RLFC	18	11	1	6	3	634	514	38
Leigh Centurions	18	10	0	8	4	448	448	34
Whitehaven RLFC	18	10	0	8	2	420	399	32
Widnes Vikings	18	10	2	6	5	453	410	30
Sheffield Eagles	18	8	1	9	3	425	530	29
Featherstone Rovers	18	6	1	11	6	452	515	26
Batley Bulldogs	18	5	0	13	8	387	538	23
Dewsbury Rams	18	2	0	16	7	315	612	13

2008 The Co-operative Conference National

Bramley Buffaloes	18	15	1	2	2	668	268	49
Crusaders Colts	18	15	1	2	1	723	316	48
Warrington Wizards	18	15	1	2	1	747	396	48
Featherstone Lions	18	9	1	8	3	438	470	32
Huddersfield U Rangers	18	6	3	9	6	586	400	30
Liverpool Buccaneers	18	6	1	11	4	432	583	24
Gateshead Storm	18	6	2	10	2	436	677	24
Hemel Stags	18	6	0	12	4	532	630	22
Dewsbury Celtic	18	5	0	13	3	441	622	18
East Lancashire Lions	18	2	0	16	2	325	966	8

2009 engage Super League

	P	W	D	L	F	A	Pts
Leeds Rhinos	27	21	0	6	805	453	42
St Helens	27	19	0	8	733	466	38
Huddersfield Giants	27	18	0	9	690	416	36
Hull Kingston Rovers	27	17	1	9	650	516	35
Wakefield Trinity Wildcats	27	16	0	11	685	609	32
Wigan Warriors	27	15	0	12	659	551	30
Castleford Tigers	27	14	0	13	645	702	28
Catalans Dragons	27	13	0	14	613	660	26
Bradford Bulls	27	12	1	14	653	668	25
Warrington Wolves	27	12	0	15	649	705	24
Harlequins RL	27	11	0	16	591	691	22
Hull FC	27	10	0	17	502	623	20
Salford City Reds	27	7	0	20	456	754	14
Celtic Crusaders	27	3	0	24	357	874	6

2009 engage Super League Reserves

	P	W	D	L	F	A	Pts
Wigan Warriors	20	19	0	1	854	298	38
St Helens	20	17	0	3	809	376	34
Huddersfield Giants	20	14	1	5	720	410	29
Bradford Bulls	20	12	0	8	508	526	24
Warrington Wolves	20	11	0	9	555	584	22
Leeds Rhinos	20	9	1	10	632	615	19
Hull Kingston Rovers	20	9	0	11	546	474	18
Harlequins RL	20	9	0	11	624	602	18
Hull FC	20	8	1	11	572	579	17
Castleford Tigers	20	7	1	12	463	714	15
Salford City Reds	20	5	0	15	476	691	10
Wakefield Trinity Wildcats	20	5	0	15	326	812	10
Celtic Crusaders	20	3	0	17	374	778	6

2008–09 Gillette National Youth League

	P	W	D	L	F	A	Pts
Leigh Miners Rangers	20	19	1	0	637	130	39
Celtic Crusaders	20	15	3	2	454	198	33
West Cumbria	20	16	0	4	546	264	32
West Hull	20	13	1	6	401	264	27
East Leeds	20	13	0	7	420	281	26
Featherstone Lions	20	12	1	7	482	326	25
Leigh East	20	11	2	7	378	295	24
Saddleworth Rangers	20	10	0	10	429	335	20
Ince Rose Bridge	20	6	1	13	248	428	13
Keighley Cougar Cubs	20	5	2	13	400	530	12
Siddal	20	5	2	13	270	474	12
North London Stags	20	4	1	15	288	634	9
Gateshead Thunder	20	4	0	16	224	658	8
Waterhead	20	0	0	20	0	360	0

South Wales RLFC

Second Division 1996

Hull Kingston Rovers	22	21	0	1	1009	294	42
Swinton Lions	22	18	0	4	785	295	36
Hunslet Hawks	22	18	0	4	730	326	36
Carlisle	22	13	0	9	654	486	26
Doncaster Dragons	22	13	0	9	500	540	26
South Wales	22	12	0	10	528	548	24
Leigh Centurions	22	10	0	12	594	510	20
York	22	9	0	13	449	603	18
Chorley Chieftains	22	6	0	16	354	723	12
Barrow Braves	22	5	0	17	354	651	10
Bramley	22	5	0	17	360	759	10
Prescot Panthers	22	2	0	20	301	883	4

Date	Opposition	Venue	Result	Score
31 March	Hull Kingston Rovers	H	L	8–70
5 April	Prescot Panthers	A	W	24–22
8 April	Bramley	H	W	22–18
12 April	Barrow Braves	A	L	4–16
21 April	Doncaster Dragons	H	L	12–22
5 May	Leigh Centurions	A	W	23–20
12 May	Chorley Chieftains	H	W	58–0
17 May	York	A	L	26–54
26 May	Hunslet Hawks	H	L	19–26
2 June	Swinton Lions	H	L	8–26
8 June	Carlisle	H	W	37–18
16 June	Hull Kingston Rovers	A	L	16–40
23 June	Prescot Panthers	H	W	50–18
30 June	Bramley	A	W	44–6
7 July	Barrow Braves	H	W	48–16
14 July	Doncaster Dragons	A	L	18–24
21 July	Leigh Centurions	H	W	30–22
28 July	Chorley Chieftans	A	W	18–16
4 August	York	H	W	20–16
11 August	Hunslet Hawks	A	W	21–14
18 August	Swinton Lions	A	L	16–26
25 August	Carlisle	A	L	6–58

Top try scorers: Sean Marshall 15, Andy Currier 14, Ioan Bebb 7, Mike Riley 7
Top goal scorers: Ioan Bebb 45, Mike Healey 18
Top points scorers: Ioan Bebb 118, Sean Marshall 60, Andy Currier 56
Top apps: Andy Currier 22, Mike Riley 22, Anthony Hatton 21

Cardiff Demons Academy team

League results	P	W	D	L	F	A	Pts	Pos
1997 Division 2	18	12	0	6	702	440	24	4th
1998 Division 2	15	11	1	3	454	226	23	2nd
1999 Division 1	10	0	0	10	90	484	0	6th (out of 6)
2000 Division 1	14	2	1	11	241	562	5	10th (out of 12)

1998 Division 2 Grand Final – Hunslet Hawks 39 Cardiff Demons 30

Rugby League Conference

Welsh Grand Final
2003   Bridgend Blue Bulls 42 Aberavon Fighting Irish 8
2004   Bridgend Blue Bulls 26 Aberavon Fighting Irish 21
2005   Bridgend Blue Bulls 56 Torfaen Tigers 16
2006   Bridgend Blue Bulls 22 Cardiff Demons 10
2007   Bridgend Blue Bulls 24 Newport Titans 18
2008   Valley Cougars 26 Blackwood Bulldogs 12
2009   Blackwood Bulldogs 38 Bridgend Blue Bulls 22

Harry Jepson Trophy Finals (Welsh appearances)
2003   Bridgend Blue Bulls 33 Carlisle Centurions 26
2005   Bridgend Blue Bulls 60 Leeds Akkies 10

2001 RL Conference Central
Hemel Hempstead Stags	12	12	0	0	537	121	24
Gloucestershire Warriors	12	9	0	3	422	202	18
Cardiff Demons	12	8	0	4	393	210	16
Oxford Cavaliers	12	5	0	7	236	424	10
Worcestershire Saints	12	2	0	10	167	507	4

2002 RL Conference Central South
Hemel Hempstead Stags	10	8	0	2	491	140	16
Cardiff Demons	10	6	0	4	332	284	12
Gloucestershire Warriors	10	5	0	5	344	343	10
Oxford Cavaliers	10	4	0	6	290	338	8
Worcestershire Saints	10	0	0	10	120	590	0

2003 RL Conference South West
Cardiff Demons	10	9	0	1	510	123	18
Gloucestershire Warriors	10	7	0	3	468	178	14
Somerset Vikings	10	6	0	4	324	207	12
Oxford Cavaliers	10	3	0	7	247	393	6
Worcestershire Saints	10	3	0	7	133	482	6
Bristol Sonics	10	2	0	8	226	525	4

Welsh Conference 2003
Bridgend Blue Bulls	10	10	0	0	608	197	20
Aberavon Fighting Irish	10	7	0	3	500	285	14
Torfaen Tigers	10	6	0	4	363	357	12
Rumney Rhinos	10	3	0	7	344	411	6
Cynon Valley Cougars	10	2	1	7	247	552	5
Swansea Bulls	10	1	1	8	244	504	3

Welsh Conference 2004
Bridgend Blue Bulls	12	12	0	0	544	197	24
Aberavon Fighting Irish	12	9	0	3	464	291	18
Torfaen Tigers	12	7	0	5	459	289	14
Newport Titans	12	6	1	5	426	315	13
Cardiff Demons	12	3	0	9	358	442	6
Swansea Valley Miners	12	2	1	0	235	647	5
Valley Cougars	12	2	0	10	266	571	4

Welsh Conference Premier 2005

Bridgend Blue Bulls	12	11	0	1	606	210	22
Aberavon Fighting Irish	12	10	0	2	584	322	20
Torfaen Tigers	12	6	1	5	352	369	13
Newport Titans	12	5	0	7	397	400	10
Valley Cougars	12	5	0	7	304	512	10
Cardiff Demons	12	3	1	8	436	337	7
Swansea Valley Miners	12	1	0	11	257	588	2

Welsh Conference Premier East 2006

Cardiff Demons	8	5	1	2	271	201	11
Blackwood Bulldogs	8	5	1	2	265	248	11
Newport Titans	8	4	1	3	330	204	9
Torfaen Tigers	8	4	0	4	296	254	8
Valley Cougars	8	0	1	7	158	413	1

Welsh Conference Premier West 2006

Bridgend Blue Bulls	8	7	0	1	353	176	14
Aberavon Fighting Irish	8	4	0	4	274	207	8
Swansea Valley Miners	8	3	0	5	218	248	6
West Wales Sharks	8	2	0	6	108	322	4

Welsh Conference Premier 2007

Bridgend Blue Bulls	7	6	0	1	248	137	12
Torfaen Tigers	7	5	0	2	195	207	10
Newport Titans	7	4	0	3	252	154	8
Blackwood Bulldogs	7	4	0	3	261	209	8
Valley Cougars	7	3	1	3	215	198	7
Cardiff Demons	7	2	1	4	201	191	5
Neath Port Talbot Steelers	7	2	0	5	148	241	4
West Wales Sharks	7	1	0	6	133	316	2

Welsh Conference Premier 2008

Blackwood Bulldogs	7	7	0	0	326	130	14
Valley Cougars	7	5	1	1	270	204	11
Bridgend Blue Bulls	7	4	1	2	228	242	9
Torfaen Tigers	7	4	0	3	214	190	8
Cardiff Demons	7	3	0	4	186	174	6
Newport Titans	7	3	0	4	219	236	6
Neath Port Talbot Steelers	7	1	0	6	148	230	2
West Wales Sharks	7	0	0	7	166	351	0

Welsh Conference Premier 2009

Blackwood Bulldogs	8	8	0	0	328	90	16
Bridgend Blue Bulls	8	7	0	1	302	103	14
Valley Cougars	8	6	0	2	333	234	12
Cardiff Demons	8	5	0	3	220	167	10
Newport Titans	8	3	1	4	228	286	7
Neath Port Talbot Steelers	8	1	2	5	146	262	4
Torfaen Tigers	8	2	0	6	170	314	4
Dinefwr Sharks	8	1	1	6	213	320	3
St Clears Wild Boars	8	1	0	7	102	266	2

Bibliography

Books

Bateman A. and Rees P. (2002), *Allan Bateman – There and Back Again*, Edinburgh, Mainstream Press

Blain N. et al (1993), *Sport and National Identity in the European Media*, Leicester University Press

Butcher T. (2000), *The Rugby League World Cup*, Brighouse, League Publications Ltd

Butcher T., Clay G. and Spencer D. (1996-2008), *Gillette Rugby League Yearbooks 1996 to 2008*, Brighouse, League Publications Ltd

Collins T (2006), *Rugby's Great Split*, London, Routledge

Fagan S. (2005), *The Rugby Rebellion*, Sydney, RL1908

Farrar D. and Lush P. (1998), *Tries in the Valleys*, London, London League Publications

Fletcher R. and Howes D. (1981 to 1999), *Rothmans Rugby League Yearbooks from 1981 to 1999*, London, Hodder Headline

Hannan T. (2005), *Seasons in the Sun*, Halifax, Impress Sports Ltd

Harrison J. (2004), *Beyond the Heartlands - The History of the Rugby League Conference,* London, London League Publications

Haynes J. (2007), *All Blacks to All Golds*, Brighouse, League Publications Ltd

Johnes M. (2005), *A History of Sport in Wales*, Cardiff, University of Wales Press

Maguire J. (1999), *Global Sport*, Cambridge, Polity Press

Rowe D. (1999), *Sport, culture and the media: the unruly trinity*, Buckingham, Open University Press

Rylance M. (2004), *The Forbidden Game*, Brighouse, League Publications Ltd

Skinner J. and Edwards A. (2007), *Crashing through the Class Barrier* in *The Games are not the same*, Melbourne, Melbourne University Press

Wenner L. (1998), *Mediasport*, London, New York, Routledge

Magazines

Rugby League World published by League Publications Ltd.
Open Rugby published by Harry Edgar and League Publications Ltd.
Various Wales match programmes from 1990 to date

Newspapers

Archives of *Glamorgan Gazette, The Guardian, The Independent, League Weekly, Merthyr Express, Rugby League Express, South Wales Argus, South Wales Echo, South Wales Evening Post, Wales on Sunday, Western Mail*

Additional websites

http://en.wikipedia.org
http://groups.msn.com/PNGKumuls
http://worldrugbyleague.blogspot.com/2007/10/richard-lewis-10-year-international.html
http://www.bbc.co.uk
http://www.crusadersrfl.com
http://www.cymrurl.com
http://www.ffr13.com
http://www.ponty.net/rowley-mark
http://www.sportinglife.com
http://www.totalrl.com
http://www2.hunterlink.net.au/~maajjs

Television

Sky Sports, BBC, ITV, S4C, Micron Video.

Original interviews

Lee Briers, Neil Budworth, Dan Clements, Geraint Davies, James Davies, Simon Davies, John Devereux, John Dixon, Tony Duggan, Kevin Ellis, Phil Ford, Iestyn Harris, Aled James, Jordan James, Mark Lennon, Andy Lindley, Gerald McCarthy, David Mills, Justin Morgan, Roger Moore, Rowland Phillips, Matthew Pritchard, Damien Quinn, Mark Rowley, Michael Ryan, Anthony Seibold, David Watkins, Ian Watson, Brynmor Williams, Wayne Williams, Dai Young.

261

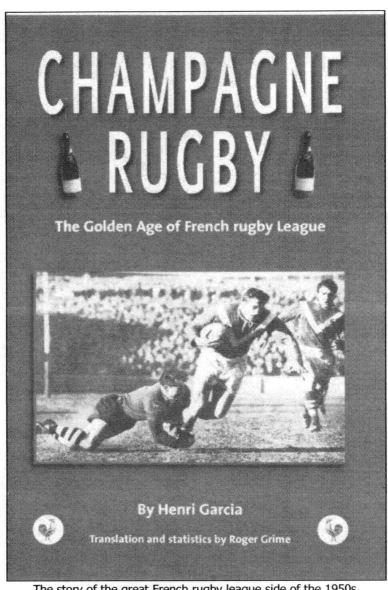

CHAMPAGNE RUGBY

The Golden Age of French rugby League

By Henri Garcia

Translation and statistics by Roger Grime

The story of the great French rugby league side of the 1950s,
and their three triumphant tours of Australia.

Published at £12.95, available for just £5.00 post free from London League
Publications Ltd. Credit card orders via www.llpshop.co.uk , or order by
cheque (payable to London League Publications Ltd) from PO Box 10441,
London E14 8WR.